BIRTH OF THE BASTARD PRINCE

Anurag Anand is a bestselling author-cum-corporate professional presently residing in the millennium city, Gurgaon. He has authored books panning across genres such as self-help, contemporary fiction and historical fiction. Some of his better known titles include *The Legend of Amrapali*, *The Quest for Nothing*, *Where the Rainbow Ends* and *Of Tattoos and Taboos*. To know more, visit *www.anuraganand.in* or check out Anurag's Facebook page: *anuraganandauthor*. You can also follow him on Twitter @ *anuraganand1978* or mail him at *contact@anuraganand.in*

Praise for *The Legend of Amrapali*

'…a captivating story that combines fact with fiction…'

—Midday

'Anand had mixed historical fact…with his imagination to weave an enchanting story'

—HT Live

'An enchanting tale of a woman, who succeeds in dethroning a megalomaniac ruler … *The Legend of Amrapali* is a discovery of a woman warrior'

—The Times of India

'Sinister plot and political wizadry of chaste love and unbridled passion run riot in Anurag Anand's *The Legend of Amrapali*'

—Deccan Herald

BIRTH
of the
BASTARD PRINCE
The Legend of Amrapali

ANURAG ANAND

RUPA

Published by
Rupa Publications India Pvt. Ltd 2014
7/16, Ansari Road, Daryaganj
New Delhi 110002

Sales centres:
Allahabad Bengaluru Chennai
Hyderabad Jaipur Kathmandu
Kolkata Mumbai

ISBN: 978-81-291-3454-7

First impression 2014
10 9 8 7 6 5 4 3 2 1

The moral right of the author has been asserted.

Typeset by Saanavi Graphics, Noida

Printed at: Gopsons Papers Ltd., Noida

To my late grandfather, Shri Birendra Kumar Singh, and his loving memories: a simple man to whom I owe my passion for stories and storytelling.

Neither sin nor a lone sinner remains,
In her embrace they are all but the same.
Like the pureness of a mother's womb,
And the pristine break of every new dawn,
In her lap, Vaishali conceals an era long gone,
One precious daughter and many wayward sons!

INTRODUCTION

With the passage of time, history, plagued by the erosion of collective memories and polluted by unrestrained human imagination, tends to lose its sheen and lustre. It is in these fading alleys that some of the most intriguing and enigmatic characters of the past can be found dwelling. The absence of accurate records from their time is usually made up for by the layers of fiction and fantasy their stories accumulate as they are passed down from generation to generation.

Amrapali, the legendary courtesan from the ancient kingdom of Vaishali, is one such name that stands tall in the labyrinth of our fast-fading past. Stories of this divine beauty's valour, her charisma, her benevolence and generosity can still be heard echoing within the households of the Indo-Gangetic plains. The echoes, though, are now waning.

Therefore I embarked upon this journey to recreate her legend, armed only with the little available information about her and my effervescent imagination. My endeavour was to tell a story that was real, devoid of the exaggeration which is responsible for blurring the divide between ancient history and mythology, and yet paint Amrapali in the same strokes and shades as her widely envisioned persona.

In the first book, *The Legend of Amrapali*, I have dwelt upon her early life, the challenges she had to face and the atrocities she had to endure by sheer virtue of being raised in a poor family at a time when women were mere slaves to the wishes of the menfolk. I have traced her forced ascension to the coveted yet morally deplorable title of the Nagarvadhu, the astuteness which enabled her to avenge her inflictions and the strength of her character that enabled her, a mere danseuse, to indelibly record her name in the glorious chapters of Aryavart's history. And this, bearing in mind that she shared her living years with men like Gautam Buddha and Lord Mahavira, men of towering stature and deeds, was no mean feat.

While this book carries on from where *The Legend of Amrapali* ends, I have attempted to make it a stand-alone read. The references to the prequel have been deliberately kept at a minimum and where unavoidable, they have been duly supplemented with details to avoid breaking the rhythm. And for those who are keen on getting a flavour of *The Legend of Amrapali* before embarking upon this journey the summary below should prove useful.

The kingdom of Vaishali was a confederacy of 7,707 small khandas, each ruled by a family belonging to one of the eight prominent Kshatriya clans of the region. The patriarchs of these families, or the Rajas, comprised the Vajji Assembly, which convened once every year to elect the Vajji Gana Parishad or the People's Council of Vaishali. This Governing Council, helmed by a democratically elected King, was responsible for the overall governance of the kingdom. While the respective Rajas maintained their own fleet of soldiers and were accountable for their own Khanda and its residents, all matters of common interest such as delivery of justice, promotion of trade with other kingdoms and defence against external aggressors fell within the purview of the Governing Council, making it the supreme authority of Vaishali. Resultantly, the elected members of the council wielded considerable influence and became the centre of attraction for the entire neighbourhood. Amrapali, to Somdutt, was not just a daughter, but the upholder who would carry his family name forward. He wanted to leave no stone unturned in giving her an upbringing that would hold her in good stead in the later years of her life. It was with this purpose in mind that he approached the city gurukuls, one after the other, to enroll his daughter, only to be unfeelingly turned down each time. The gurukuls in those days were meant to tutor boys and groom them into able men. A girl studying in a gurukul was practically unheard of and none of the gurus that Somdutt met was even willing to consider challenging the prevailing norms.

The only option left for Somdutt to explore was Rajkul—a gurukul favoured by Vaishali's nobility for educating their wards, run by Acharya Narhari, erstwhile Senapati of the Vajjian army and now a revered teacher. Somdutt was still in the guru's chamber, making his practised plea, when a commotion outside interrupted their conversation. On stepping out of the room they found Amrapali wrestling with two older boys in a bid to rescue a helpless goat from their tormenting. Seeing her valour, any doubts Acharya Narhari might have had about accepting her under his tutelage were dispelled.

'Such compassion and courage is a rare combination even in adults, let alone a small child. I would love to teach her,' the Acharya said. There was one condition however— Amrapali would not be admitted to the gurukul. Acharya Narhari would instead visit Somdutt's house to tutor her. Thus, at the tender age of four, Amrapali began her education under one of the shrewdest minds and most accomplished teachers in the whole of Aryavart.

Life, meanwhile, had other plans for little Amrapali.

It is said that those who benefit from the offerings of Mother Nature are also susceptible to her ire every once in a while. The city of Vaishali blessed by its proximity to the amalgam of two great rivers, was to experience this first-hand. The city that had withstood several raging floods over the past years was gravely threatened by the tumultuous Ganga that, like a beast on the verge of breaking its shackles, was gushing at dangerously high levels. To safeguard the citizens against the impending floods, the King ordered immediate evacuation of the city. The residents were urgently herded off to makeshift camps away from the banks of the raging river.

The camp remained Amrapali's home for months to follow and it was here that she forged some of the bonds that were to serve her well in times to come. Key among them were Prabha, a girl her own age and hailing from the same neighbourhood in Vaishali as her; Pushpkumar, a boy who was to later become a particularly significant constituent of her life; and Baba Yesubal, an elderly soldier in the Vajjian army and a part of the regiment deputed for the security of the makeshift encampment.

Eventually when the waters receded, the citizenry returned to Vaishali, only to be greeted by a picture of extreme devastation. The city, with muck and rotting animal carcasses lining its streets, was now a shadow of its erstwhile joyous and jubilant self. As an aftermath of the floods, it was gripped by a strange fever that even the most accomplished among Vaidyas failed to counter with their aushadhis (herbal medicines). Among the thousands who lost their lives to this deadly disease was Saudamini, Amrapali's beloved mother.

Amrapali was devastated, but the loss proved even more severe for Somdutt who, unable to bear this cruel twist of fate, slipped into an insidious trap of gloom and despair. Resultantly, the task of managing the household fell on Amrapali's amateur shoulders, propelling her into instant maturity. She rose up to the challenge, slipping into her new role as the lady of the house with apparent ease, keeping the sting of her pain to herself. Saudamini's absence had left a void in Amrapali's life that could never be filled, but time did well to return her life to the tracks of normalcy. Her private lessons with Acharya Narhari resumed and while she learnt subjects like rajneeti and arthashastra from the Guru, she also started visiting ladies from the neighbourhood who imparted training in skills like dancing, music and embroidery. The one activity that she had a natural flair for and took to with a surprising display of passion and commitment, was dancing.

Whatever steps Amrapali learnt in her dance class, she would practise for hours in the garden behind the Old Palace of Vaishali while Pushp would silently watch with a look of admiration and extreme affection in his eyes. Since King Manudeva's family had shifted to the newly constructed royal palace, an epitome of grandeur that stood close to the city centre, the Old Palace had remained vacant but for an old caretaker. Pushp's father had worked as a gardener there, and by the virtue of his familiarity with the caretaker, Pushp was permitted to visit the garden with Amrapali as and when they desired. Amrapali, now a stunning young lady with features that even the most accomplished sculptors envied, was being unknowingly steered by her heart into hitherto unfamiliar frontiers and she couldn't find it within herself to resist. Amrapali's relationship with Pushp was now transgressing into a zone she didn't entirely comprehend. Lately, she had begun to feel a strange flutter within her in his proximity and had been hesitant to share this development even with Prabha. She enjoyed Pushp's company and he in turn seemed equally eager to accompany her to the haat, the temple or anywhere else she happened to be heading.

One evening, on Pushp's insistence, Amrapali accompanied him to hear a discourse by the Shakya Muni, a young prince who had renounced his worldly stature and material comforts in search of nirvana. Some even claimed that he had succeeded in his quest. Pushp, using his connections, had managed to procure a seat for them in the first row facing the podium. Right from the time that the Muni stepped on to the stage, flanked by King Manudeva, Mahamatya Tamra Bhadra and other prominent members of the Vajji council, Amrapali was unable to peel her eyes off him. There was something magnetic about the man—his words perhaps, or his glowing persona—that made it impossible for anyone to ignore him.

As Amrapali's consciousness drifted along the ripples created by the ascetic's words, she remained oblivious to another set of eyes, eager and probing, affixed upon her own youthful self. A man whose desires mattered more than anyone else's in the entire kingdom of Vaishali, the King—Manudeva. The divine beauty had unknowingly triggered a chain of events that evening which were to take her further from the normalcy of her life towards the designs of destiny.

Manudeva, thoroughly smitten and unable to keep his mind off Amrapali, summoned Somdutt to seek his daughter's hand in marriage. The offer, though generous, sent tremors of fear and shock down Somdutt's spine. Manudeva was already married and nearly twice as old as Amrapali. Yes, there was the lure of watching his daughter become the Queen of Vaishali, but Somdutt knew his daughter better. Amrapali would never trade her freedom and the desires of her heart for anything material, not willingly at least. Moreover, her feelings for Pushp might not yet be apparent to her, but Somdutt could see them as clearly as he saw his own reflection in the clear waters of the Ganga. He knew that it was only with Pushp that Amrapali could remain happy, and Somdutt could not deprive her of this happiness. Unable to muster the courage to say no to Manudeva's face, Somdutt returned, seeking time to deliberate over the proposition. It was evident to Amrapali that something was weighing on the old man's mind, but despite her repeated questioning he did not reveal his concerns to her.

Tamra Bhadra, the elderly prime minister was entrusted with the task of paying Somdutt a visit and convincing him to give away Amrapali to Manudeva. A virtuous and impassioned man, Tamra Bhadra could not help being struck by a wave of empathy for Somdutt and his daughter. During the course of his discussions, he not only warned Somdutt about 'the law', the most likely resort for Manudeva in the wake of a refusal, but also touched upon a glaring loophole that Somdutt could make use of to steer clear of it. The law, an archaic decree by one of the earlier Kings of Vaishali, allowed for the most beautiful girl in the entire kingdom to be appointed the Nagarvadhu or the city's bride through a vote by the Governing Council. It was said that the King had come up with the decree when the girl he desired had snubbed his advances. He might have succeeded in his motives then, but an unprecedented backlash by the populace and members of the Vajji Assembly ensured that it was never put to use again. Hence, the law, like a rusting sword waiting to be picked up for claiming its next victim, lay dormant in the rulebooks of Vaishali, waiting for its invocation.

Indeed, Somdutt's hesitation irked Manudeva enough for him to contemplate using the law. Aware of the discontentment it had led to in the past, he set in motion a series of clandestine measures to prepare the grounds for the law being invoked unopposed. Covert operatives, men from Vaishali's secret service, were deployed to mingle with the public and create enough curiosity about Amrapali's exquisiteness and her celestial beauty, leading to a communal longing and desire that would bend the public opinion in favour of the law. This sinister plan for Amrapali's appointment as the Nagarvadhu was underway when a disturbing piece of news forced Manudeva to revisit his original strategy. He learnt that Somdutt intended to get Amrapali married to Pushp in three days' time, the day she turned eighteen. As per the provisions of the law, only an unmarried girl over eighteen years of age could be nominated for the Nagarvadhu's election. If something was not done urgently, Amrapali was likely to slip from his grasp, forever.

On the day of her wedding Amrapali had woken up jubilant and expectant. Little did she know about the cruel twists that the passing hours held in their folds. The first devastating news to reach her was of Pushp's demise. He had been arrested on charges of treason the previous day, she was told, and in a brazen attempt to escape from prison he lost his life. Amrapali, who was aware of the ensuing tussle between her Baba and the mighty King of Vaishali over her, knew better than to believe the story. Later that day, even as she struggled to come to terms with her loss, a messenger delivered a parchment at her doorstep. It was an order from King Manudeva for her to present herself before the Governing Council of Vaishali, which was to take a vote on her appointment as Vaishali's Nagarvadhu.

Somdutt was inconsolable. The lone battle he had been waging was lopsided from the very beginning, but he could not shake the feeling that he had betrayed not only himself but also his beloved daughter. It was when he began treading on the borders of irrationality, suggesting steps like taking Amrapali's and his own life, that Amrapali was once again compelled to take charge of the situation. In an amazing and somewhat curious display of courage, she accepted Manudeva's invite to attend the specially convened session of the Governing Council. The casting of votes was a mere formality, as no sooner had Amrapali stepped out of her chariot that she gauged the mood of the assembled gentry. There was little doubt that most of the lust-laden eyes she saw darting towards her had already envisioned her as the Nagarvadhu—their collective bride. It wasn't a surprise then that the Governing Council, in a rare near-consensus, voted in favour of her appointment. Tamra Bhadra's hand remained the only unmoving one during the show of hands by the council members to cast their vote.

Amrapali agreed to take on the mantle of the Nagarvadhu, but not before the Council agreed to three of her conditions. First, she wanted gold to the measure of her weight and the Old Palace of Vaishali to be given to her. This, she explained, was to ensure that she led a life befitting the Nagarvadhu of a kingdom as prosperous and mighty as Vaishali. Next, she wished for the right to choose the patrons she would entertain. And thirdly, she wanted a dedicated troop of soldiers, detached from the command of the Vajji army, to be entrusted with the security of the old palace. In turn, she said, she would hold a public dance performance every full moon night which would be open for all citizens of Vaishali to attend. On the other days, she would privately entertain a selection of guests, at a price, of course. The ploy behind her demands, especially the right to choose her patrons, was not hidden from Manudeva and he vehemently opposed their acceptance by the council. But the council members, their vision blurred by a thick film of lust, were in no mood to risk the opportunity from slipping out. Deftly maneuvered by Tamra Bhadra, they unanimously vetoed the king's reservations and accepted all of Amrapali's demands.

A few days later, in a ceremony of unrivalled grandeur and opulence, Amrapali, after taking a dip in the Abhishek Pushkarini, was anointed the Nagarvadhu of Vaishali. Accompanied by her Baba and Prabha, she was escorted to the old palace by a sea of jubilant and rejoicing men. It was a moment of mixed emotions for Somdutt. While he was aware of the sacrifices Amrapali had had to make, he couldn't help but bask in the attention that the residents of Vaishali were showering upon his daughter. The shower of petals and Akshat, the incessantly cheering crowds, it was nothing short of a dream for him. For a fleeting moment Saudamini's smiling face appeared before his eyes and a solitary tear ran down his cheek.

The next full-moon night, as promised, Amrapali enthralled the populace of Vaishali with a scintillating dance performance. Her dance left the audience spellbound. She hardly appeared human, it was more like an apsara from the heavens had descended on earth.

As the musical notes hit their crescendo and Amrapali, after a vigorous spin, elegantly dropped on the stage, the crowd burst into frenzy. They showered their beloved Nagarvadhu with the gifts they had brought, piling up precious gems, jewellery and the finest of fabrics at her feet. Amrapali stood in complete silence, her hands folded and head bowed slightly, heedless of the tempest that was waiting to consume her once she stepped off stage. The scene was indeed gruesome—Somdutt's lifeless body hanging from a dhoti, the other end of which was fastened to the wooden beam of his room. The sight of his daughter walking into a hall filled with hooting and jeering men, inebriated by the heady mix of madhu and lust, had proved too much for the old man to digest.

The blow was severe, but Amrapali took it in her stride, diverting her focus instead on fulfilling the promise she had made to the citizenry of Vaishali and using her newfound power to alleviate the sufferings of the downtrodden. She started several schools, those where girls were as welcome as the boys, commissioned roads to link remote corners of the kingdom to the city, dug wells and canals to ensure sustained supply of water to shortage prone areas. Her magnanimity was an escape for her, from an existence that constantly gnawed at her from within. Another thing she successfully managed was to keep Manudeva at bay.

With each passing day Manudeva's obsession for Amrapali continued to mount and it was soon threatening to breach even the frontiers of his sanity. The tales he heard other nobles recount of Amrapali's dexterity, her unparalleled beauty, left him feeling spurned and furious. His numerous attempts to woo the Nagarvadhu with expensive gifts and lovelorn messages were not acknowledged. One day, his reason clouded and his emotions heightened by a liberal dose of opium, Manudeva decided to take the bull by its horns and put an end to his misery. He paid the Nagarvadhu a visit, hoping to impress her into surrendering to his whims. The discussion, however, didn't go as he had planned and it had soon crossed the boundaries of civility. All he managed was to prick Amrapali's old sores, mostly of his own inflictions. When he left, Amrapali was seething and in her eyes was an unshakable resolve to make her tormentor pay for his sins. Pushp's death, Somdutt's demise, both were losses that needed to be avenged and Manudeva had pushed her to a point where she had finally decided to make him pay for his misdeeds.

Manudeva's visit acted as the trigger for Amrapali to chart out one of the most ambitious and portentous schemes ever enacted—a cleverly devised blueprint to topple the leadership of the world's first known democracy. Armed with the blessings and guidance of her guru, Acharya Narhari, and the loyalty of Prabha and the six Xingnou warriors, a gift to her from Baba Yesubal, she set out to stage one of the most astounding political coups in the history of Aryavart. If Manudeva had to be brought down, her first strike had to be at the very fulcrum of his power and authority— the throne of Vaishali. With the next council elections barely a few months away, Amrapali had to devise a way to rid him of his kingship. The immediate hurdle facing her was that the Lichchavi votes combined with those of Manudeva's ardent supports were sufficient to ensure smooth victory for the incumbent king. If Amrapali was to dethrone the king, she needed to somehow carve a fissure in this assured vote-bank.

She found her solution in Yudhveer, a young Lichchavi noble and the deputy king. Playing on his ambitions, Amrapali was able to ally with Yudhveer, taking the first step towards the realization of her objective. In the days to follow, loyalties were bought, blood was spilled and crafty ploys to earn the allegiance of Rajas were put into play. All was proceeding as per plan, but for Kalkinath, the Ichchavaku Raja.

With the way the numbers appeared to be stacking up, it was essential for Amrapali that the rajas of the Ichchavaku clan voted in favour of Yudhveer instead of Manudeva. Prabha, who Kalkinath had been wooing for a while, had dropped several hints to him with the purpose of influencing his allegiance, but the Raja had failed to take the bait. The votes he controlled were going to be the deciding factor in the elections and Amrapali could not afford any ambiguity with respect to them.

It was at this point that a mysterious visitor, a man named Bindusen, came to visit Amrapali. Bindusen claimed he was a trader, but his bearing and appearance reeked of nobility. Much to the Nagarvadhu's dismay, Bindusen was not only aware of her machinations, but also suggested a way for her to emerge from her quandary. The task was simple: Kalkinath needed to be eliminated. Kalkinath meanwhile, was not as impervious to the developments as he appeared to be. A shrewd politician, he was only biding time before committing his allegiance, so as to ensure that he sided with the most likely victor. In the end he choose to align himself with Manudeva, revealing to him the vague outline of Amrapali's plan he had managed to piece together, in return for a promise to be appointed the next deputy King.

A tussle of epic proportions ensued. A man with all the resources of the kingdom at his disposal was pitted against a mere woman. The odds were stacked heavily against Amrapali, but to her, defeat was never an option. In a brazen display of astuteness and courage, she was able to tilt the scales in her favour by getting Kalkinath eliminated.

Manudeva responded by ordering Amrapali and Prabha's arrest on charges of the Raja's murder. Once again, by a clever manipulation of evidence, Amrapali was not only able to prove her innocence in the courtroom, but also managed to cast a shadow of doubt over the King's own conduct. Such public disparagement, just days before the election, further worsened Manudeva's standing. The Rajas who were still undecided about their votes were suddenly faced with a compelling reason to make up their mind.

The votes were cast and the results announced. As Amrapali had hoped, Yudhveer was declared victorious with a healthy margin of votes.

The next morning, while she was idling in the garden of the old palace, she received a parchment signed by Yudhveer. It was through this that Amrapali learnt about Manudeva's demise. The outgoing King, the letter claimed, was so shocked and humiliated by his defeat that he had chosen to end his life by hanging himself within his chamber sometime during the night. Yudhveer had kept his word. Amrapali had exacted the revenge she desired, but there remained an unfathomable burden weighing down on her heart. Her life as the Nagarvadhu of Vaishali had just begun. Who knew what other insidious traps her destiny had already laid in her path...

1

Like an oasis in the middle of an arid wasteland, the Old Palace of Vaishali stood shimmering in its regalia—a sharp contrast to the unnerving tranquility that had besieged rest of the city. Men, nagar seths and peasants alike, were gushing in through the gates like droplets of a torrential downpour.

A plush red carpet had been rolled out from the palace entrance right through the path that led to the Aam Sabhagriha—an accessory fated to be trampled upon by the very feet it guided to the shrine of sins. The milky candescence of the moon mingled with the golden glint of fiery torches that lined the boundary walls and lent an exultant tactility to the surroundings.

Dasis clad in bright orange dhotis and glistering white dupattas adorned the entrance, sprinkling scented water and a mix of rose and marigold petals upon the alighting patrons. In the backdrop, beyond the immediate glare of the torches, were heavily armed guards, menacing in their stillness and their darting eyes betraying the alertness of their state.

The patrons, blind to the reception that was laid out for them, were jostling against each other—pushing, tugging and pulling—to enter the Aam Sabhagriha before those around them could manage to do so. The intricately carved door to the enclosure stood like a grandiloquent, ceaseless pit, swallowing all life forms that arrived at its threshold.

Tonight was a full moon night; a night when their Nagarvadhu, Amrapali, would mesmerize them with her celestial dance moves and the tempest of anticipatory anxiety was getting the better of them. 'Apsaras from the heavens descend to the Old Palace in disguise to witness Amrapali's performance, in a bid to learn her bhavas and mudras,' it was proclaimed and widely believed by the citizenry of Vaishali.

While accepting the mantle of the Nagarvadhu, Amrapali had made a pact with the Vajji council whereby she had agreed to hold a public dance performance every full moon night, which was open for all citizens of the kingdom to attend. She had lived up to her part of the deal and once every fortnight, for the past three years, the palace had been adorned like a bride to be, shimmering, glittering and welcoming her patrons with open arms, as it did today.

The audience section of the Aam Sabhagriha comprised clearly demarcated sections for seating attendees on the basis of their social standing and antecedents. While the nobles and moneyed traders enjoyed the closest proximity to the stage and had dasis tending to their needs, the peasants, artisans and other non-affluent patrons were relegated to the farther ends of the enclosure.

Unlike other nights when the Nagarvadhu entertained only a small set of chosen guests in the significantly smaller and private chamber known as the Swapna Kakshika, there were no favourites, preferences or reservations on the night of her public performance. Each citizen of Vaishali had as much right to be party to this carousal as the other and thus the seats in each of the sections of the Aam Sabhagriha were left to be occupied on a first-come first-serve basis.

After every public dance performance by Amrapali, the citizens of the kingdom anxiously started counting days to the next full moon night when they would once again permit their senses to run astray and unbind their hearts to the angelic presence of their beloved. When the day finally arrived, the city streets, brimming with vim, vigour and vitality, buzzed with the nervous anticipation of an eager virgin. Men, young and old, could be seen tending to their daily chores with a sense of heightened urgency, making a beeline for the barber's shop in an attempt to enhance their appearance or simply whiling away time in wait of the appointed hour.

At sundown they headed towards the Old Palace, laughing, dancing, drinking and making merry, leaving behind a deserted maze of bricks and discomfited family members who had long resigned to their own fate and learnt to live with the meandering desires of their loved ones. Those left behind, the wives, mothers and daughters, found solace in the fact that their dear ones would eventually return and remain with them, at least till the next full moon night dawned.

The revellers, too absorbed in their excitement to worry about anything but Amrapali, would wait for hours for the palace gates to open and once they did, rush to the Aam Sabhagriha to grab a seat that would keep them in the closest permissible proximity of the danseuse for the rest of the evening. Today was one such day; a fortnightly celebration of love, longing and licentiousness that the city had become accustomed to.

'Maharajdhiraj, Magadh Naresh, Shrenik Bimbisara padhaar rahe hain,' the sentry stationed outside the chamber announced the arrival of King Bimbisara in a basal, chill-laden tone. At once all eyes, eleven pairs of them, darted towards the entrance and the physical frames of those present in the chamber stiffened to rapt attention.

After a brief pause, the sudden silence that enveloped the setting was broken by the sound of approaching footsteps—rhythmic, measured and weighty. A towering figure soon emerged on the scene, hands folded, lips curled in a smile and black wavy hair bouncing on his shoulders with each step he took. 'Pranam,' he said, greeting the gathering in general. Such was the man's aura that those in his proximity, generals and ministers alike—men of remarkable stature themselves, found themselves tongue-tied, struggling to weave words into sentences they had already framed in their minds.

He seemed neither domineering nor imperious; on the contrary he seemed to be a man of compassion, continence and solitude. With sharp, chiselled features, intelligent eyes, calm composure and a smile which appeared to have a regular presence on his visage, he resembled any handsome, well-bred man one could expect to come across at a stall in one of those exclusive haats dealing in wares shipped from faraway lands or behind the counters of stores dealing in expensive gems and jewellery.

Often a mention of his name was all it took to shed the devious veil of affability his appearance presented and reveal the man whose brutality and ruthlessness had made his name synonymous with dread and fear across the length and breadth of Aryavart. This too was distortion of actual facts, for those in his propinquity could vouch for the meticulous planner, thinking strategist, shrewd statesman, ambitious and mildly conceited ruler, doting father and passionate lover that was Bimbisara, the illustrious King of Magadh.

Bimbisara, a scion of the Haryanka Dynasty, had taken over the reins of the kingdom at the tender age of fifteen, and since then he had tirelessly worked towards realizing his treasured dream of expanding the Magadh Empire to cover the entire breadth of

Aryavart, from Dantapur on the east bank to where the Sindhu River merged with the ocean in the west. He used diplomacy, marital alliances and when nothing else worked, the might of his sword to further his ambitions.

When he marched with his enormous army, his weaker adversaries, in a bid to avoid confrontation and certain annihilation, often chose to flee, abandoning their territories. And those who opted to stand their ground seldom survived to witness the obliterated state of their provinces and the reign of wolves and ravens in a hitherto populous area after Bimbisara's forces had receded. His exploits had earned him the title of 'shrenik' (the one who commands a massive army), a bulging treasury, a fearsome repute and left him with an expansive kingdom and half a dozen wives to tend to.

With brisk steps Bimbisara walked through the group towards the other end of the chamber where a large gilded throne, carved in marble and decorated with brocaded silk in crimson and fiery-orange hues, laid in wait. With a sway of the hand he signalled for the others to take their seats before alighting on the seat himself.

A young boy, detaching himself from the assembled group, reached forward and touched the King's feet to obtain his blessings before parking himself on the smaller throne to Bimbisara's right. By now the others too were comfortably perched on their designated chairs from the two columns ahead of the throne.

This was the Mantrana Kaksha or consultation chamber of Bimbisara's palace in Rajgriha, the capital city of Magadh. The assembled gentry comprised his top generals, ministers and a young man whose name, much like Bimbisara's, was destined to be enshrined in the historical memory of mankind.

'This is a proud moment for me, for you, for the whole of Magadh,' he began his address gently, almost imperceptibly.

'The kingdom of Anga is now a part of the Magadh Empire, a feat possible only with your toil, sweat and blood. I salute you, your loyalty, and each and every commander, warrior and foot soldier from your legions who have made this victory possible and enabled Magadh's expansion to the far west. Each victory brings with it a surge of joy and abundant rewards for those who live to cherish them, but we must not blind ourselves to the pain and sufferings of those who have staked their lives in earning for us this happiness. The royal treasury has been instructed to send two hundred gold mohurs each to the families of deceased soldiers and fifty for each one grievously injured in the war,' he continued, only to be interrupted by sharp laudatory cries of *'Maharaj Shrenik Bimbisara ki jai ho!'*

Other than the King there were only eleven dignitaries present in the room but their thunderous bellowing was deafening, perhaps fuelled by the intoxication of recent victory. After a battle that had lasted for just under a year and claimed thousands of victims, the ruler of Anga had surrendered to the might of Magadh. The victorious army had returned home barely a few days back.

As always, the city of Rajgriha had greeted its victorious children with open arms, pampering them and tending to their every need, however wayward they might have been, like a doting mother giving in to the whims of her errant offspring. The streets, spic and span, were decorated and lined up with stalls serving choicest of delicacies and various forms of inebriants—wines, bhang and tadi (toddy).

Women clad in dazzling outfits, most of them brought in from nearby cities, could be seen smiling at potential customers or negotiating with them for the right price to quench their long-suppressed carnal thirsts. Soldiers laughing, singing, dancing and making merry could be found in every nook of the city and the denizens could only but lend a blind eye to the festive dissoluteness that had shrouded the city.

It was when the continuing festivities had lasted over two days that the King had summoned his top aides for the meeting that was underway at the Mantrana Kaksha of the royal palace.

'The decisions pertaining to the governance of the newly acquired territories will be taken soon. Meanwhile, you too can collect the rewards for your troops and your own selves from the treasury,' he continued once the cheers had waned, only to incite a fresh volley with his declaration.

This time, instead of waiting for the ovation to subside on its own, he lifted both his hands in the air and as if by the swirl of a magic wand, silence was instantly restored to the chamber.

'But the one thing that overwhelms me, not only as a king but also as a father, is the fact that the campaign was ably led by Yuvraj Abhay Kumar,' he said, gesticulating towards the young man sitting by his side. A blaze of pride could be seen simmering in his eyes as he glanced at his son. The young man, barely sixteen or seventeen years of age, quickly emerged from his seat and stood facing the King, hands folded and head bowed in acknowledgement.

'My son, you have made not only your father, but the entire Haryanka Dynasty proud of your vim and valour. I am assured that one day I would be leaving behind the reigns of Magadh in able hands and that your gallantry will ensure that no enemy shall ever muster the courage to stand opposing you. Hence my son, I confer upon you the title of Ajatshatru—the one with no enemies,' he said, reaching out and drawing his sword from the case bound to his waist.

As Abhay Kumar went down on one knee and Bimbisara anointed him, ritualistically dabbing his shoulders with the tip of the sword, once again the chamber burst out in loud cheers. Only this time the words echoing praised the Yuvraj, '*Yuvraj Ajatshatru ki jai ho! Yuvraj Ajatshatru amar rahen!*'

'Thank you, Maharaj. I am blessed to have been born as a scion of the Haryanka Dynasty and more so as a son to a great man and an even greater ruler like you. I assure you that Anga was only the first of many victories that we shall cherish together and I will leave no stone unturned to realize your dream of making Magadh the most expansive empire on land,' the young man replied in measured words.

A mirror image of his father, he had even taken on Bimbisara's tranquil composure. Utterly unfazed, he accepted the praise and adulation being bestowed upon him by the King with grace and poise worthy of a seasoned crusader—glimpses of which he had displayed while carving the heroic victory against Anga in the first ever campaign he had spearheaded for Magadh.

'Doubtlessly my son, doubtlessly,' the proud father beamed. Sifting his gaze towards the other occupants of the room, he continued, 'My comrades, it is you who constitute the formidable and dreaded might of Magadh and it is you who have been the steady pillar behind every glorious triumph we have tasted. But there remains a long way to go before we can rest and peacefully reflect upon our past accomplishments. Our motherland calls upon us to earn for her the promised glories that we set out to and it is for her sake that we must keep on going.'

Bimbisara paused and with a sweep of the eye he searched his confidantes for any streak of dissent or hostility. Having encountered none, he continued, 'Vaishali! Our dream of making Magadh the most expansive kingdom under the sun can only be realized once the Vajji Confederacy and its capital city, Vaishali are brought within its folds. The riches from Vaishali's treasury and precious stones and gems from its mines will help us reinforce our troops and fund our further campaigns.'

His voice was now rising and falling with poetic fervour. The words, though spoken matter-of-factly, had a dramatic effect on the audience as they looked at each other, attempting to analyse the implications and organize their own chain of thoughts.

Devdutt, a middle-aged minister, was the first to speak. 'Maharaj, Vaishali has been gaining in repute and significance due to its trade links with other kingdoms and it may someday stand as a threat to the Magadh Empire. We must not permit such a threat to prosper in our own backyard and hence it is imperative that the Lichchavis be cut down to size immediately. We must invade Vaishali at once.' The impatience in his tone, whether emerging from the eagerness to concur with the King or his own musings, made him sound callow and infantile.

Prasenjit, the Senapati of Magadh and a reputed strategist who had saved many lives and claimed many more with his shrewdly crafted incursions, was quick to cut into Devdutt's monologue. 'Agreed Maharaj, our aspirations cannot be met until Vaishali is annexed,' he began, addressing Bimbisara and completely ignoring the glares from the slighted Devdutt.

The pivotal role of militia in Bimbisara's scheme of governance had elevated the Senapati to a pedestal where none but the King himself could dare to affront him. Even the Yuvraj treaded with a fair degree of prudence while dealing with Prasenjit and Devdutt was left with no option but to pucker his face into a frown and listen to what the Senapati had to say.

'But Vaishali is a completely different story. It isn't like any of the kingdoms we have annexed in the past. Waging a war with Vaishali would mean taking on the combined might of the 7,707 Rajas that make up the confederacy. Moreover, Vaishali with its gargantuan walls on three sides and protection of the Mahavana on the fourth, is insulated from enemy attacks. As you are aware many Emperors have tried to annex the city in the past but have failed miserably. If you will excuse my transgression, Maharaj, I am not sure if we are ready to take on the Lichchavis just as yet.'

Unexpectedly Bimbisara responded to his Senapati's submission with a discerning smile. He waited for a few moments, as though deliberately weaving a shroud of suspense around his reaction, before addressing Prasenjit.

'Undermining the enemy is one of the most common reasons for defeat in battle and often it is the undaunted, confident ones who fall into this trap. I am glad, Senapati, that your strong shoulders bear a head that is rational and balanced,' he began. Mockery or adulation, the words could have meant just about anything, but the King continued without pausing to explicate.

'We shall not commit the same blunders that the earlier invaders of Vaishali have committed. Our forces will not attempt to scale the city's walls making us vulnerable to the enemy arrows and nor shall we make an effort to cross the Mahavana and face the wrath of lurking predators. When the time comes, we shall march into Vaishali and affect its siege from within.'

Once again Bimbisara paused for effect, but this time round the curious Yuvraj did not permit the silence to last long. 'How will that happen, Maharaj?'

'My son, while you were away earning your battle honours, I have initiated the manoeuvrings that will enable this. However, further details can only be revealed at the opportune moment,' Bimbisara responded before sifting his gaze towards others.

'The protectors of Vaishali, much like its citizenry, are invalidated in their shared fascination for the beautiful Nagarvadhu. Of late the city has transformed into a habitat for love-crazed neurotics and the intrepid and deadly Lichchavi warriors are busy polishing their suavity rather than their swords. The inevitable curse of their riotous folly lies in their defeat and we must not let this opportunity go begging.'

'I understand that our soldiers have only just returned from battle and they need time to recuperate and also our battle reserves will need to be replenished. Though we will not be going to war with Vaishali immediately, we don't have the luxury of much time either. So, unless there are any concerns that remain to be addressed, I suggest that you start working on getting the forces ready for battle,' he said, his eyes eventually locking with those of the Senapati.

'Very well, Maharaj. I will need about ten days to get everything in order and ready for your inspection,' Prasenjit replied, bowing his head in accordance.

'Great! So gentlemen, let us all brace ourselves for one of the most onerous campaigns of our lifetime. Together we shall alter the writings on the walls of history—the unconquerable shall be conquered, Vaishali shall be annexed,' Bimbisara concluded and left the room amid chants of praise and blessings for him and the kingdom of Magadh.

The Aam Sabhagriha, in the golden haze of its interior adorned with precious stone and mosaics, and under a dome that blazed like the vault of heaven, was bursting on its seams, crammed with as many human forms as it could accommodate. Those who had endured a longer wait had been rewarded with seats they were now occupying while others were compelled to remain on their feet. Dasis scuttled through the aisles, filling and refilling their glasses with madhu and engaging the patrons in small talk.

Clouds of smoke emanated from the incense burners and the stage, lit with hundreds of blazing torches, reflected the glittering pieces of the chandelier dangling from its ceiling, giving the illusion of a gargantuan ball on fire.

Suddenly, the drone of the tanpura abruptly arrested the ongoing hustle and bustle. With craned necks and pounding hearts the spectators watched, as slowly, step after step, Amrapali walked to the centre of the stage. She looked divine.

Clad in a yellow dhoti embroidered with golden lace, a golden blouse, and a netted dupatta draped over the top-knot of her hair, Amrapali walked with the glossy elegance of a dewdrop sliding over a lotus leaf. As she turned to face the audience, her hands folded and face aglow with radiance befitting the noon sun, the hall burst out with deafening cheers. Such was the resounding applause with which Vaishali greeted its Nagarvadhu that even the solid walls of the Aam Sabhagriha appeared to be trembling in buoyancy.

The cheers eventually subsided, making audible the music which had gained in tempo since Amrapali had first stepped on stage. Matching her moves to the tune, she went about the Mangalacharana (invocation piece) seeking forgiveness from mother earth for stamping on her and offering salutations to the gods, gurus and the audience before taking on the chouka bhanga or the square stance.

As she stood still, like a statue, the music once again changed tones and her troupe of support dancers took to the stage. Leading the six dancers was Prabha, Amrapali's childhood friend and confidante who, since her friend's appointment as the Nagarvadhu, had remained by her side like a guardian angel.

Amrapali had seen fate snatch away each of her loved ones—her mother Saudamini, her father Somdutt and Pushp, the only man she had ever loved. Prabha was the only one left that she could call her own now, and she in turn had persistently remained by Amrapali's side through all her tribulations and exaltations, ever willing to overcome obstacles of any nature for her sake. Among the hundreds of lives the Nagarvadhu touched on an everyday basis and the thousands who claimed to have bequeathed their hearts to her, if there was one person who Amrapali truly loved it was Prabha.

With the dancers having taken their positions, the music once again switched flavours and through a highly developed language of gestures the dancers proceeded to unfold the story of Nala Charitam for their audience. Through their abhinaya, a moustache-adorned Prabha portraying Nishadraj Nal, and Amrapali as the beautiful Princess of Kundinapur, Damyanti, transported their audience into a world of pure, unbridled love.

As Amrapali relived the life of Damyanti, rejecting proposals from gods and men alike and using her bhavas and mudras to profess her unequivocal love for Nal, she could not help but think about Pushp. Her own story bore an uncanny resemblance to Damyanti's except that her determination, instead of uniting her with the subject of her affection, had taken him away from her forever. Jerking away her thoughts, she once again scanned the audience gallery hoping to find the one familiar face she was looking for. Once again she was disappointed.

The spectators, at least those who had not compromised their senses to the free-flowing madhu, unmindful of her musings, seemed to be in a state of catatonic trance. While some were completely absorbed in the saga of Nal and Damyanti, others had embarked upon their own flights of fantasy interpreting Amrapali's expressions of love as a personalized communication meant especially and exclusively for them. It was only in the third pehar of the night when the two lovers, with the musical notes hitting a crescendo, were united on stage that the performance came to its conclusion, ending the spell it had cast on the audience.

'Pali, what was playing on your mind tonight?' Prabha enquired. They had just receded from the stage and were busy untying their ghunghroos in the anteroom.

'Nothing. Why? Did I commit some mistake?' Amrapali replied nonchalantly.

'A mistake in your dance performance, I am sure even Muni Bharat will struggle to find,' she said, looking at her friend with an arched brow and a proud smile. 'But you surely are hiding something from me. You can fool everyone but not me. It was Bindusen you were searching for, were you not?'

Bindusen, a wandering trader, had first visited her when Amrapali was in the midst of executing her plan to replace the then king of Vaishali, Manudeva, with her ally and the present ruler, Yudhveer.

The plan, a closely guarded one, was known only to a handful of people and when Bindusen in his first meeting with her had referred to it, Amrapali was left baffled and shaken. Her fears that the scheme had been compromised were, however, dispelled eventually and she succeeded in enabling Yudhveer's ascent to the throne of Vaishali.

She had achieved what she had set out to, but her lingering doubts about Bindusen and the sources of his information had not left her. Bindusen had visited her thrice since their first meeting and though he had been charming and amiable as ever, all she had managed to learn about him was that he was a trader and his work brought him to Vaishali every now and then.

During each of his visits the two had spoken at length, touching upon varied and contrasting subjects and each time he had surprised her with his topical knowledge, acumen and eloquence. He would talk about cultures and people from foreign shores and with equal ease shift to discussing musical notes and tunes; it were as though there was nothing under the sun that had escaped his attentive and intense eyes.

Unlike her other patrons, Bindusen never expressed discomfiting desires or attempted to gain undue proximity to Amrapali, making her completely at ease in his company. He had managed to cast an impression on the Nagarvadhu, but more overbearing was the shroud of curiosity that Amrapali found herself grappling with every time she met him.

During each of their meetings she had attempted to make him talk about himself, but to no avail. He had remained guarded like a shelled tortoise and using his skilled articulacy, managed to steer clear of the trap of words she laid out for him. And when she did pose a question directly, all she got in return was an evidently rehearsed reply that left her in no better stead.

Amrapali had even got her guards to clandestinely follow Bindusen on his way out of the palace and each time they had returned empty handed, having lost sight of him somewhere along the way. The design of his disappearances seemed deliberate rather than merely coincidental and this left the Nagarvadhu further perturbed and agitated.

The last time she had met him was about a month back and in the privacy of the Swapna Kakshika he had expressed his desire to see her in her full regalia, dancing to the cheering crowds and enthralling them to ecstasy on the night of her public performance. He hadn't specifically said when he would visit, but for some reason Amrapali was half expecting him to be in attendance today.

Prabha had somehow managed to latch onto her thoughts, but she certainly did not intend to own up to her internal deliberations.

'Bindusen? And just why would I be trying to locate him among the audience?' she shot back at her friend. Just as Prabha, with a half-smile, was about to retaliate, their conversation was cut short by the sudden knock on the door.

The intruder was Bhaichunk, better known as Ballabh, a Xingnou warrior and also the commander of Amrapali's personal bodyguard unit. Ballabh, along with five of his comrades had scaled mountains, jungles and vast breadths of land looking for Amrapali in a bid to repay the favours of an ageing warrior, Baba Yesubal.

Baba Yesubal, a man who had known Amrapali as a little girl and had looked upon her as the daughter that he never had, had protected Ballabh's clan from a bunch of nomadic raiders. Up in the mountains, when he heard about the ruthless plot that had resulted in Amrapali's appointment as the Nagarvadhu of Vaishali, he was quick to exercise the influence of his obligations and dispatch Ballabh and his men for her protection. Since then Ballabh had remained with her, faithful and dedicated as the Xingnou are known to be.

Some quick words were exchanged between the two and Prabha saw expressions of incredulity and surprise followed by compassion and understanding fleet across Amrapali's face before Ballabh bowed down and made a hasty retreat. Baba Yesubal, among other things, had taught Amrapali the language of the mountains and as a result only she, in the whole of Vaishali, was equipped to understand the native tongue of Ballabh and his men. Due to the limited communication they engaged in with others, the six warriors still relied heavily on the language of gestures and the few broken bits of the local dialect that they had managed to pick up.

'He says there is an old man who has been waiting all evening to see me. The guards at the gate tried to dissuade him, asking him to return tomorrow morning, but he is adamant on meeting me right away. He claims that it is a matter of life and death. Ballabh too has seen the man and to him he seemed genuinely needy,' Amrapali explained for the benefit of Prabha.

'You must be tired so you carry on to your chambers. I shall meet the visitor and figure out what the matter is,' she added as an afterthought.

'No, I am fine. I shall wait too,' Prabha replied firmly. Amrapali knew better than to argue with her, so she simply nodded her head in accordance.

2

The man, old and frail, was futilely trying to conceal himself behind Ballabh's tiny frame. Ironic, Amrapali thought, that the man would attempt to hide from the very person whose audience he had been seeking all evening. He looked frightened. Perhaps it was the grandeur of the Old Palace or the aura of the Nagarvadhu that had smitten him to muteness.

'I am informed that you wished to see me. Tell me, what can I do for you?' she enquired politely. The man did not appear particularly wealthy, but he was not a pauper either. His countenance, clouded by shades of fear, fatigue and pain, exuded a sense of intellect and dignity gathered through years of steering past life's vagaries.

'I... I...' he mumbled, trying to lend words to his supplication, slowly emerging from behind the makeshift human shield.

'Help me, devi. Please help me save my son,' he finally blurted, falling on the floor to grab her feet.

Over the past few years Amrapali's benevolence had earned her a repute which saw the needy and deprived lining up at the gates of the Old Palace, some in need of alms to meet personal exigencies and others to seek her interference in getting access to basic amenities like water, schools and roads. She had been spending a significant portion of her time in listening and tending to the woes of common people.

She had set up pathshalas which, against the age-old tradition of educating only the male children, imparted quality education to young girls and boys alike. Roads to the unconnected hinterlands of the kingdom and wells to provide the populace with fresh supply of water, she had done all within her resources to help the poor and needy. On a few instances she had even used her good offices with King Yudhveer to get the state to take on the more extensive of the welfare projects that came her way.

'It is these people who make us what we are and without their love and adulation we would forever remain incomplete. It is an honour that they place their faith in me and come to the palace with their problems. We must therefore strive to meet their expectations at all times,' she often told Prabha.

This of course was a plausible explanation for her kindness and consideration, but the more pressing motivation was not hidden from Prabha's eyes. She knew that in ridding others of their pain, her friend looked for an outlet to let go of some of her own sufferings. It was by bringing a smile to someone else's face that Amrapali momentarily closed herself to the torment and losses that she had had to endure. Charity for her was not merely a gracious act; it was the energy source that enabled her to bear the lusty gaze of her patrons till this day.

It was her familiarity in dealing with the destitute that told her that the old man befallen at her feet was different. He was not helpless by character, but someone who had been rendered helpless by the throes of destiny, circumstances or the designs of others. She was perplexed and the fact that his request was wayward, something she could not make head or tail of, only added to her bafflement.

'Baba, please get up and tell me the whole story. I promise you, I will do whatever I can to save your son. Who are you?

Where is your son? What is the danger that he faces?' she said, gently holding the old man's shoulders to help him get up before leading him to one of the vacant stools.

'I am Parimal, a trader from Ukkacala,' he began, weighing the first few words to escape his lips. 'My son, Suraj Mal, who works with me, had entered into a business deal with Raja Udit, the King of Ukkacala Khanda. As per the deal we were to get for him ten well-bred Kabuli horses against a consideration of one thousand gold mohurs. These horses can be bought for anywhere between seventy and eighty mohurs at the haats of Gandhar, and after accounting for our expenses, we stood to make about ten to fifteen mohurs per horse as profit. The Raja had even given us an advance of six hundred mohurs.'

While Amrapali listened to Parimal's story intently, tedium started seeping into Prabha's demeanour. The third pehar of the night, succeeding an exhausting dance performance, wasn't the most ideal setting for a discussion on commercial transactions involving horses, Kabuli or otherwise.

'We spent about a month travelling to Gandhar, looking for the best horses to buy, and returning back. However, along the way a landslide struck our entourage, burying two of the horses and much of the other merchandise we were bringing back with us. We were able to deliver only eight live horses to the Raja,' the old man continued absorbedly.

'The financial loss was monumental, but we were hoping to recover the cost of the two dead horses from the remaining two hundred mohurs that the Raja owed us. But when we asked him for the money, he flatly refused and instead started demanding a return of the advance he had paid to us. He said that the deal was for delivery of ten horses and since we could not fulfill our part of the obligation, it stood cancelled.

'When, despite our begging and pleading, he refused to budge, we even settled to return the advance and asked him for some time so that we could sell the beasts in the local haat and raise the money. But once again he refused. He said that he would not let go of the horses until the entire amount he had paid to us was returned. When Suraj protested, he had him arrested on charges of trickery and fraud.'

'Absurd. The Viniccaya Mahamatta will never permit him to get away with this. It is he who is trying to use the mishap to his advantage and swindle you,' the Nagarvadhu retorted.

'At the time of giving us the advance, he had made us sign on some parchments that we had failed to study. What were we to do, it was a sizeable deal and we trusted him. He is the Raja after all,' the old man expressed in his defence and continued after a brief pause.

'Raja Udit is also Senapati Chetak's maternal uncle and the Mahamatta will surely put his word above mine. As you are aware, if found guilty of treachery, my son could face a punishment as severe as having his arms amputated or even death.' His eyes once again welled up.

The situation was indeed grave. Amrapali was not ignorant of Raja Udit's crooked contrivances. The Raja was known to impose arbitrary taxes on his subjects and engage in questionable business transactions, machinations that had elevated him into one of the wealthiest Rajas out of the 7,707 that made up the Vajji Confederacy.

Raja Udit, post Yudhveer's ascension to the throne had aligned himself to the King and was even said to be one of the principal financiers for his election campaigns. Given the circumstances, she could not rely on Yudhveer to intervene on behalf of Parimal and annoy one of his prime allies. Not to mention, Udit's association with the Senapati, a man on whom the King's reliance had increased considerably over the passing years.

Moreover, Chetak's detestation for the Nagarvadhu was a well-known fact. Though Amrapali had never personally met the Senapati, she had heard of several instances where he had publicly proclaimed her to be the root cause behind most evils plaguing the kingdom. 'Men beat their wives, forcibly take away their jewellery and even resort to illegal means of accumulating wealth, all to be able to squander it at the wretch's behest,' he had often been heard alleging.

The implication was simple, the Nagarvadhu was left with no one to lean on and if the innocent man was to be saved, she would have to fashion it single-handedly. She tried to think of other options that she might have overlooked, but exhaustion prevented her from doing so. Although she was mentally and physically drained, she knew that she could not allow herself to break the old man's faith and permit his son to be sacrificed at the whims of a merciless man. She had to figure out a way.

'Tomorrow, at the break of dawn, I shall meet you at the Raja's palace. Go home, Baba, and stop worrying about Suraj Mal. Nothing will happen to him,' she comforted Parimal, while herself remaining unsure of how the feat would be managed. 'And ask your wife to put together his favourite fares for lunch. Her son will be hungry when he returns home,' she added for good measure.

Elsewhere, in the royal palace of Rajgriha, in an aphotic chamber barely illuminated by the flickering flames of a lone torch, a man paced up and down, lost in deep deliberations. The eerie silence breached only by his rhythmic footsteps, the abstractions conjured on the walls by dancing shadows and the solemn atmosphere were adding an ominous touch to the setting.

Suddenly, with a mild creak, the door to the chamber was tugged open, its metallic studs glittering momentarily in the abysmal lighting. The man paused to glance towards the door and upon recognizing the intruder, walked towards her and bent down to touch her feet. 'Pranam Matashri, you have heard too, haven't you?' he enquired.

'Yes, my son, I heard and when I did, I couldn't stop myself from rushing here to see you,' she said, pulling out the lone lit torch from its sconce and using it to light the others. In no time the room came back to life, its golden and silver upholstery dazzling in full regalia and the two human forms adequately discernible. The lady, still holding the flickering torch in her hand, was Rani Nanda, eldest among Bimbisara's six wives and facing her was her son, Rajkumar Vihalla Kumar.

'Why, mother, why? First he lets that Vaidehi Putra lead the Magadh army to battle and now he bestows him with the title of Ajatshatru and in the presence of all his court officials proclaims him to be the next King of Magadh. Am I not his eldest son, and in being so, is the throne of Magadh not my birth right?' he said, pouring out his anxiety in the comforting presence of his mother. His droopy, blood-shot eyes and quivering voice betrayed a liberal ingestion of opium.

'Despite being his eldest Queen, I was never accorded my rightful title of Maharani and now he is attempting the same sleight with you. I will never allow him to trample over the rights of my son,' she responded, visibly enraged with the developments.

'But what can we do, Mother? He is the King and we, his mere subjects. As always, he will give some unreasonable explanation for his actions and we will have no option but to accept it. Just like, while justifying his decision to let Abhay lead the troops in the battle of Anga he had said it was because Abhay was physically more capable of enduring the afflictions of war than I was.'

'I know, but brute strength cannot be the basis for declaring the heir to the throne. Leading the forces to battle is one thing, but succession to the throne of Magadh is completely another. He can't get away with such frivolous excuses this time. And if he is so obdurate about his beloved Vaidehi Putra's crowning as the King, he is free to divide the kingdom into equal parts and distribute the reigns among all his sons,' the Rani replied, voicing her dissidence with her husband's wishes.

'Mother, you know as well as I do that father is never going to agree to that. He is too absorbed in his conceit to allow even the delivery of justice for his own son stand in the way of his dream to expand the Kingdom of Magadh across the breadth of Aryavart. This option is ruled out. Magadh will remain united and there will only be one King to occupy its throne after Bimbisara,' he rebutted her.

'So then, what is the way out? Is there nothing we can do?' she said, emerging from her fit of fury.

'This is what I have been deliberating all evening and finally a plan seems to be taking form,' he said, flashing a crooked smile. It had taken double his usual dose of opium, but the inebriating smoke had eventually managed to shred the veil of uncertainty and indecision that had been clouding his mind. He now knew exactly what needed to be done and his mother's outburst of compassion had fuelled him with the courage to go ahead with his plan.

'It might not be the most ethical thing to do, but in asserting ones claim to the throne, ethics and morality are not always the best virtues to be guided by. Don't worry mother, leave it to me and you shall witness your son being crowned as the undisputed King of Magadh,' he assured Rani Nanda.

'Whatever it takes, my son, whatever it takes,' she replied.

It was a small entourage, eight people in all. She had deliberately decided against being escorted by her usual faction of guards lest the visit came to be seen as an intimidation attempt by Raja Udit. It was in her interest and that of Suraj Mal for the matter to reach an amicable settlement with the Raja and hence apart from Prabha, she had opted to be accompanied only by Ballabh and his five comrades.

The ride from Vaishali to Ukkacala wasn't particularly short; the Khanda was located at a distance of about twelve kosas from the city gates and an additional kosa and half from the Old Palace. But the pleasant early morning breeze and the scenic backdrop that greeted them—bright green rice plants, bathed fresh in the overnight dew, swaying musically to the tune of chirping birds— took away most of the tedium from the journey.

Amrapali had been evaluating various arguments that could be presented to Raja Udit, but none of them appeared to be powerful enough to make him yield. 'We will have to take it as it comes,' she told Prabha when quizzed about the intended plan of action, before once again losing herself to the elemental magnificence of the surroundings.

As instructed, Parimal was waiting outside the Raja's palace and he greeted them with a smile as the chariot and horsemen pulled up ahead of him. He looked different from what Amrapali remembered, more composed and alive, perhaps resurrected by the ray of hope he envisioned her to be. While Prabha announced the Nagarvadhu's arrival and shouted out to the sentries, instructing them to inform their master of this unexpected visit, Amrapali said a silent prayer seeking divine intervention to help her live up to the old man's expectations.

The exceptional hour of the visit and the eminence of the visiting dignitary led to a brief flurry among the sentries, post which the guests were duly escorted to the meeting room inside Raja Udit's palace. The palace was a modest one, nothing ostentatious or extravagant. 'He must like his mohurs safely put away in the treasury,' Amrapali thought, scrutinizing the cane, jute and clay artifacts that decorated the room.

It wasn't long before the Raja joined them, still struggling to emerge fully from the grasp of sleep, his puffy eyes and moist forehead standing testimony to the haste with which he had readied himself to greet the Nagarvadhu. 'Welcome, Devi, to my humble abode. It is an immense honour for me and the people of my Khanda that you decided to grace our lands with your kind presence. Only, had I been aware of your impending visit, I would have made preparations worthy of the occasion,' he said courteously, completely ignoring the presence of the old man who stood staring at him with amber eyes.

'Thank you, Raja Saheb, for the gracious words and do accept my sincere apologies for landing up unannounced at this inappropriate hour,' she replied, reciprocating her host's geniality. 'But the matter was such that it appropriated an urgent visit rather than following the protracted path of conventions and custom. I come to you with great anticipation and hope that you would heed to my humble request.'

'Now you are embarrassing me, Devi. All that is mine is yours too, so pray tell, what can this modest servant of yours do for you?' he replied.

'I am given to understand that this man here,' she said, pointing towards Parimal, 'has unwisely offended your kind self and that his son lies imprisoned in your custody. All I seek of you is the release of the young man against a personal assurance from my side that whatever their misdeeds, they will not be repeated again.'

'You are too naïve, my lady, to trust these scoundrels. They have cheated me of my money and now they are going about pretending as though I am the one being unreasonable. I am a law abiding man and let me assure you that they will be dealt with suitably and in accordance with the laws of the land. Now, you don't expect me to obstruct the proceedings of law for their sake, do you?' His voice remained as polite as it had been, but his true intentions now stood exposed, staring back at her in their repulsive nakedness.

She had known enough men of influence—Kings, nobles and ministers—to be cognizant of the rampant modus operandi within the political corridors. She was well aware that in the aisles of power a man's word is bound to him only by the viscosity of convenience and yet she couldn't help but feel indignant. Perhaps the sugary demeanour of the Raja had allowed her guard to slip and expectations to mount.

Immediately checking the flow of her emotions she said, 'Please don't get me wrong, I harbour no intentions of obstructing the path of justice and neither do I wish for you to do so. Your losses must most certainly be replenished and in fact topped with adequate compensation for the inconvenience their actions have caused you. My only wish is for an amicable settlement to be arrived at so that the elderly parents are spared the plight of having to grieve for their young son.'

Sensing the opportunity for a windfall, the Raja signalled one of his sentries to fetch the imprisoned Suraj Mal.

'You are big-hearted and extremely generous my lady. Though I believe that only with the harshest imaginable punishment will we be able to dissuade such criminals, I cannot muster the audacity to deny you this simple wish. But how do you intend to make good my losses? What is it that you have in mind?'

While Amrapali was still attuning herself to the chameleon-like flickering hues of her host, a slight commotion drew her attention towards the entrance. A young man, hazel-eyed, tall and proportionately sculptured like a carved statue, was dragged in by two guards. He had chains dangling from his wrist and feet which the sentries were tugging on to guide him. But despite his debilitated state he was walking with a proud swagger, as though refusing to subjugate himself to the constraints of bondage.

'A mirror image of his father, only a much younger and fitter version,' the Nagarvadhu thought, before shifting her gaze back towards Raja Udit. 'I have a proposition for you. You can keep the eight horses that Parimal has delivered to you and additionally I shall give you two of the finest horses from my stables. You don't even need to pay the two hundred mohurs that Parimal had been seeking,' she began.

'In turn you will release Suraj Mal. And since the two have lost most of their belongings in the landslide, you will also give them some provisions to help sustain their family till the time they are able to get back on their feet. Is this acceptable?' she asked. The look of utter astonishment and anguish that had emerged on Parimal's face due to her offer did not escape her but she avoided locking her gaze with the old man.

'Sounds reasonable, but what exactly would I need to pay for their sustenance? I would prefer to have that categorically defined rather than leave loose ends that are open to individual interpretation,' Udit was quick to concur. Originally he had sought only to save the two hundred mohurs that were due to the traders, but now, with a stroke of good fortune, he was not only saving his money but getting two more well-bred horses.

'We have had a decent crop of potatoes this year, so why don't you pay them in terms of potatoes and they can consume what they want and exchange the rest for other items of need? There can be a simple measure of quantity as well; say you pay them potatoes against each nail on the horseshoes of the two horses I give you. On the first day you pay them one potato for the first nail, on the second day two for the second and so on. The number of potatoes payable against each nail will keep doubling from the previous one so that by the end they have some potatoes left with them to be traded for grains and pulses. Also, the time it will take to account for all the nails should be enough for them to get their business back on track. With your generosity they will thus be spared the plight of starvation,' she suggested.

Udit engaged in some hasty mental arithmetic—two horses with four horseshoes each and each horseshoe having six nails; only forty eight nails to account for! 'No wonder they say women should limit their influence to matters regarding the kitchen and not venture beyond. What a deal! True that beauty and brains can't coexist; this woman is much more dim-witted than she looks,' he thought, nodding his head in agreement.

'And as you had suggested, we must not leave any scope for ambiguity in the matter. So I suggest that we all go to the Mahamatta's office right away and document our acceptance of the deal in his presence,' she recommended to the eager Raja. Not only Parimal, but Prabha too had a dazed look in her eyes. Neither could comprehend the meaning or motivation behind her actions, but both refrained from voicing their concerns. Only Suraj Mal stood looking at her with a perceptive smile as the sentries got down to freeing him from his shackles.

'It was your faith that made you come to me, now don't lose it just as yet. Have patience and believe in your belief, it will not let you down,' she said to the old man as they left the Mahamatta's office and embarked on the return journey to Vaishali.

The mid-afternoon sun was beating down; its scorching rays threatening to smoulder anything that stood in its way. The earth, holding its own against the blazing tyrant, seemed to be counteracting by releasing the heat pent up in its belly through the tiny cracks that had materialized on its surface.

The constituents of the landscape hadn't altered much since they had last passed them, only now, the roads, with their hearth-like disposition were no longer pleasant or agreeable to travel. The ride back to Vaishali was turning out to be a nightmare, much against Amrapali's anticipations.

Her dry lips were stiffening and her tongue, with its depleting wetness, was no longer able to moisten them. The coarseness in her throat too had become unbearable and was even threatening to hurt. She looked at Prabha. Her friend and companion was faring no better. She then scanned the faces of the six riders riding alongside the chariot—though they looked alert, thirst and fatigue had eroded the firmness of their postures. Even the tired horses were trotting along at a sluggish and lethargic pace.

Once again she looked around, as she had been doing for the past several miles of the journey, but still she couldn't sight a single breathing soul in the distance. Farmers had retreated to the comfort of their homes leaving the vegetation in their fields to endure the summer heat and practised travellers had long deserted the roads in a bid to return at a more favourable hour. Amrapali recalled from her ride earlier in the day that there were no settlements lining up this particular stretch of the road, not even a solitary hut where they could hope to get some drinking water, till the very last leg of their journey.

'We should at least have carried some water with us. If not while starting from the palace, we could have picked up a surahi or two in Ukkacala. Now we will only come across the next settlement close to the city gates and that still is a fair distance away. I hope I am able to survive for that long,' she murmured, showering her thirst induced frustration upon no one in particular. And just then, as if by the will of God, she saw a group of monks walking right ahead of them.

'Stop, stop,' she yelled, waving frantically at the hermits, almost startling a few of them. They were about a dozen in all; young men wrapped in long saffron-coloured dhotis, perspiration on their shaven heads glittering in the fierce sunlight, cloth sling-bags dangling from each one's shoulders, they seemed like perfect replicas of one another. It was incredible how, despite being barefoot, the monks looked completely at ease with the vagaries of nature.

'Be with Buddha, Devi,' one of the monks broke away from the pack and greeted her by placing his palms together. 'What assistance can we be of to you?'

'We have been travelling for a while, O Holy One, and are immensely thirsty. We were wondering if you would have some water that you can spare for us?' she appealed to him.

The monk pulled out a small wooden container from his bag and handed it to her. It was only with the first few sips of water permeating within her that she felt her conscious regain charge of her senses. She looked around and found Prabha, Ballabh and the other guards sipping hungrily from similar containers. The other monks too had followed suit and handed over their water containers to the thirsty seekers.

'O Generous One, who are you and what makes you travel barefoot, braving this scorching heat?' she enquired.

'I am Anand, a humble disciple of the Shakya Muni Gautam,' he began, as Amrapali continued to sip the remaining water from the container in her hand. 'Heat or chill, winds or the rain, these are only exiguous elements and have limited role to play in the manner we bhikshuks lead our lives. Each day we travel from the city to distant villages and towns seeking alms for our sustenance and the monastery's upkeep,' he said.

'But why would you do that? You are all young and have a sizeable part of your lives ahead of you. Why then would you, of your own will, wish to lead the life of an ascetic? You can get married, have children and lead a peaceful and content life with your families. Why would you want to wander about leaving your hunger and thirst at the mercy of others?' Amrapali could not control herself from voicing her astonishment.

She had attended one of the Shakya Muni's sermons, at Pushp's behest, sitting by her beloved's side, on a day that was to become the turning point of her life—a day that seemed so far back in time and yet so recent. That day she had found herself concurring with the sage and his teachings. But as destiny began to reveal its cruel designs, claiming her most prized possessions one after the other, she had found her views taking an entirely divergent track.

All her life she had strived hard to be congenial and considerate towards others, one of the earliest teachings of her Baba that she recalled even today, yet fate had left her to be used and abused by complete strangers. If the notion of natural justice was absolute, why had it failed to make even a passing appearance in her world?

She had seen power and wealth accomplish strange feats— from earning loyalties of people to making them trade their souls—she had witnessed the entire spectrum of humanity, from its grimiest underbelly to the radiant crest, prostrating themselves in the aisles of authority. She firmly believed that the ultimate path to salvation lay not in renunciation but in accession and it was this belief that had prompted her to question the monk.

'I was once married, my lady, to a beautiful young girl and we had just the sort of life you mentioned. But for how long could that possibly have lasted? The happiness derived from worldly associations is merely transient. It is the deeper meaning of life and eternal bliss that we bhikshuks seek,' he replied sympathetically.

'I don't understand this. Don't you crave the companionship and love of your wife any longer? And even if you don't, have you ever thought of the endurance you have subjected her to by walking out on her?' she argued.

'I don't crave her love, as I know I am still the subject of it. The very essence of marriage is in understanding and respecting each other's beliefs and privacy and in doing so my wife has lived her part. Of course my joining the order of monks did result in sizeable sorrow and grief for my family initially, but that is a small price to pay for the more precious spiritual treasures they stand to gain by way of my tryst—their share of the spiritual treasures I am able to unearth. As for the other bodily longings, it is in those that we sow the seeds of misery and pain. Riddance from worldly desires is indeed one of the most significant gifts that the Buddha has blessed us sentient beings with,' he said, closing his eyes in reverence upon naming his teacher.

'And just in the quest of some eternal truth, some spiritual treasures that one can neither see nor feel, you are prepared to forego all the beautiful things that life has to offer to you today? Look around you, the world is brimming with opportunities that you are letting go of,' Amrapali was persistent. Her beliefs, gathered through years of her own sorrows and sufferings, were not so brittle that she could give in to the monk's abstract reasoning.

The monk too had realized the futility of continuing with the debate. It was interminable. 'I understand your appreciation for all the beauty that surrounds us, but it is only a sprinkle on the shroud of misery and suffering that plagues mankind. Today I am unable to convince you with my words, but a day will come when my words will not sound so hollow and your concerns too will stand addressed. It is then, with the blessings of the Buddha, that I shall visit you next,' he said, with the same composure that he had embarked upon the discussion.

'Just one little request,' he continued, pausing to dig out something from his sling bag. It was a ripe mango fruit. 'Here, can you please keep this mango in your safe custody? I shall collect it when we meet again,' he said, handing the fruit to Amrapali.

Amused, she looked at the fruit, rolled it in her hands and satisfied that it was just what the bhikshuk had said—a common mango fruit—she handed it over to Prabha. 'Be with Buddha,' Anand said, raising his hand in blessings before retreating towards the other waiting monks. Confused, dazed, but no longer thirsty, the Nagarvadhu signalled to Ballabh and the contingent was once again on its way to the Old Palace of Vaishali.

3

'He shall be here any moment now. Please be patient,' the old man said. He was tense. The three men flanking him, each about a couple of decades younger than him, were already exhibiting signs of mounting impatience. While two of them remained glued to their seats, twitching their feet ardently, the third had risen and was now anxiously pacing across the breadth of the dung smeared floor.

It was a small hut, a square plot of cleared land enclosed within a frail thatched-roof structure made of bamboo sticks, straws and dried grass. There were no signs to indicate whether it was actually being lived in; no utensils, no garments, not even beddings. The only furnishings consisted of six wooden stools, three of which were presently vacant, and two wall-mounted torch holders sans any torches. There was a distinct smell in the air, perhaps emanating from the dung-paste coating on the floor which still looked moist in certain patches.

'The sun is setting, it is getting dark,' the man, who had been walking for about half a ghati now, paused to address the elder one. 'If we leave this place after sundown, the chances of somebody spotting us, a patrolling unit or a wandering traveller, will increase manifold. We can reconvene on another…'

His voice dissolved mid-sentence amid the sudden clatter of horses' hooves that was growing louder and louder. A bunch of riders appeared to be approaching the hut. Immediately all eyes darted towards the entrance and while the elderly man stepped forward to greet the visitors, others stood up in rapt, nervous attention. The visitors, or at least one among them, had to be of such towering stature that the occupants of the room had shed their mental preoccupations to fixedly await his ingression.

They were three, clad in simple everyday clothes—dhoti and kurta in paling shades of white, topped with bright, bulky turbans—hardly conspicuous in their appearance. In nearly rhythmic leaps they disembarked from their mounts, and while one of them seized the halters and proceeded to tether the horses, the other two marched towards the hut.

'Pranam, Maharaj,' the old man greeted the man in the orange turban as he released the section of the garment used to cover the lower half of his face from behind his ears. The visitor was tall and stout with a contrastingly genial, almost boyish, countenance. He reciprocated with a nod, briskly stepping inside the room and heading towards the centre where the others stood motionlessly.

'*Maharaj ki jai ho*,' the man who, barely a few palas back, was voicing his concerns about the delay was now bending as low in obeisance as his spine would permit. The other two were quick to follow suit.

'I hope you were not greatly inconvenienced due to the delay?' the intruder courteously enquired once the three had regained their natural postures. 'Not at all, Maharaj,' the older man, who had stepped up to within a few steps of the visitor, was quick to respond.

'It is only in your allegiance that I see my dreams taking concrete shape and the day, one of the most momentous ones in the history of Aryavart, is no longer distant. Soon, the kingdom of Vaishali shall become a jewel in the crown of the Magadh Empire and you shall be justly rewarded for your contributions towards it. But first it is imperative that for the one last time we understand our respective roles and clear any doubts that might still be lingering in our minds,' the visitor, Bimbisara, the King of Magadh, spoke.

Facing him were Bhadresh and Amanverma, two distinguished members of the Vajji council and Ramdev, a commander from the Vajji army. Narsinh Dev, the elderly prime minister of Magadh was the one who had been waiting with them for Bimbisara's arrival. The quorum was extraordinary and even surprising, but more astonishing was the venue for the meeting—a hastily erected cabin in the scantily populated section of Vaishali where the Mahavana brushed the city's periphery.

A ruler of Bimbisara's stature could seldom be seen without his usual detachment of royal guards even in Rajgriha, let alone in the heart of enemy territory. The congression certainly warranted the shroud of secrecy it was being held under and perhaps this explained Amanverma's discomfort due to the unexpected delay in proceedings. While Bimbisara ran a risk on his life upon identification, the others too could easily find themselves heading for the gallows if their rendezvous with him was even remotely established.

The precariousness of their state was only heightened since they, given their high-ranking positions in the governance hierarchy of Vaishali, were highly prone to identification by the common residents of the city, much unlike their esteemed visitor. A noble or a prominent official from the Vajji army, riding alone, minus even the most basic adornments, from a secluded section of the city was bound to arouse curiosity—an avoidable eventuality, to say the least.

'Bhadresh, you need to ensure that Senapati Chetak assigns Ramdev's unit to man the three gates of Vaishali on the fourth night from today. This is clearly the trickiest part of the mission since Chetak's loyalty to Vaishali and King Yudhveer is beyond any doubt. If you say or do anything to arouse his suspicion, the outcome might be catastrophic,' the King continued, his words ringing in alarm.

This was for the last time before the invasion of Vaishali that Bimbisara was addressing this particular group and he knew how crucial it was for his allies to be aware of the dangers they faced. He knew that the three were neck deep in the plan and there was no chance that they could back out now, out of fear, panic or otherwise. So, there was certainly no harm in allowing his words to instill some fear in their minds. If the dread managed to add even an iota of caution to the manner they approached their assigned tasks, the ploy would have served its purpose.

'I am well aware of the challenges, Maharaj, but I have worked out a fool-proof strategy to ensure that the Senapati does just what we want him to do. Of the six units currently deployed for internal security of the city, two are in-charge of the morning and night shifts for this week. I have made arrangements to ensure that two of the remaining commanders are compelled to pull out from their duties by the end of this week,' he said, pausing briefly to allow a brief smirk to emerge on his lips.

'Due to personal exigencies of course!' Once again he paused, fleetingly scanning his audience before continuing. 'So Ramdev's unit will automatically be summoned to relievé the present on-duty units along with the only other available one. All that will then be left for him to do is to volunteer for the night shift and I don't see why Chetak will not heed to the request.'

'Excellent!' Bimbisara acknowledged. 'Ramdev, upon receiving my signal, you need to open the southern gates and allow our troops to enter the city. Amanverma, you shall continue to provide us with tactical and ground support as you have been doing thus far. Over the next couple of days, selected members from our elite commando force shall seek refuge in your Khanda.

They will be guised as common traders and you need to ensure that your border guards don't pry much into the merchandise they would have in their possession.'

'But Maharaj, my Khanda is situated beyond the eastern gates of the city. If the Magadh army will be entering Vaishali from the southern gate, why is there a need to position additional commandos in my territory?' Amanverma quizzed.

Narsinh Dev noticed a transient shade of annoyance emerge on the King's visage and vanish as quickly as it had appeared. The King, a monarch, was not accustomed to the questioning ways of the Vajji Confederacy, an established democracy. 'The Vajji Rajas would need to learn a thing or two about the Magadhan ways, and very quickly,' the elderly prime minister mused.

When Bimbisara eventually spoke, his voice was as cordial as it had been earlier. 'They will be stationed there just in case the need to open another front for battle arises. In case our primary plan fails and we are not able to take the city from within, we need to have an alternative in hand. Once the war begins, it will become increasingly difficult for us to steer past the fortifications of Vaishali and send our troops to the interiors of the kingdom. The eastern gate is especially crucial since that is where the reinforcements from other Khandas will be reaching the city, but don't worry, if all goes as per plan, the need to actuate these commandos shall never arise,' he patiently clarified.

With a slight nod of the head Amanverma affirmed his comprehension. Bimbisara surveyed the other two, looking for any concerns that remained to be addressed and mentally evaluating the strength of his allies' resolve.

Satisfied at not having come across shreds of indecision, panic or frailty, he continued, 'So gentlemen, if there is nothing that you wish to add, we must conclude this meeting and disperse at once. Needless to say that the next few days will be particularly trying, but if we remain focussed, nothing can stand between victory and us. You in particular, the craftsmen to have shaped this triumph, will be amply rewarded with what has been promised and more. So go my friends; go and envision the enormous fortunes that shall soon come knocking on your doors and cherish the promise of an ecstatic existence that it shall usher along. Go and dream of the leap that your lives are about to take, for when you open your eyes you would have risen to a stature that presently remains beyond the realms of your wildest imagination.'

Bimbisara once again paused, this time to scrutinize the romantic smiles appearing on the faces of his listeners, before folding his hands and making a hasty retreat from the scene.

It was a pleasant morning with silver-lined clouds floating on the horizon, shielding the terrain from the summer sun's fury. The rain gods, it seemed had dilatorily emerged from their slumber and decided to rescue the humble subjects from their fiery plight. Eager anticipation was all pervasive—in the dry cracks that had emerged to perforate the earth's crust, in the melodious carousal of birds and in the trees swaying to the moisture-laden breeze.

It was this staging of nature that Amrapali was absorbed in, nestled in the balcony adjoining her room that jutted into the backyard of the Old Palace. The gardens of the palace had been the stage where some of her most treasured memories had been enacted in the past—a distant one, another lifetime almost—and she could see a screen of mist permeating from the clouds to assume forms from the bygone era. Of Pushp, of the longing in his eyes as he watched her dance to the silent tunes of nature and of the life she had begun to conjure up in the preserve of her fantasies.

The Old Palace, desolate then, but for a solitary caretaker, was where her love had truly blossomed. It was where the seeds of a cursed story, one that was destined to remain incomplete, were first sown. This was where she had spent numerous afternoons dancing for Pushp and when tired, resting her head in his lap and staring into his deep-set eyes as he lovingly stroked her hair.

Though she was now the rightful owner of the palace and with it the gardens, she often mused on whether the decision had been prudent. She was not sure if her proximity to the scene would ever permit her to escape from pangs of reminiscences and the tearing pain that accompanied them, but she also knew that there was nowhere else for her to go. If these moments—the times when she could run away from her wretched existence of today to the comforting embrace of her past—were to be snatched away from her, the world would be left with little to interest her.

'Pali… Pali…' she was jolted back from her reverie by Prabha. Still tugging on to Amrapali's arm, she continued, 'Again you are lost in your dreams! I tell you, you need to stop getting out onto the balcony…or the garden…or…oh, forget it; you are beyond repair now. Anyway there is someone at the door. The poor fellow has been knocking incessantly.'

Just then there was another measured knock on the door of her room. 'Come on in,' Amrapali responded, raising her voice for the benefit of the caller.

'Pranam, Devi,' a guard entered, bending in reverence to greet the Nagarvadhu. 'A gentleman has come to see you. He is waiting in the audience parlour and his name, he says, is Bindusen.'

The words had a magical effect on her. As soon as she heard the name, a flicker of joy emerged on her face, expanding to a full-blown smile, twisting the corners of her mouth slightly. With a slight nod of the head she dismissed the guard and made a dash for the far side of the room where a shiny wall-mounted metal disc was waiting to greet her.

Bindusen, knowing or unknowingly, had been sneaking into her thoughts at a disquieting frequency of late. She had often found herself replaying conversations from their past meetings in her mind and on most days she woke up with the hope that he would surprise her with a sudden visit as he had always done. And today, when Bindusen was waiting to see her, much to her dismay, she found herself grappling with a childlike nervous anxiety.

She also felt a twinge of guilt at how Bindusen's arrival had plucked her from the world of her dreams, a world which to her was more real than the one she inhabited. It was a strange feeling, as though her sudden excitement was casting a shadow on the piousness of her love for Pushp.

She brushed these thoughts aside, she loved Pushp and she would continue to do so till time immemorial. The excitement and anxiety were merely results of her deficient mortal existence, a state that Pushp had long abandoned and she was left to put up with. Moreover if she found reprieve, an escape, even some joy out of something, shouldn't she permit herself the slight indulgence? Wouldn't Pushp have wanted the same for her— peace and happiness—till such time that they remained apart?

As Amrapali hurriedly changed into the turquoise dhoti, her current favourite, and began fidgeting with her jewellery box, pulling out an ornament, placing it on her neck or forehead and unceremoniously dropping it back after viewing her reflection in the polished metal mirror, Prabha remained perched on the bed observing her with a tender smile. She could hear the thundering roar of happy tides that were charging towards Amrapali and she found herself unable to contain the little droplets of joy from trickling down her cheeks.

'Here, try these,' dabbing her eyes with her dupatta, she came to her friend's rescue and held a necklace she had picked up from the jewellery box against Amrapali's chest. With a sheepish grin

Amrapali accepted the ornament and put it around her neck. This time she didn't bother to check her reflection in the mirror. As Prabha knotted the threads of the necklace for her, Amrapali missed taking note of the volley of emotions wrestling within her friend's moist eyes.

Satisfied with her appearance, Amrapali scampered off to greet her visitor, failing to invite Prabha along. Their relationship did not provide room for trivial formalities and Prabha knew that she could have tagged along if she so wished. But not wanting to become a pricking thorn amidst the velvety amalgam of aching hearts, she had preferred to stay back. Lost in her thoughts she was treading towards her own room when another guard materialized before her.

'*Devi Prabha ki jai ho,*' he greeted. 'There is another visitor who wishes an audience with Devi Amrapali. But since the Devi is in the Swapna Kakshika, I thought I will check with you on whether we should disturb her.'

'Amrapali has gone to the Swapna Kakshika?' she muttered, more of a musing than a question. The guard nevertheless nodded his head in the affirmative, perplexed over the wily smile that had suddenly contorted her lips.

'Who did you say has come?'

'Some trader, he says his name is Suraj Mal and that he is here to return Devi Amrapali's horses,' the guard replied. Instantly an image swept past her eyes—the image of a proud, well-built, hazel-eyed, handsome, young man.

'No, don't disturb Pali right now. Have the visitor seated in the audience parlour and I shall be there to see him shortly,' she said after a thoughtful pause.

'Return the horses? But how did he ever manage to get them out of the Raja's clutches?' she thought as she approached her room. Allowing enough time for the visitor to settle, she proceeded towards the parlour to meet him.

Suraj Mal was a very different sight from the time she had last met him, and a much improved one at that. He was wearing a white dhoti and a pale tunic, open at the chest and held in its place by chords tied in front of his stomach. The garment did well to accentuate his shapely torso. He was an attractive man, much more alluring than what she remembered him to be.

As she approached him, she saw his hazel-eyes turn towards her and ignite with a flicker of recognition. *'Devi Prabha ko Suraj ka pranam,'* he greeted her, getting up from his seat and folding his hands. There was an odd mix of courtesy and arrogance in the greeting, especially the manner in which he had referred to his own self in third person. Prabha could not help but appreciate his approach as she folded her own hands in response.

'Your visit comes as a pleasant surprise. I hope Raja Udit has not been troubling you again?' she said with a smile.

'Well, with the arrangement he had dimwittedly consented to, he wasn't really left with much to trouble us with. Devi Amrapali ensured that justice was delivered in its true spirit, and though I can never repay her kindness, I thought I must definitely pay her a visit. And of course, I needed to return the two horses that she had given to the Raja.'

Prabha was even more perplexed now. Of what she recalled of the arrangement with the Raja, he was to be given two horses from the Nagarvadhu's stables and in turn he had to pay Suraj Mal and his father an agreed quantity of potatoes. 'For their sustenance,' Amrapali has said, while proposing the payment terms. Even back then Prabha had felt that potatoes were a strange medium for repayment and that the deal was not a very clever one to have been struck. But she had refrained from mentioning her reservations since their immediate objective of getting Suraj Mal released had been met and it wasn't particularly material whether the Raja was going to pay them in terms of gold mohurs or potatoes. She was still unable to fathom as to how the deal had ensured the delivery of justice.

'But what made the Raja decide to return the horses?' she asked.

'Oh, he could not afford the potatoes that he had agreed to pay and after about ten days of your visit, he came to us, pleading for the agreement to be nullified. He not only returned the two extra horses but also paid the two hundred mohurs he owed us,' he replied.

'Now you are teasing me!' she exclaimed, purposely adding a tinge of annoyance to her tone. 'Why would a Raja, a wealthy one at that, not be able to afford a paltry payout of potatoes?'

Suraj smiled at her naïvety, allowing her to build on her feigned infuriation before unravelling the trap hidden beneath the seemingly innocuous arrangement that Raja Udit and of course Prabha had failed to detect. 'The arrangement required him to pay us potatoes for each nail in the horseshoes of the two horses, forty-eight of them in all, at a nail a day. The repayment would have lasted over a period of forty-eight days, and beginning with one potato for the first day, the number of potatoes would continue to have doubled with each passing day,' he explained with the patience of a Guru introducing his pupils to complex astronomical patterns.

Prabha listened absorbedly, oscillating between the desire to unravel the mystery behind Raja Udit's sudden change of heart and a sinewy yearning to keep looking at and listening to Suraj. The man's conduct had been absorbing even while he was in captivity, and now, unshackled and liberated, his persona appeared to be dragging her towards him. And like a feeble nail drawn by a powerful magnet, she felt powerless in front of her own surging emotions.

His eyes, with every careless blink, appeared to be inviting her into their alluring depths and a part of her was eager, almost desperate, to concede. It was a strange feeling, not like anything she had ever experienced, and she was struggling to resist the temptation to allow it to overpower her senses.

'Well, by the tenth day he had already paid us 1,023 or about 180 sers of potatoes and on the eleventh day he owed us 1,024 more. It was perhaps then that he would have engaged in some serious calculations, only to realize that to live up to his side of the bargain he would need to shell out approximately four hundred kharab sers of potatoes in all—a quantity he couldn't possibly procure even by selling his entire Khanda multiple times over. The beauty of the Devi's proposal was that it appeared so simple and straightforward that he would not in his wildest dream have anticipated this. Oh, how I would have loved to see his expressions when he finally became aware of the crisis he had landed himself in.'

It took a little more explaining for her to come to terms with the magical web of numbers her friend had woven to entrap the Raja and he had not only taken the bait, but entangled himself to a point of no return. She felt her heart swell with pride at Amrapali's ingenuity and gumption.

'And since the agreement had been validated by the Viniccaya Mahamatta, he didn't even have the option of refuting it. Brilliant!' she said. 'Great, so you got not only your money back, but also the sweet taste of revenge?'

'Yes, and it was all thanks to the Nagarvadhu's intervention. Else I don't know how we would have ever emerged from the crisis. Perhaps I would have grown old within the confines of the Raja's prison with mosquitoes and flies as the only form of company,' he replied with a grin.

'Well, I am sure the poor mosquitoes are missing your company already,' she said in a placidly playful tone.

She was enjoying her tête-à-tête with Suraj Mal. It had been long, longer than the years her memory could trace, that she had indulged in such casual, unrestrained and artless banter with a man. With each passing moment she felt the chord tugging her towards him strengthening and her own control over her senses diminishing.

It wasn't love, she was certain, at least not as yet. She had loved her parents and she loved her friend Amrapali. She knew what the emotion felt like and this certainly was not it. What she was experiencing now was more basic, a raw and untamed spurt of emotion oozing from her heart to swathe her absolute being.

'I don't know about the mosquitoes, but I am not missing them for sure. And if I was still holed up with them, keeping them company, wouldn't I be deprived of the pleasure of sitting here in your charming presence?' he said.

Prabha felt that his words, though innocuous, were sprinkled with flirtatious beads. Blushing slightly and somewhat baffled by her own reaction, she replied, 'Well, I am overwhelmed and also glad that you prefer my company over that of the mosquitoes.'

The two continued to chit-chat like long lost friends, in the process discovering more about each other, losing all sense of time and occasion. Suraj was the first to draw them back to reality.

'Devi Amrapali seems to be tied up with something compelling. I guess I will have to depart without her darshan or blessings,' he said, looking questioningly into Prabha's eyes. As she realized that their meeting was bound by the winding clasp of time and sooner or later Suraj would have to return to where he came from, Prabha felt a sudden weightiness within, as though she had swallowed maunds of heavy metal balls.

She didn't want their conversation to end. She didn't want him to leave. But once again, restraining her emotions, she said, 'Yes, it might not be possible for you to meet her today. But now that you have returned the horses, it doesn't mean that you are not welcome to visit the palace. You can come and see her anytime that you wish to.'

'Really? And am I also welcome if it is not the Devi, but you that I wish to see?' For a split second her eyes locked with his and in that moment she gauged that he meant every word he had said. But even before she could think of an apt response, he had averted his gaze and was back to being his jovial and flippant self. 'I know, I know, I have troubled you enough already and the last thing you would want is to see me anytime soon,' he added.

'No, no, you are most welcome to visit me too,' she was quick to refute. The urgency in her tone was palpable and she found herself smiling at the futility of her reaction. And soon, without a further word being spoken between them, the two were laughing out aloud—an unrestrained and capricious laughter, one originating from somewhere deep within their hearts.

As Suraj Mal rode out of the palace gates, lifting his face to soak in the raindrops dripping down his face, Prabha stood waving to him and silently praying for him to return soon. The emotions she was now grappling with were completely alien to her and she couldn't decide on what to do with them—whether to grimace with the pain of parting with Suraj or to beam with the glimmer of anticipation that he had left behind.

It was in this confused state that she headed back towards her chamber. Amrapali had still not emerged from the Swapna Kakshika.

The sun was setting, retiring for the night when Amrapali finally emerged from the Swapna Kakshika. There was a definite spring to her strides and she bore the look of an urchin after a hearty meal, pleased and satiated. As she passed Prabha's chamber, she paused briefly, in two minds on whether or not to share the happenings of the day with her friend.

Eventually she would. There was nothing that remained concealed between the two, but she was not sure if she was prepared for the narration just as yet. First she herself needed to make sense of the developments and only then could she think of articulating it into words. Her pulse was racing faster than a herd of purebred horses and her heart was thumping like a series of earthquakes rummaging the inside of her chest.

Deciding in favour of temporary seclusion, she rushed to her room and slumped down on the bed. Her head flanked by two satin-laced pillows, she closed herself to the outside world and began to recapitulate the sequence of events from the time she had gone to the parlour to welcome Bindusen.

He had looked his usual self—poised, calm and suave—and greeted her with his characteristic magnetic smile. She was mildly annoyed at not finding even a trace of desperation or anxiety, oodles of which she had been containing within herself since she had learnt of his arrival, in her guest's deportment. It seemed as though he was clueless about the agonizing wait she had endured or the eagerness with which she had been looking forward to his visit. He seemed to be on a regular social stopover, unmindful of the undercurrents of longing and fondness that had begun to bind them together, at least as far as Amrapali was concerned.

'Welcome Bindusen Ji,' she said, attempting to sound as nonchalant and unperturbed as she could. 'I thought it would be on one of my performance nights that I would get to see you next. This comes as a pleasant surprise.'

'My apologies, Devi, for despite my deep-felt desire to witness your public performance I haven't yet had the good fortune to do so. Business has been extremely demanding and I haven't been to Vaishali in a while. This time too I am here only for a brief period and hence I thought of paying you a visit today,' he replied. There was a certain glint in his eyes as he addressed Amrapali, but his posture remained passive and discreet.

With an understanding nod, Amrapali led him to the Swapna Kakshika—the chamber of dreams—oblivious to the euphoric event that was to unfold within its closed doors.

They chit-chatted for a while, talking about the weather, Bindusen's business, the Nagarvadhu's dance performance from the last full moon night and other matters before Amrapali dwelt upon a thought that had occurred to her during one of her mindless reveries. 'Your work takes you around the world and I assume you would be faring well enough too. But don't you ever feel the need to set anchor and settle down? I mean, get married, have babies and lead a normal life?'

It was a simple question, artlessly posed, but the effect it had on Bindusen was profound. His expressions suddenly turned sombre and he slipped into a contemplative silence. Amrapali persisted, allowing the silence to prevail, intently staring into his brooding eyes until he gave in and decided to talk. His tone was measured and words appeared to be originating from some distant source.

'Not all men are sanctified with the luxury of a normal life. Normalcy is purely a matter of perceptions. What appears normal to some might seem bizarre to others and vice versa. But I do agree that men need to strike the right balance between their ambitions and the callings of their heart. The heart is much too vital an organ to be overlooked,' he said, drifting from abstraction towards reality. 'And it is but my heart's doing that finds me sitting here, alongside you,' he said, locking his gaze with hers.

She could feel his eyes boring into her, discharging a wave of intense heat within her that threatened to consume not only her body but also her mind. This unexpected assault of the senses left her baffled and gasping and as he continued to delve into her eyes, she knew that she was losing herself to the intensity of the moment and there was little she could do to prevent the inevitable. Instinctively, she shut her eyes and her voluptuous lips broke into a welcoming pout.

The moment of indecision had passed, the barriers of containment had been breached and the conclusion had been drawn. The wait of barely a few pals, which seemed like eternity to Amrapali, ended when she felt Bindusen's breath ricochet against her own. His lips, burning with desire, hungrily descended on hers and his hands began searching her with a sense of desperate urgency.

Her hair, the loosely pinned bun over her head, was now cast adrift and flailing delicately with each passionate shuffle, and the fine, teal-coloured strap of her blouse rested precariously on her smooth, ivory shoulders, threatening to fall at the slightest cue. Bindusen whispered something incoherent and she felt his smooth lips gently brushing past the sinewy lines of her neck. His breath was hot, like small puffs of fire on her skin, and she found herself gasping each time his skin connected with hers. And just then, a loud thunderous roar startled them, making Amrapali tighten her embrace around Bindusen.

The clouds on the horizon had surrendered with the loud rumble and droplets of rain were rushing down to crash against the first surface they found. Strong winds were whipping the trees outside and thumping against any other object that attempted resisting their unrestrained rush. The collective intonation of nature's emissaries sounded like a musical crescendo stretched to eternity. It was as though the gods had decided to shower their blessings on the mortal union that was being consummated within the walls of the Swapna Kakshika.

4

His forehead was creased and hands clasped tightly behind his back as he paced up and down the length of his chamber. Intermittently he would sneak a glance at the heavy sheesham door, as though he were anxiously waiting for an important visitor to step through. Senapati Chetak was known to be an astute strategist, sometimes rash and impulsive, but an extolled warrior nevertheless. It was seldom that he engaged in such deep considerations as he now appeared to be, and when he did so, it expectedly had to involve a matter of utmost importance and exigency.

It was only yesterday that the messenger had arrived. Though his request was out of the ordinary and the parchment he carried, unmarked, bearing not even the sender's insignia, there was something within the words of the letter that had made him cede.

'Greetings to Senapati Chetak from Vihalla Kumar, the Rajkumar of Magadh,' the letter began. The name of the correspondent was enough to draw his complete attention.

A few paragraphs of praises followed, for Vaishali, its rulers and particularly for the Senapati's valour and gallantry. Chetak was not impressed and hurried through the words, keen to discover the underlying purpose of the message.

'I have some vital piece of information for you, news that can only be shared in person and is bound to have a considerable bearing on the future of Vaishali. It is crucial that I see you by the second pehar of tomorrow, and the reason for this urgency I will only be in a position to explain when we meet. Hence, I request you to inform the messenger of a convenient time tomorrow when I can pay you a visit.' Chetak paused to look at the messenger. The man—a slender and petite youth, hardly the image of a servant to be entrusted with a message as crucial as it was claimed to be—stood expressionless with his eyes affixed to the floor.

'Of course, given the nature and purpose of my visit, it is important that due secrecy be preserved and that this communication remains strictly between your kind self and me. At the appointed hour I shall reach your palace directly, and since this is not a state visit I would urge you to refrain from any kind of welcome that could draw suspicious attention,' he read on. After a few more lines of general courtesy, the letter was signed by its purported dispatcher.

Chetak flipped the letter in his hand to check if there were any marks on its rear that could help establish its source. He found none.

'How do I know that it is indeed Rajkumar Vihalla Kumar who has sent you? Let alone the royal seal of Magadh, this letter contains not even a single identification mark. It could have been penned down by just about anyone,' he said, eyeing the messenger suspiciously. In the past he had used this glare to break some of the most hardened spies he had come across, watching them belt out secrets concealed in remotest compartments of their brains without a tinge of vacillation. A menacing glower by the Senapati, it was said, was more trying than a hundred whip-strikes on one's posterior. But today his stare appeared to be wavering, as though it was bouncing off a glass sheet.

'A day's wait and you will know that it was indeed the Rajkumar who has penned this message,' the young man, placid and composed, stated matter-of-factly.

The Senapati felt a flashing urge to strangulate the arrogant young man with his bare hands, a thought he brushed off in due regard to the immunity he enjoyed in his capacity of a messenger. The Senapati didn't instantly take to the man, in fact his audacity and nonchalance were unnerving, but what he had just said did make some sense.

The Rajkumar had offered to pay a visit rather than invite him over, so it couldn't be a ploy by one of his many enemies to take him down. It would be a ludicrous idea for them to even contemplate assaulting him in his own backyard. By granting the man an audience there was nothing he stood to lose and, as the messenger had said, in just a days' time all curiosity that the letter had generated would be settled.

'And yes, not to forget the subtle traces of impudence in the language of the letter. It could very well have been written by one of those dynastic brats, born with a silver spoon in his mouth,' he thought before consenting to meet the Rajkumar. Now that the designated time for the meeting had arrived, he found himself anxiously waiting for his visitor.

When he finally heard a knock on the door, he scurried towards his chair and once comfortably seated, yelled out to the guards to let the visitors in. The door opened and almost simultaneously two frail figures stepped in. Chetak recognized the first, he was the same messenger who had paid him a visit the preceding day, but it was the man accompanying him who immediately commanded his interest.

Skinny, as though a sheet of skin had been tightly wrapped around a structure of bones, and with hollow, bloodshot eyes, he looked more a starving, landless peasant than a man of royal ancestry. It was through his ostentatious clothes and adornments that he was attempting to make up for his beguiling appearance. A heavily embroided silk tunic hung on his torso with matching brocaded padukas on his feet. A pair of long earrings, embedded with precious stones, was dangling from his ears and the countless chains and lockets around his neck were entangled with each other, as though struggling to establish their preciousness over the other.

Chetak was left with little doubt that the man he was facing was indeed the Rajkumar of Magadh. 'None but a spoilt Prince from a dynastic monarchy like Magadh could bear to be seen in public dressed like that. And didn't he want to keep this meeting discreet? I bet half of Vaishali is talking about the strangely attired man heading towards my palace,' he thought, stepping forward to welcome the Rajkumar. It was only in the course of their discussions that the Senapati would learn that his visitor had used a palanquin for commuting, and also that his claim about the matter he wished to discuss being a grave one wasn't entirely unfounded.

'So, Rajkumar, what was the vital piece of information you wished to share with me?' he shot out as soon as they were seated. He had deliberately chosen to ignore Vihalla Kumar's companion. He was yet to take a liking to the man.

'It is a matter that concerns the security of Vaishali and who better to discuss it with than you,' the Rajkumar began, momentarily locking his eyes with that of his host. Noticing early traces of impatience in Chetak's eyes, he decided to omit the opening segment of his well-rehearsed speech, liberally laden with accolades for the Senapati, and come straight to the point.

'On the second night from today, the city of Vaishali will be under attack…and as I see it, I don't think your existing defence mechanism will be adequate to ward off the offensive and prevent the city from being taken,' he said.

'Under attack! Who is going to attack us? And how do you know about it?' Though the Senapati had complete faith in the multilayered defence system of Vaishali that he had personally set-up, the revelation had left him startled. 'And what makes you think that our defences will not be able to ward off the threat?' he added as an afterthought.

'The plot has been hatched within the walls of the Rajgriha Palace and it is the Magadh army that will launch the offensive. I know about it since I overheard a conversation to that effect between my father, King Bimbisara and Narsinh Dev, our prime minister. And I say that your defences will prove inadequate since the plot is to siege Vaishali from within, an eventuality I assume even you wouldn't have accounted for,' Vihalla Kumar replied. His words were measured, and there was an unmistakable resonance of truth to them.

'How would they ever get into the city to siege it from within? Moreover, if the conspiracy has been hatched by your own people, why are you here to warn us?'

'Senapati Ji, if I were in your place, I would be more concerned about the information I bring to you rather than my underlying motives. Let's just say that I have some personal agenda which does not provide for Vaishali being annexed, at least not just as yet. And if you are thinking that I am here to strike a deal and that I would want something in return for this information, you are mistaken. Just consider this a gesture from a friend, a well-wisher, and use the little time you have to strengthen your defences,' he said, smiling for the first time since having entered the room, the partly decaying and thoroughly stained teeth adding to his awfulness.

'And how do they intend to get their soldiers past the city gates?' Chetak enquired once again. There was concern in his voice and his mind was racing ahead, mentally evaluating the actions he could take to secure the boundaries of Vaishali given the constraint of time.

'Now, this is where I am constrained by the limited information I possess. In the conversation I overheard, though my father spoke about our forces entering the city unobstructed through one of its gates, he did not elaborate much on which of the three gates he was referring to or how the clear passage was to be made available to them,' he said, pausing briefly to make sure his host understood his limitations.

'But there has to be an insider, someone who wields enough authority to order opening of at least one of the city gates without being questioned, who is hand in glove with my father. If it means anything to you, there was a name that my father took a couple of times during the dialogue—Amanverma!'

'Raja Amanverma,' the Senapati repeated, his eyes simmering with rage. He got up abruptly, not bothering to engage in trivial expressions of gratitude, due indication for his visitors that the meeting was over. The Rajkumar and his companion followed suit, getting up and folding their hands. 'Pranam Senapati,' Vihalla Kumar said, attempting to draw Chetak from the contemplative daze he appeared to have slipped into, and take his leave.

Chetak folded his own hands in return and walked his guests out of the room to their waiting palanquin. 'I don't know your motivation behind making the effort to warn us against this imminent strike, but the populace of Vaishali, myself included, shall remain ever indebted to you for this gesture. Through this act of yours, you have earned yourself a loyal ally in the kingdom of Vaishali for the time that you occupy the throne of Magadh, a day I pray comes soon,' were the Senapati's parting words to the Rajkumar before he rushed back to his palace, screaming out to the guards to urgently summon his most trusted lieutenants.

Within a matter of ghatis the entire administrative and military machinery of Vaishali was lubricated and churning. The Senapati had informed the King, Maharaja Yudhveer, of the recent developments and with his consent had divided the crucial and more urgent tasks among his trusted aides. Each aide was assigned specific responsibilities with clearly outlined deliverables, without being made privy to the larger purpose they were cumulatively working towards.

Chetak knew that the enemy had managed to penetrate deep within their governance structure and till such time that they were able to identify and weed out all coconspirators from amidst them, it was crucial that any available information was percolated only on a need-to-know basis. It had thus been agreed between the Maharaja and him that details of the looming threat would be shared with none, at least for the time being. Creating ripples of undue anxiety among the ranks was best avoidable for now.

While one Vajji commander was instantly dispatched with clear instructions to bring in Raja Amanverma, exercising utmost discretion and urgency in the process, another was assigned the task of securing all three gates of the city, ensuring that the privileges of entry and exit were limited to only those who could satisfactorily establish their credentials and purpose. Members of Vaishali's secret service were called upon to deploy their operatives at every point of vantage and the slightest anomaly or deviation from the usual was to be reported to the Senapati at once.

Messengers, bearing scrolls personally signed by King Yudhveer, were sent to rulers of the kingdom's prominent Khandas. These scrolls carried specific instructions on the number of foot soldiers, riders and archers the Rajas were immediately required to dispatch for Vaishali. They were also told to stock up their granaries, scale up the border-vigil and ready themselves and their frontiers for any unforeseen eventuality in the very near future. Once again, the scrolls refrained from revealing much, but the solemnity of the words scribed on them compelled the recipients to treat them with utmost caution and sincerity.

Hope transforms into delight when expectations are realized ahead of their time. Prabha too was delighted—ecstatic even—as she sat alongside Amrapali watching Suraj Mal bow down to pay his respects to the Nagarvadhu. It was only the previous evening that she had seen him ride away from the palace. His mount, like a savage tyrant, fleeing away with a part of her, leaving her expurgated and miserable.

She had spent whatever remained of the day and a better part of the night replaying, over and over again, fragments of their conversation in her mind, smiling at nothing in particular or bursting into abrupt chuckles. She tried to get him off her mind, but the harder she tried, the deeper she found herself drifting away in his thoughts. A part of her longed to see him again, there and then, and the uncertainty shrouding the fulfillment of this longing left her feeling miserable.

In the morning, her head throbbing due to exhaustion and lack of sleep, she headed to Amrapali's chamber meaning to vent her aching emotions. 'You remember Suraj Mal, the trader whom we had freed from Raja Udit's captivity? He was here yesterday… to return the two horses you had given to the Raja.'

She paused, waiting for her friend to ask a question—How had Suraj got hold of the horses? What else did he have to say? When had he come or when did he leave?—Just about anything that could get the conversation going. But Amrapali continued to stare back, oblivious to the tempest brewing within Prabha. She was listening, assimilating and even responding, but her heart and soul appeared detached from the exchange. The Nagarvadhu was lost in a world of her own, and Prabha, in her own state of unease had been too preoccupied to take note.

And when, at the lunch table, one of the guards interrupted them to announce Suraj Mal's arrival, she felt her heart skip a beat. Amrapali instructed the guard to seat the guest till they were done with their meal, but Prabha felt as though the delicacies in her plate that she was savouring just moments ago had suddenly lost their entire flavour. With great difficulty she managed to gulp down a few handfuls before alighting from the table to wash her hands.

Amrapali's plate was still full and there were no signs of any efforts being made to disgorge the contents hurriedly, and this somewhat peeved Prabha. To her, each passing moment felt like an agonizing lifetime and when the Nagarvadhu eventually got up, she was quick to lead her down the corridors that led to the audience parlour.

'Devi Amrapali, Devi Prabha, my salutations,' he said, a coy smile emerging as his eyes locked fleetingly with Prabha's. She found herself blushing.

'Devi, my father and I are indebted to you for the rest of our lives,' he addressed Amrapali. 'It is but for your benevolence and generosity that I stand here a free man today. And it is the opportunity to thank you in person, for a favour that I can never dream of repaying, that drew me to the Old Palace once again today.'

Suraj Mal had a way with words. His eloquence, wit and confident demeanour did not go unnoticed by the Nagarvadhu. She was impressed. Also noticed were the fleeting glances the visitor occasionally stole towards Prabha and the fond attention she was bestowing upon each word that escaped his lips in turn. The Nagarvadhu's lips curled in a faint smile, so faint that it failed to register with any of the other occupants of the room.

After entertaining Suraj for a while and feeling the undercurrents of desire pendulate between him and Prabha, Amrapali exited the scene citing some personal errand as a flimsy but effective excuse. 'In the meantime why don't you show our guest around the palace?' she suggested to her friend who nodded in meek accordance.

It was an unabashed display of being blinded by love, a condition often associated with aching hearts, as Prabha remained oblivious to the fact that her friend had implicitly acknowledged her innermost emotions. It was a definite aberration that the Nagarvadhu had offered for one of the guests of the Old Palace to be shown around. And it wasn't merely his good fortune or even a matter of chance that Suraj Mal was the recipient of this privilege.

Yudhveer and Chetak were both present during Amanverma's interrogation and it didn't take long for the Raja to begin singing. An allegiance forged with material gains as its fundamental basis is by nature frail, and the Maharaja and Senapati of Vaishali being in attendance further diluted any determination to adhere to it that Amanverma could possibly have mustered. In a matter of ghatis his coconspirators, Bhadresh and Ramdev, too, were chained alongside him and divulging minutest of details about Bimbisara's plans and all they had done to assist him.

'Forgive me Maharaj, I had been greedy and was misled...' Bhadresh pleaded as he glanced towards Amanverma. His eyes were crimson with fear and his face pale as a blank parchment. His limbs were trembling, flailing helplessly almost, overcome by a profound sense of dread and trepidation. His present state, like that of the other two, was indeed pitiable, but that did little to soften the stone-cold expression on the Senapati's face.

'Greed, you think that is reason enough to explain your treacherous and malignant conduct? If a peasant, a poor man, had reasoned so, it would have made sense, but you, esteemed members of the Vajji council…' Chetak's trailing voice was soaked in a cruel, piercing jet of hatred and his bloodshot eyes were pouring ambers upon the three reprobates.

'A mistake Senapati, a terrible mistake I have made,' Bhadresh replied, shaking his head vigorously. 'Forgive me just this once and you will not regret your decision, I swear… Yes, the Magadhan commandos… Bimbisara had mentioned that a unit of his commando force will infiltrate our borders before the siege begins, and remain on standby to assist the main army in case of any unforeseen eventuality.' Like a lethally wounded boar, Bhadresh was scampering hither and thither, looking for any avenue that could help save his life. And in his sway he had managed to blurt out words that caught both Yudhveer and Chetak's fancy.

'Commandos! Where are they?' Yudhveer shot back anxiously.

'Maharaj, they were to take refuge in Amanverma's Khanda… posing as a bunch of traders. That is all I know, I swear. Please forgive me…' tears were streaming down his eyes and, with his hands folded, Bhadresh was pleading for clemency.

Yudhveer was quick to shift his focus towards Amanverma. 'So, you are still hoping that by concealing facts you will enable Vaishali's annexation?'

'No Maharaj, Bimbisara had only said that his men would take refuge in my territory and that I should instruct my security personnel to allow them passage without much ado. I was waiting to hear from them, but I never did. I don't think they ever came,' he replied. Though the Raja sounded convincingly honest, Chetak moved forward to question the prisoner. Not meaning to take any chances, he went on to quiz Amanverma on the exact words that had been exchanged with Bimbisara, verifying the accuracy of his responses with Bhadresh and Ramdev, and probing him on any actions that he knowingly or unknowingly might have taken to facilitate the entry of enemy troops into the kingdom.

Convinced that no further information could be extracted from the prisoners, he got up, briefly locking his gaze with the King, and after a slight nod of the head made an exit from the room. In barely a few moments, time that the prisoners fruitlessly expended in begging for Yudhveer's mercy, Chetak returned and whispered something in the King's ear. Yudhveer nodded in affirmation.

Glancing at the three prisoners with a look of contempt and disgust, he once again addressed the King, 'Maharaj, what do you suggest we do with them?'

'Their mistake is unpardonable. To my mind, they deserve a punishment so harsh that it sends shudders down the spine of anyone harbouring ill thoughts about our motherland. By placing a wager on Vaishali's sovereignty they have lost their right to breathe in its pristine air.' After a brief pause, Yudhveer continued, 'But I fear that any such action will act as a warning signal for our enemies. They will realize that their ploy has been compromised and that might prompt them to alter their plans or put them on hold for now.'

Chetak heard his king's concern, weighing each word as it was spoken. His response too was measured. 'Indeed, they would know. But I don't think they will have enough time to put in place an alternate plan so hurriedly. At best the knowledge that we are aware of their plot and perhaps prepared for it, might prompt them to fall back for now. And I see no harm in doing that,' he said.

'Are you suggesting that we should avoid confronting the enemy?'

The anxiety in the eyes of the three spectators, as they followed each minute syllable of the debate with bated breath, was palpable. After all, it was on the eventual outcome of this argument that their lives perilously hung.

'Maharaj, please don't get me wrong, but a battleground is not always the best platform to display one's valour. It takes no less courage to exercise restraint and wait till the opportune time for taking action. We are prepared, and I am sure our men are more than capable of thwarting any enemy overtures, but we must not lose sight of the fact that Magadh has been planning this assault for a while now. We can expect them to be geared up to the hilt and though there is little doubt about our victory, it will come at a substantial price. However, if we play it right and defer the confrontation to a later date, we might be able to cut this loss of life and property drastically,' Chetak argued.

The discussion did not stretch for long and a decision on the treatment to be meted out to Amanverma, Bhadresh and Ramdev was soon arrived at. The Viniccaya Mahamatta was urgently summoned to the royal palace and following a quick briefing, was made to put his stamp of approval on the order that would seal their fates forever.

That very afternoon the residents of Vaishali were presented with the first of many distressing sights to follow—half-naked bodies of the three traitors hanging from hastily erected poles at the city centre. Hands bound behind their backs, eyes bulging grotesquely and twisted tongues wagging like curtains screening their craning necks, they looked likes gargoyles designed by an architect with a penchant for the ludicrous.

The scene was too stark to be ignored and soon hoards of people were thronging the site, wanting to witness the dreadfulness with their very own eyes. As word spread, the gathering continued to expand like a blot of ink on a cotton garment, concealing in their midst the two sign-boards flanking the bodies that read—Better dead than to betray your motherland—Governing Council of Vaishali. A cryptic note for the uninitiated, but a resounding message for those it was intended for.

The atmosphere within the Mantrana Kaksha of Bimbisara's palace was heavy, weighed down by the tension prevailing in the air. The King, seated on his usual gilded throne, was lost in his own thoughts. The young Prince, Ajatshatru was anxiously pacing up and down the chamber's breadth while Senapati Prasenjit and Pradhan Mantri Narsinh Dev had their gazes affixed on the King, waiting for him to break the silence.

Following Bimbisara's instructions, Prasenjit had got the Magadh army battle-ready in no time. Officers were recalled from the leaves they had embarked upon following the battle for the conquest of Anga. Ironsmiths were made to blow their hearths night and day to forge swords, shields and spear-heads to replenish the depleted armoury and soldiers were summoned back to Rajgriha with the promise of another bountiful booty.

Ajatshatru had assumed the responsibility of maximizing military support from the smaller vassal states of Magadh. Together, the Senapati and the Prince had put together a formidable army comprising five thousand war elephants, ten thousand chariots, fifty thousand cavalry and over hundred and fifty thousand foot soldiers.

A massive camp had been set up outside the outer walls of the city to accommodate the army, shielded from prying eyes by the delightful Chaitya, the largest of the five hills surrounding

Rajgriha. A sense of restlessness prevailed at the site as the soldiers sharpened their weapons in anticipation of battle.

Only the previous evening, Bimbisara had visited the campsite for an inspection and had expressed satisfaction, commending Prasenjit and Ajatshatru for a task well accomplished. It was then that he had shared with them the details of his strategy to infiltrate Vaishali's ranks, which was now successfully in place. He had gleefully announced that on the second night from then, the Magadh forces would march right into Vaishali, unhindered, through the southern gate of the city.

Ajatshatru, though excited about the prospects of an effortless victory, had voiced his displeasure at being kept in the dark for so long. 'In that case, we will not need all the troops that we have so painstakingly gathered. We could have done with a much smaller army,' he had grumbled.

'That, my son, is precisely the reason why I refrained from sharing my plans with you and Prasenjit till today. The preparations preceding a war usually determine its eventual outcome, and we cannot afford any laxity in that aspect. Don't forget, it is the mighty kingdom of Vaishali that we look to annex,' the King had replied.

And today, with barely a pehar to go before the army began marching towards Vaishali, one of Narsinh Dev's spies had returned with terrible news. 'The dead bodies of Amanverma, Bhadresh and Ramdev—all three—are hanging in the very centre of the city of Vaishali. Our plan has been compromised. They know all about it. I am even unable to establish contact with the group of commandos who had been garrisoned in Amanverma's Khanda,' the spy had conveyed.

The prime minister had hurriedly convened the meeting that was currently underway. It was this piece of disturbing news that had propelled Bimbisara into a contemplative trance.

'Senapati, how do you view this development?' the King finally spoke.

'Maharaj, the enemy being forewarned surely takes away the element of surprise from the attack, but still we are well prepared to take them on. Moreover, if we disperse the army we have put together now, it will become increasingly difficult to gather them all over again in the near future. I think, we must look at this only as a minor skirmish and proceed with the attack,' Prasenjit replied.

'Yes, we had not made the preparations knowing that we would be able to scale Vaishali's walls without a confrontation. This development does not alter our position in any significant manner. I am forced to concur with the Senapati on this Maharaj, we must order the army to march as planned,' Ajatshatru added.

Next, Bimbisara looked at Narsinh Dev, who nodded his concurrence.

'Very well, gentlemen. Though I would have liked to step back and evaluate other possible alternatives to improve our chances of victory, I do understand that time is not on our hands. Given the circumstances, we are left with little option but to proceed with the assault. So, tonight it is when the siege of Vaishali begins! In the name of Magadh, victory shall be ours,' Bimbisara proclaimed.

Shifting his focus to more tactical concerns, he continued, 'With the odds of gaining an uncontested entry into the city having diminished considerably, the single most pressing worry for us would be to find a campsite capable of lodging our entire army. The approach to Vaishali, as we are all aware, is flanked by the Ganga and the Mahavana on either side, not leaving us with the luxury of much open space to set camp away from the firing range of their archers.'

'Yes, Maharaj, size will also act as a hindrance for the agility and manoeuvrability of our forces. We therefore intend to sail with only half the troops at the onset, the remaining to be split between a make-shift base in Patligram and Rajgriha. This will not only ensure constant replenishments for the advance camp, but will also make sure that Rajgriha remains protected from the unscrupulous designs of our other enemies,' Ajatshatru responded.

'We have also identified the place for setting up the advance camp. It is not too far from the city gates, but well shielded from enemy sight by the Mahavana,' Prasenjit added.

'Very well then,' a visibly reassured Bimbisara nodded. 'I am impressed with your meticulous planning. There is little doubt that under your able leadership, victory will soon be ours, and eager to witness this historic moment personally, I intend to accompany you to the battlefront. In my absence Narsinh Dev will act as a custodian for the seat at Rajgriha,' he said, alternating his gaze between Ajatshatru and Prasenjit.

Bimbisara's astuteness and perspicacity was beyond doubt and he had been the sole architect behind many Magadhan victories of the past. But of late he had been steering clear of the battleground, depending either on Prasenjit or Ajatshatru or both to reign in the battle honours. His preference for rush of adrenaline, it appeared, had subsided with age and he was happy to immerse himself in administrative matters and certain other engagements which he preferred to retain close to his heart, revealing their nature to none but his closest confidante, the prime minister.

Prasenjit and Ajatshatru exchanged an imperceptible glance. They were both perplexed with Bimbisara's desire to be present at the battlefront. It wasn't usual for the King to be present in the battlefield and not be in command of his troops. The situation was surely precarious for the present commanders of the Magadh army. Bimbisara's motivations—whether the momentousness of the occasion, or the faith in his own abilities over all else, or something altogether diverse—they could not pinpoint, but the fact was that the King had spoken and there was little they could do to make him change his mind.

5

As trade between the kingdoms of the Gangetic plains flourished, the Ganga emerged as one of its most significant facilitators. Wooden dinghies and vessels cruising along its usually tepid waters offered not only a cheap but also a significantly quicker alternative for transportation than the lazy-paced and often rickety bullock-carts.

Safety was another important reason for preferring the water-route over land. Dreaded bandits inhabiting the dense forests along the river basin found bullock-carts, with their sluggish pace, to be soft targets for their plundering pursuits. Though the states boasted of total security cover for traders passing through their territories, vast stretches of desolate roads made effective policing an impossible task. Packs of marauding brigands would materialize from nowhere and in a flash return to the safety of dense woods with anything of value they could lay their hands on, leaving behind ravaged convoys with tattered and mostly lifeless bodies of hapless traders strewn around. The practised precision of such raids left the authorities with little time to even react.

Traders, unable to muster either the will or the might to protect their interests against pillaging dacoits, had resorted to hauling their wares through the water route leading to numerous ghats and port towns, small and big, mushrooming along the coastline. One such settlement was the Mahendru ghat on the outskirts of Patligram, a small Magadhan town north of Rajgriha.

Mahendru ghat wasn't a planned settlement and had simply emerged as a vital inland port due to its axial location—located on the south bank close to where the Gandak emptied itself into the Ganga from the north, and axially opposite the teeming port of Vaishali, it served as a conduit for Magadh into maritime trade.

In the daytime the ghat bore the look of a busy port that it was—labourers toiling in the sun, bodies glistering with beads of sweat, loading or unloading cargo from anchoring vessels, vendors crying out to draw attention to their wares, mostly sugary syrup in earthen pots being passed off as tea and rounded moulds of baked dough (littee), the preferred snack of the natives. There were middlemen and agents who approached unsuspecting tourists and recommended one or the other lodging option in Patligram, promising to fulfill all needs that might arise during their brief halt. Groups of boatmen, oars resting close at hand, could be seen idling away time, waiting to embark upon yet another journey along the course of the river—a bustling cornucopia of human activity and commerce.

But that was the daytime. The nights, ominous and threatening, continued to belong to outlaws and brigands, if not for their presence than for the fear they had managed to instill in the minds of people, ensuring that all frenzy of business settled into a peaceful slumber much before sundown. Further insulating the ghat from any nocturnal human presence was the adjacent cremation ground which bore the genesis for many stories inundated with mystical characters and paranormal events.

The last set of boats left the port by third pehar of the day so as to ensure that they reached their destinations while the sun still remained on the horizon. Arrivals continued for a little while longer, but with the brush of nightfall all activities ceased and people retired to the safety of Patligrama, leaving the ghat to the mercy of beasts descending to claim their right on the day's spoils—packs of wild dogs, pigs, hyenas and wolves.

The scavengers too had their schedules well charted out and wrapped up their foraging within the early hours of the night, retreating to where they had descended from. The sounds of their angry growls and ravenous munching eventually dissolved into the eerie hum and incessant gurgle of dribbling water, punctuated sporadically by distant sounds, too faint for perception.

Tonight however was anything but usual. It was a new moon night and the darkness was all pervasive, as though a veil of black velvet had been carelessly dropped over the Mahendru ghat. In this pitch black night, shadows—not one or two but hundreds and hundreds of them—were emerging from nowhere and in a practised, almost mechanical fashion heading towards the eastern end of the ghat. It was the Magadh army, ready to embark upon a journey that would last much longer than their most conservative estimates.

The marching shadows were heading towards several large boats anchored at the far end of the ghat. As soon as the lead contingent reached first of the boats, the men broke out of formation and began boarding without waiting for a command. This continued sequentially till the first five boats were brimming to capacity with soldiers, about four hundred in each, before their anchors were pulled up. The remaining hands noiselessly pushed the five boats, easing them from the sandy shallow banks into the water, till the currents seized the baton and began drifting them downstream.

This was the Forward Contingent, a platoon sent in advance of the main army to test the waters. Their purpose was to unearth any concealed enemy traps and forewarn their comrades of impending dangers. Yet, the forward contingent was not merely the proverbial sacrificial lamb but a full-fledged platoon comprising two thousand armed soldiers. They were fully equipped to tackle any minor skirmishes along the way and also served to give the enemy an impression that the main army was on the move, forcing them to reveal their concealed hands.

The main body of the army continued to assemble at the Mahendru ghat—elephants, charioteers and horsemen now joining the cavalry—as they waited for the forward contingent to anchor safely on the enemy banks. The gathering was swelling constantly like a wild jungle fire, as the constituents of the enormous army continued to trickle in.

The five boats, after allowing the currents to take them adrift till half the river's breadth, now had oars splashing into the waters, guiding them purposefully towards a clearing on the opposite bank. The clearing was little under a kos in distance from the eastern periphery of Vaishali's port, but the dense forest that separated it from the city walls gave them the requisite cover to reach within striking distance of the southern gate with minimal risk of being spotted.

In about a ghati from when they had set sail, the forward contingent touched down on the northern banks of the river without an incident. And as if on cue, those left behind began lowering large rafts, made by binding symmetrical logs under a platform of wooden planks, into the water. The horses, elephants and chariots were then loaded onto them with trademark Magadhan efficiency under the joint command of Senapati Prasenjit and Yuvraj Ajatshatru.

The rafts, flanked by a succession of boats were next to leave the shore. They followed the already established pattern, allowing the currents to lug them midstream before seizing control and steering themselves to their destination. A procession of boats followed, the empty ones returning to ferry more passengers in the meantime. The relay was being undertaken with clockwork precision and the soldiers, upon being deposited on enemy soil, were quickly and noiselessly joining their comrades in setting up the makeshift camp.

Meanwhile, the forward contingent had already secured the site's periphery and the alert soldiers were ready to thwart any unexpected enemy advances. Their roles were meticulously laid out and instructions precisely conveyed. As soon as the last boat cast anchor, they were to mount the first offensive and try to gain entry into the city through its southern gate.

'*Om namo bhagwate rudraya karnapishachaya swaha,*' the basal chant rang through the stillness of the night followed by a sudden eruption of flames as spoonfuls of ghee dribbled into the havan kunda. The blaze briefly bathed the figures surrounding the kunda—four in all, staring into the fire with crimson, kohl-smeared eyes—before withdrawing back.

The verse echoed again and yet again with practised precision as the four lifted their wooden ladles in unison and allowed the ghee to drip into the ceremonial fire, sending the flames into recurring frenzied bouts. There was nothing peculiar about the scene. It could have been unfolding in the patio of any god-fearing household in Rajgriha, with prayers and offerings being made to the deities for fulfillment of avaricious objectives ranging from good health and fortune to matrimonial alliances and plentiful rains. But it was not.

The site for the havan was the cremation ground located on the southeastern periphery of the city, safely insulated from habitation by a stretch of tamed forestland. A curved path, more of a trail carved by the scraping soles of those escorting the dead to their final destination, cut through the woods leading to the cremation ground. The living otherwise seldom found reason to venture into the forest and beyond.

It wasn't just the venue of the ceremony that was unusual. The four men, all bare-chested and clad in identical black dhotis were a curious sight too. Three of them—the skinnier ones—had large unkempt beards and their disheveled hair, dangling in matted dreadlocks, gave them the look of otherworldly menace, enough to send shivers down the sturdiest of spines. Rosewood and rudraksha beads dangled from two of their necks while the third, visibly more accomplished in whatever it was they had set out to accomplish in their lives, had bones strung together by dried vine for a neckpiece. Whether or not the bones were human one couldn't tell, but the skull ominously placed between him and the fire altar had most definitely belonged to a fully grown man or woman once.

'Repeat after me,' the sadhu with the bone necklace instructed the man sitting across him—the fourth member of the coterie and one starkly dissimilar to his companions. His well-groomed appearance—neatly combed hair, clean-shaven visage and the layers of fat around his waistline—spoke of a privileged background and life, very unlike that of his ascetic accomplices. He was wearing a necklace of polished pearls and matching rings dangled from his ears. Though, like the other three, he had horizontal streaks of sandalwood paste lining his forehead, his body was not smeared with ashes from the cremation ground.

'I—, son of—, of —gotra,' the Sadhu began.

'I, Devdutt, son of Vishnu Dutt, of Marichi gotra…' the man followed suit, filling the blanks with the obligatory facts.

Once the pledge was recited, at the sadhu's cue Devdutt dropped the akshat and petals he had been holding into the havan kunda. His features distorted in concentration once again, as he settled his gaze on the flames emerging from the fire altar.

It was another fire, one in a different dimension of time and space that had altered not only his trajectory of life but also the manner in which he approached it. The images were etched so deep that they constantly abraded his soul and he, till this day, could vividly recall that night from many years back. He must have been five or six years old at most—just the age when a child starts accumulating memories to last an entire lifetime. And the first memory that he had been compelled to deposit in this bank had relentlessly continued to hound him till date.

They were about two dozen of them or even more—men, armed with bamboos, sickles and rods—who had come knocking on their door. His father, Vishnu Dutt, an accomplished tantrik who was known to use his knowledge of occult arts to heal the ailing and weak, had been busy with his ritualistic evening prayers then. They hadn't offered an explanation or waited for Vishnu Dutt to arise from his prayer mat. Instead they had dragged him out, like a sack of potatoes, holding him by the shoulders and arms, allowing his legs to flail.

His mother, too stunned by the assault to react immediately, had rushed out behind them and so had he. But they were both held back, interrupted mid-flight by men overbearing in stature and intent. He could still feel the gashes from his wasted struggle, on his soul rather than the body, as he had haplessly watched the mob grope and feel his mother's body and pound his father's fallen one with fists, legs and anything else they could lay their hands on. Their mingled cries, desperate and pleading, like a pack of animals being led for slaughter, continued to resonate within his head till this day, denying him even a single night's sound sleep.

The pack, tired, after having beaten Vishnu Dutt out of consciousness, finally decided to put an end to their perverted game. Devdutt had watched in horror as the assailants poked his father's unconscious body with blazing torches, passing on the flames to his still frame. His dhoti was the first to catch fire and in no time the flames had spiralled into a razing inferno, swallowing Vishnu Dutt's entire body. The fetid, piercing stench of burning flesh permeated the air, but the mob remained relentless. They began to throw dry leaves and twigs into the fire, as though, blinded by their monstrosity, his father's pyre appeared to them like a celebratory bonfire of the harvest season.

Still wailing and clamped in a firm grip, he had glanced towards his mother who had passed out in the hands of her captor, her mind refusing to bear the brutality of the unfolding scene. Her body, covered in shreds of what had previously been an intact garment, hung loose, held around the chest by a pair of burly hands. This was the last he could recall of the dreadful night, for his little eyes had slowly shut too, doing their bit to steer him away from the trauma and suffering.

The trauma had never left him though. He still felt it, running in his veins, throbbing in his temples and jolting him from within like a bolt of lightning. His mother, bereaved and humiliated, had lost all reasons to live but him. So, the very next day, with a small bundle containing their most prized possessions and a kalash with her husband's asthi, little Devdutt in tow, she left their home and the city of Vaishali for her father's house in Rajgriha.

Devdutt's maternal grandfather was the royal astrologer of Magadh and he spared no means to ensure that his daughter and grandson were provided with all possible luxuries and privileges that money could buy. Devdutt had the best of toys to play with, he was admitted to one of the most illustrious gurukuls of the region, and his playmates belonged to the most revered of Magadhan clans. And yet, the mother-son duo led their lives in the most mechanical fashion, the joys of luxuries failing to assuage the ghosts from their tumultuous past.

The horror of having watched his father being charred alive had left an indelible dent in little Devdutt's personality, making him wary of everybody around him. Overnight, from a lively and playful child he had transformed into a reclusive loner. Whether at the gurukul or in the company of his friends, he limited his speech to necessities and seldom participated in the frolic and banter that other children thrived on. It was in the company of parchments and granths, or while gazing at the night sky with his grandfather that he appeared most at ease.

It was later, when he was old enough to understand the vices—greed, lust and power—that formed the core of the world around, that his mother confided in him the cause of his father's brutal murder. Vishnu Dutt was a simple man, a Brahmin, who, after mastering the Vedas had been unceremoniously drawn to the deeper and darker manifestations of dharma. Seeking knowledge, causes and effects that governed the phenomenal universe or brahmanda, he had travelled far and wide, through the southern plains and across the Himalayan mountains.

Devdutt's mother, a newly-wed bride then, had been fully sympathetic towards his quest and had never stood in the way of his travels, deftly tending to the needs of the household during his elongated spells of absence. When he returned home he would be the Brahmin he was, performing priestly duties at religious ceremonies and depending on the alms he received for his livelihood. But soon he would begin to get restless, often when he had saved enough to fund his travels and sustain the household in his absence, and start readying himself for yet another journey.

It was a few months after Devdutt's birth that Vishnu Dutt found his calling in the tutelage of a wandering sadhu he met at a shrine in Vaishali. The sage, accompanied by a small entourage of followers, hermits like his own self, was camping in the city en route to Mount Kailash. It was by pure chance that Vishnu Dutt happened to be visiting the very same shrine and decided to pay homage to the holy man.

'Son, the answers you seek are all around you, but you are unable to spot them. Life is a veritable maze and it is only when your sight is trained to guide you to the fissures in the hedge separating the world we know from the one we don't that you will find true peace of mind,' was the abstract response he received for his greeting from the sadhu. The man appeared to be mumbling in a deep state of trance, but the words struck a chord with Vishnu Dutt. Intuitively he knew that it was not by a random act of chance that he had met the sadhu and that it was the sadhu who would serve as a conduit for the salvation he sought. There and then Vishnu Dutt decided that he would join the sadhu's entourage in their journey to Mount Kailash.

'It wasn't easy. You were barely a few months old and even the thought of managing everything without him around was most unnerving, but for the first time I could see an unmistakable glint in his eyes. I simply couldn't bring myself to deny him the opportunity he seemed so excited about, and so, once again, I happily consented. He was gone for over six months, but when he returned he was a changed man...' his mother had said, slipping into some distant crevice of her memories.

A changed man Vishnu Dutt was. In the six months he spent on the mountains he had mastered three of the ten mahavidyas or goddesses of wisdom and in the process gained a host of supernatural powers including a miraculous healing touch.

Within days of his return to Vaishali, stories of his magical powers began to spread like wildfire and sick and ailing people began queuing up outside his house. Vishnu Dutt was happy to serve as a medium for alleviating people's sufferings and began to spend a better part of his day chanting mantras—sacred utterances—into ears of the hopefuls and blowing at wounds of the injured.

His evenings were devoted to prayers, a ritual that occasionally extended well into the night. 'It is like drawing water from a vessel. Unless the water is replenished, the vessel will eventually run dry. My sadhna is the source of my powers and I need to keep to it if I am to continue helping people,' he would often say. It was on certain nights, usually Amavasya and Purnima that he would leave the house clutching his prayer beads and a small bag replete with items for use during puja, only to return with the next dawn. His wife never questioned him on his whereabouts and he never volunteered an explanation.

There were many beneficiaries of Vishnu Dutt's renewed avatar, but there was also a man who was gravely pained by his rising popularity—the Nagar Vaidya of Vaishali. Vishnu Dutt had managed to heal many patients that the Vaidya had failed to, a fact that was eating into not only the Vaidya's popularity but also his earnings. His patients were migrating in hordes, seeking Vishnu Dutt's healing touch—a more effective and economical alternative to the Vaidya's sour potions.

The Nagar Vaidya had used his proximity to the Raja of the Khanda as a means to threaten Vishnu Dutt on numerous occasions. The Raja's soldiers had even arrested him once on charges of fraud and misleading the public, but were forced to let him go in wake of the public uproar their action had incited. The Vaidya had sent emissaries meaning to strike a deal with Vishnu Dutt, but the divergence of their objectives forbade any common ground between them. Each time, the Nagar Vaidya's failed efforts to salvage his vocation only resulted in burgeoning frustration for him, until fate provided him just the weapon he had been looking for.

It seemed, a curse of the gods had befallen the expecting mothers of Vaishali. One out of every two children to take birth in the city was being born still, dead even before breathing in the first gasp of air. This had been happening over a period long enough to establish a pattern and create a sense of panic among the populace. Even Vishnu Dutt, their saviour, had found his powers dwarfed against the established cycle of human mortality. His healing touch had failed to ignite a spark of life in any of the dead infants.

The inexplicable nature of the calamity made people attribute it to an act of vengeance by the gods and other such. It was this confused and anxious state of the masses that the Vaidya used to his advantage, feeding stories to the rumour mills about how this was god's way of getting back at them for allowing Vishnu Dutt to interfere with his wishes.

At once Vishnu Dutt was branded an envoy of the devil, a practitioner of dark and forbidden arts who was solely responsible for the misfortunes to have engulfed the city. The people—gullible and naïve—the same ones, who had once queued up outside Vishnu Dutt's house jostling for a mere touch of his, were quick to lap up the story. Anything, just about anything that could offer even a near-plausible explanation for their predicament was welcome, and they not only stopped visiting Vishnu Dutt but he also became the sole focus of the aggravated fury welling up within them.

The telling blow came, when, urged by the Vaidya, some of them followed Vishnu Dutt on one of his nocturnal jaunts and were shockingly led to the local cremation ground. The men returned to inform others of their discovery—the account further dramatized each time it was recounted—till it reached the ears of those still grieving the loss of their little ones. The opening was sufficient and the evidence enough. They were quick to latch on to the theory of Vishnu Dutt being the sorcerer who had claimed their unborn children, since it provided them with a much needed opportunity to vent out their bottled rage. And armed with sticks, rods, sickles and whatever else they could lay their hands on, they had headed towards his house seeking vengeance.

The disclosure by his mother had only worked in augmenting the feeling of loss for Devdutt. He was infuriated at the irrationality and crookedness behind what had transpired. One sane mind, just one sane mind among the lot of marauders and his father could have been breathing still. He was vengeful towards the wily Vaidya in particular and the populace of Vaishali in general; he wanted to burn them all, the entire city, like they had burnt his father. But a helpless child, with neither the means nor the courage to shape his vengeance, he had chosen to channel his emotions elsewhere—towards the written word.

Devdutt had taken to his books with punishing intensity and used his time to understand theories, revise them, memorize them and then revise them again. Though still an introvert who could not withstand even a concentrated gaze, his academic proficiency soon became a frequent topic of conversation among those in know. In no time he had earned himself the repute of being an astute strategist, in theory at least, and a thinker par excellence. He seldom participated in debates, avoiding them like a mud pit, but when he did present an argument, it came backed with so much evidence that even the wisest of men found themselves ill-equipped to counter him.

He had inherited from his grandfather an in-depth understanding of stars and the effects their alignment and interplay had on humankind. He could bury himself in complex astrological calculations for pehars together and emerge with predictions that stood ground up to a reasonable degree of accuracy.

His inclination towards tantra, perhaps a genetic acquisition from his father, was not known to many, but had been continually nurtured nevertheless. He would lose himself in his father's parchments, understanding the complex and sometimes bizarre tantrik rituals and practicing them whenever he could. However, this was one pursuit he was obligated to engage in without the knowledge of his mother or grandfather. He was aware that somewhere in their subconscious they blamed his father's vocation for his untimely demise and he feared a reprisal from them to no end.

Therefore it came as little surprise when the young king of Magadh, Bimbisara, who, at the tender age of fifteen had ascended upon the kingdom's throne, invited him to become a minister in his council. Bimbisara had gone to the same gurukul where Devdutt, about five years prior, had been educated. Accounts of his unrivalled knowledge and extreme intelligence had not escaped the ears of the would-be king. So, while looking for fresh talent to revitalize his ministerial council Bimbisara had sought him out, and a purposeless Devdutt, still nurturing the flames of hatred within, had been quick to accept.

The path had not proven easy for him. A ministerial berth came with its inherent need to manoeuvre and manipulate people, an ability that Devdutt did not possess. His personality, a taciturn and docile one, did not help much either, and Devdutt had difficulties in establishing himself in the same league as his more dominant peers. Though Bimbisara continued to consult him on crucial matters, he got the feeling that his words, drawing more from theory than gumption, were not given their due regard.

The prejudice, usually involuntary and unintended, struck Devdutt like an excruciating stab each time, forcing him to recoil further into the familiarity of his seclusion. He seldom reacted or voiced a protest.

Devdutt had learnt to shroud his emotions well, in fact it wouldn't be wrong to say that he had grown up recognizing only a limited array of emotions, the predominant ones being loathing and rage. He was a bitter, cold and ruthless soul encased in a body stupefied by his continued sequestration. His feeble and neglected exterior and his demure persona gave him the impression of being a placid pushover, a man who was highly unlikely to display aggression. Consequently, for most of his life he had borne taunts and jibes from his colleagues, mastering the art of transforming his pain into revulsion and depositing it into the reservoir within. The taunts and jibes had ceased with his elevation to the ministerial council, but the internal pool of hatred had continued to thrive. It was distressing, the degree of agony and hatred that had accumulated within him, eating into the more humane emotions of compassion and consideration, principally because he did not know how or where to vent them. He was drifting along, offering least resistance to the tides of time and oblations of life when a sudden development jolted him from his slumber, giving his life both, a purpose and a new lease.

Bimbisara was planning an offensive on Vaishali, a city that Devdutt had neither forgotten nor forgiven. Perhaps this was the opening he had been waiting for all his life and maybe the time had come for justice to be delivered and Vishnu Dutt's cold-blooded murder to be avenged. In form of the Magadh army he could see just the force capable of vanquishing the formidable city of Vaishali. Total annihilation of the city, no less, he sought, and the stars too were aligning themselves to make this a reality.

All that Devdutt now had to do was wait and watch, and perhaps garner support for his missionaries from any likely quarters. And that is precisely what he was doing at the cremation ground in the company of three strange men—invoking dark malevolent powers to cast a spell of doom on the city of Vaishali.

The ceremony was nearing its conclusion and the one rite remaining was that of the bali—a sacrificial offering to propitiate the deity. Devdutt and two of the sadhus were now standing on the same side of the altar. All three had their eyes tightly shut and the sadhus were chanting mantras in a tone so vicious and urgent that Devdutt was getting goose bumps by simply listening to them.

Before long the third sadhu returned, holding a sword in one hand and dragging something with the other. As he approached the altar, piercing the circumference of luminosity, the article he was tugging became more perceptible—it was a small boy, one who couldn't have seen more than two autumns in this life, fearful and reluctant. His mouth was gagged and hands tied in front of his body. It was the knot on his hands that the sadhu was using as a grip to drag him. The need for him to be dragged came partly from the mild resistance he was offering and partly because of the small rope that dangled as a bridge between his ankles.

Upon reaching the altar, the sadhu handed the sword to Devdutt and forcibly made the boy kneel down, strategically placing his neck on a wooden slab. The other two sadhus continued with their chanting, only more ferociously. The boy tried to look up, struggling to raise his neck, but the sadhu was quick to push him back using his palm to restrain his head. In that fleeting moment, anyone who dared to look into the little boy's eyes—but for the four who mattered—would have seen a desperate plea, a world of promise and a flurry of questions that were condemned to remain unanswered.

The main sadhu, the one adorning a bone necklace, opened his eyes and with a gesture of the hand instructed Devdutt to proceed, while he continued with his demonic recitation. Instantly Devdutt clasped the sword with both hands, drew it over his head, and without any hesitation brought it slicing down to meet the boy at the back of his neck. The blade cut through the frail body with ease and connected with the wood emanating a slight thud.

A muffled scream and another thud followed, as the body and the head hit the ground. The lifeless head rolled a few paces, leaving a thick trail of blood behind, a pair of dazed eyes staring back from it, before coming to an abrupt halt. The wasted body continued to convulse, oodles of blood gushing out from severed arteries, as the four men watched with the indifference of a woodcutter having chopped yet another tree. Their chanting had ended, drawing a curtain of silence over the scene.

Though Bimbisara's crafty scheme had been compromised, somewhere in the recess of his heart he continued to hope that a delightful twist of fate would have the colossal gates of Vaishali open up to his forces, magically. His mind understood the futility of such thoughts, but he was simply unable to shake them away. As he watched Ajatshatru mount his regal Badakhshan stallion to lead the advance contingent, he felt his heart swell with a nervous pride and his hopes went soaring further into the dominion of irrationality. It was for the first time that he was witnessing his young son lead the army into battle from such close quarters, and like any doting father, his sense of repletion was struggling to emerge from the debris of absorbing anxiety and concerns for his son's well-being.

Ajatshatru had taken it upon himself to lead the vanguard while Prasenjit was entrusted with the task of readying the backup battalion. With chariots and war-elephants, the backup unit was more expansive than the unit under Ajatshatru's command—a mix of only foot soldiers and cavalry. The backup's purpose was to remain on standby and reinforce the lead unit when needed—

customarily under the contrary events of the lead unit managing a fissure and entering deeper into enemy territory or encountering a formidable resistance that left them minified.

Bimbisara stood outside the royal tent, a lavish conical structure located right in the centre of the encampment, surrounded by about half a dozen bodyguards. He gazed up at the sky, peering into the seemingly ominous darkness. Even the stars, at least the few that had been visible earlier, appeared to have found some pretext to make a quiet exit. A creepy stillness, much unlike the muted bustle surrounding him, had spread over the horizon, signalling that the night was stretching along its final leg.

His reverie was broken by the sound of approaching horse hooves. It was his son Abhay or the Prince—Ajatshatru, handsome, regal and fearless as Bimbisara had always wished of him. With a tug on the reins Ajatshatru brought the beast to halt a few paces ahead of Bimbisara and like a skilled rider, disembarked in a single sweeping motion of his right leg. Walking up to Bimbisara and rendering a gentle salute he said, 'Father, the time for us to realize our dream has come. I am here to seek your blessings and God willing, you shall soon see the Magadh flag fluttering over Vaishali's gates.'

Overcome by a soaring surge of paternal affection Bimbisara pulled his son into a tight embrace. He didn't utter a word, sliding his palm over Ajatshatru's head instead, and for the brief moment that their gazes locked, emotions concealed within the deepest crevices of their hearts were bared to the other. Ajatshatru was the first to retract and, bowing slightly, he marched back to his mount and galloped away in the direction he had come from.

Ajatshatru's unit had less than a kos to cover before they emerged on the eastern end of the Vaishali ghat, not a sizeable stretch, but made tumultuous by the dense vegetation they had to wade through. The river bank and the surrounding shrubbery was not used to being trampled upon by a couple of thousand feet and hooves at one go, and stood like the natural, first-level defence for the city that it was meant to be. Soldiers had to hack through overgrown weeds and uproot plants to leave behind a trail wide enough for the backup unit to reach them urgently if the need ever arose.

Consequently it took over three ghatis for them to cover a distance that they ordinarily would have scaled in less than one. When they did emerge on the ghat, exposed and vulnerable without the protective covering of trees, they were compelled to pause and regroup since the arduous journey had left their original battle formations ruffled and confused.

The frontline had only just begun to take guard when a swooshing noise, persistent like the annoying buzz of a mosquito, tore through the silence. The sky, ready to emerge from the long night, was instantaneously plunged back into complete darkness.

'Cover,' Ajatshatru screamed, but just a little late. Before his men could even react, a barrage of arrows descended upon them piercing through anything they came in contact with. Cries, human and animal, rang across the horizon, piercing the remaining stillness of the night as men rushed for cover using trees, shields, bodies of their dead comrades and beasts, to shield them from the raining death.

Deftly sliding his body to one side and using his mount's frame to protect himself, Ajatshatru steered the horse towards a bunch of trees at the mouth of the forest. The well-drilled beast, nimbly avoiding the falling arrows, rushed his master to the safety of the bushes. Ajatshatru felt the conch shell tied to his waistband, but immediately pulled his hand back. There was no point in summoning backup. More exposed troops would only result in more enemy arrows finding their mark.

He peeped from his point of vantage to take stock of the situation. Arrows continued to rain relentlessly, but they were now hitting the earth or depositing themselves on the many lifeless bodies strewn around. The scene was one of utter carnage. Ajatshatru had lost hundreds of men without even setting an eye on the enemy. The sight was unnerving and he felt a muscle twitch somewhere in his chest. With an excruciating sigh he turned his sight from the dead to those who were still living.

To his relief his remaining men had managed to pull out of harm's way and were now huddled up behind trees, much like his own self, or had receded away from the archers' range and were standing ankle-deep in the river, shields held high to intercept any roving arrow that had overshot its peers. Mentally he evaluated the options he was left with.

They could not mount an attack from their current position. Vaishali's archers had the advantage of elevation; they were shooting their arrows from atop the city walls, while his men were incapable of finding their mark unless they stepped forward and exposed themselves. Returning wasn't an option either. That would mean a waste of all lives that had already been laid down and dampen the morale of the troops to no end. Moreover the situation wasn't likely to alter much if the assault was postponed to a different time or day. Vaishali would continue to exercise the advantage their fortifications offered and their archers, doubtlessly, would be ready and waiting to shower their arrows on any advancing party.

The only feasible alternative he was left with was to march ahead, to a point where his own archers and spear-throwers would come into play. That, he knew, would not breach Vaishali's fortifications, but if he was able to disturb their order, he could summon his backup troops, and aided by the elephants, they could attempt to force their way in.

Screaming orders to the sergeants who had assembled around him, he got the remaining battalion to regroup near the edge of the river. Their formation, unimaginatively christened the 'turtle' formation, had three rows of foot soldiers holding their shields, horizontally linked to each other, forming layers, one atop the other, to form a shell-like outer covering for the marching battalion. The cavalry followed, holding their shields in similar fashion, followed by the remaining infantry who held theirs above their head to form a roof-like covering.

The contingent, when it began its march, appeared like one large homogeneous mass enclosed in a shell of shields, slowly but surely trudging towards its prey. The archers from Vaishali once again began exercising their bow strings, but this time they heard no screams or cries. The only sound was that of repeated thuds as metal arrow-tips crashed against the wooden shields, sometimes lodging themselves in the resulting fissure and sometimes bouncing back worthlessly.

Once they were close enough, Ajatshatru ordered the unit to halt. The task ahead was rather simple—sections of the casing would momentarily collapse, allowing just enough time for the archers to release their shots, before covering them back. The act would be repeated over and over again, thoroughly confusing the enemy as random sections of the outer layer would suddenly cave in to release a flurry of deadly arrows. But one element that Ajatshatru had missed taking into consideration was the astuteness of the adversary he faced.

As the first set of shields went down to allow a bunch of archers, bow strings tout and fingers itching, to release their first shot, an alarming spectacle materialized before them. The panels of the large wooden door ahead had begun to drift apart, revealing in the aperture a battalion of mounted soldiers, ready and rearing to go. The Magadhan archers released their arrows anyway, but only with trembling fingers, and the sound of their arrows cutting through the air was immediately dissolved by the clatter of hooves from thousands of galloping horses.

Ajatshatru was left with just enough time to sound the conch shell and summon help before the horsemen came crashing into his advance battle line, their swords, maces and spears striking his men hard. Caught off guard yet again, his men had to pay for their inertia with their lives. Even before his cavalry could step up to the challenge, hundreds of his soldiers had fallen, slain or wounded gravely. Wielding his own sword and encircled by about half a dozen bodyguards, Ajatshatru charged towards the horse that appeared to be carrying the raiding unit's leader, slashing at and obliterating any obstruction along the way.

Chetak could see Ajatshatru heading towards him, clearing his path with skilled movements of his sword, his deep-set eyes glittering with hostility. The resentment was mutual. Chetak felt a strong urge to charge at the Magadh Prince and teach the pompous youngster a lesson, but he was quick to check himself. From his experience he knew that brash and impulsive actions were the difference between those who survived a battle and those who didn't. There was a plan he needed to adhere to and it allowed little room for such reckless transgressions, so, with a slight nudge of his heels he instructed his horse to turn around and the beast instantly obeyed.

Ajatshatru was stunned. He had heard stories of the Lichchavis' gallantry and what he was witnessing was a far cry from the enemy's impression he had conjured in his mind. The warrior he had been regarding for a duel had retreated even before his approach. In fact he seemed to be abandoning the battleground and heading back towards the city gates. Exasperated, he looked around, perhaps hoping to catch the eye of another Lichchavi fighter who had been witness to his comrade's cowardice. But he found none.

Instead, to his utter chagrin, he realized that the entire battalion to have unexpectedly emerged from Vaishali's gate was drawing back just as unexpectedly. He considered the option of giving them a chase, but only fleetingly. The sudden ambush had left his own contingent in tatters and his men were hardly in a position to pursue the fleeing enemy. In fact he could see a deliberately suppressed look of relief on some of the faces around.

So ordering his troops to fall back, he continued brooding over the possible reasons for his adversaries' mysterious exit. The Lichchavis were in a position of command and they could have inflicted much greater damage on the Magadhan army by simply allowing the battle to continue unabated, why then did they choose to withdraw? Was this a part of some larger scheme that he was unable to see through and one that he needed to be weary of?

A sudden, unmistakable reverberation of a large army on the move—one emanating from thousands of marching and screaming beings, human and animal—broke his reverie. His backup contingent, helmed by a visibly anxious Prasenjit perched on a howdah at the back of his favourite elephant was slowly emerging from the jungle. That was when the thought struck Ajatshatru like a bolt of lightning. The Lichchavis were cognizant of support reaching him and had thus planned their blitzkrieg in a manner that enabled them to return to safety after inflicting a sizeable damage to the vanguard.

The enemy had outmanoeuvred him and the realization left him feeling sore, strengthening his resolve to capture Vaishali in turn. The battle had just begun and he had an ominous feeling that it was going to last long.

Just then another thought struck him and kicking his horse to a gallop, he rushed towards Prasenjit, holding the rein with one hand and waving furiously with the other. The vanguard had made the mistake of stepping into the open unprepared and had to bear the ruthless assault by Vaishali's archers. The same mistake could not be committed twice. He needed to steer Prasenjit's troops towards the river, away from the firing range, and there they would regroup and plan the next offensive.

6

Love, like a wild flower, does not rely on favourable surface conditions to sprout and bloom. It simply materializes out of nowhere, like mushrooms after heavy rains, to slowly but surely make its presence felt. And when in full bloom, it scatters its delightful fragrance, clouding the body, heart and soul of its subjects to propel them into a rapturous frenzy of peculiar proportions.

Such was the frenzy that Amrapali was struggling to contain, except, instead of the happiness that is known to radiate from those in the sway of love, she was enveloped by a sort of befuddled melancholy. This state was but a manifestation of the mêlée ensuing within her—between the pragmatic Nagarvadhu of Vaishali and the longings of a love-struck young woman—a battle, which, irrespective of the side emerging victorious, was bound to leave her hurt and lamenting.

Nearly two months had passed since Bindusen's last visit, the rainy day that remained so vivid in her memories that she could weave an illusionary world from it to escape into whenever her heart so desired. There had been no news of him since then and her angst had been mounting with each passing day.

She was conscious that her beloved city, Vaishali, was at war and that the city gates had remained closed to ordinary passers-by for over a month now. She had heard that the enemy, an insatiable Emperor from the nearby kingdom of Magadh, was camped outside the city with a grand army and that skirmishes were being reported almost on a daily basis between the two warring factions. The valiant warriors of Vaishali had been spilling their sweat and blood to protect the city and her heart went out to them.

She could envisage a helpless Bindusen, also afflicted by the trauma of their separation, perturbed and aggrieved at his inability to severe the shackles of fortuity and scramble to meet his beloved. The rational side to her even empathized with Bindusen's powerlessness, but it was her heart that simply refused to pay heed to deductions, judicious or otherwise, that condoned the distance between them. She was suffering at the hands of love—a minute, tearing agony that remained wedged to her like a bloodthirsty parasite.

Normally she would share her longings and her distresses with Prabha, her confidante and childhood friend, but her villainous destiny appeared to have covered all its bases. Lately Prabha had been spending a lot of time outside the palace and when around she appeared preoccupied with musings of her own. A development, the cause and effect of which Amrapali was in the know of, that had taken away her only medium to vent out the repressed anguish.

But Amrapali was glad for Prabha. Her selfish dependency on her friend notwithstanding, she knew that Prabha deserved better. She needed to experience love first-hand, the feeling that many had attempted to define but had failed in doing so. Amrapali was happy that Suraj, a man discernibly honest and worthy, had walked into Prabha's life at the opportune moment to sweep her off her feet. She had seen a glint of sincerity in his eyes, and in hers, a sparkle of emotions she had never witnessed previously.

Prabha would confide in her, sharing the most intimate of conversations Suraj and she had, blushing or fidgeting with her dupatta, and she would listen with the affectionate curiosity of an indulging parent. She had neither found the opening nor the inclination to burden Prabha with the tribulations of her own heart at a time when her life was passing through this extremely special phase.

Today wasn't particularly different from the other days this time of the year. The morning breeze was carrying a certain nip giving an indication of the fast approaching winter season. After finishing their breakfast, Amrapali and Prabha had strolled out to the palace garden hoping to bask in the unobstructed radiance of the morning sun when a guard had approached them to announce Suraj's arrival.

'Ironic,' Amrapali thought, 'while we sit here and wait for one Suraj, an entirely different one shows up.' She was somewhat bothered by the unexpected intrusion, but she did not allow it to show. Instead, smiling at her own trite pun, she watched Prabha rush out to greet the visitor. Once again, she was left alone, as she had so often been along the path of her life. She stayed back in the garden for a while, admiring its natural comeliness, but when, fuelled by her desolation, her mind began to drift into a precinct she had come to dread, she summoned Ballabh and instructed him to ready her chariot.

Her destination was the same mango grove where she had been found as a child, lonely and abandoned but brimming with vitality. Many years had passed ever since, and it was only recently that she had once again felt drawn to the place. Perhaps it was a connection of the mind, a similarity in the emotions she was experiencing now to those she would have had as a wailing, derelict infant, that made her feel at ease in the shade of the mango trees. It was this search for momentary relief that had been frequently summoning her to the orchard of late.

As the chariot, escorted by her trotting troupe of guards, snaked through the city roads, she could see the fallout of war on the faces and lives of the people she passed. Fear and uncertainty had cast a shadow of gloom on the otherwise vibrant streets and people, wary and confused, appeared to have retreated into some invisible shell, going about their lives in a manner of melancholic monotony. The chaupals were deserted and the marketplace, though not yet lacking in essential supplies, was missing its usual early morning hustle-bustle. Although the city remained connected with rest of the kingdom, its sudden barricading against external trade had stymied the primary income source for some, while most others were hit by the spiralling effect of the downturn. Manufacturers were left laden with unsold stocks while transporters had their fleets of idle wagons accumulating dust. To curtail their losses, many businesses had ceased production of their wares, leading to job cuts and further adding to the prevailing economic insecurity.

The mood had not spared even the rich and wealthy, making them overtly cautious about their spending. This, coupled with the imbuing, battle-induced despair, had suppressed any appetite for recreation among the populace of Vaishali. Consequently the Old Palace, which, not particularly long ago would be bustling with eager patrons desirous of gaining admission into the Swapna Kakshika, was left unfrequented and desolate. Gauging the pulse of the people Amrapali had even suspended her fortnightly public performances, leaving her with a gaping void of time that her anxiety often rushed to fill.

Today also, like her recent visits to the grove, Amrapali wandered aimlessly—gazing at the trees, attempting to follow the melodious dialect of chirping birds and retiring under the spreading canopy of one of the trees when she was tired—till the sun began to drop, leaving the sky bathed in a pale pink radiance. Getting up, she brushed the persistent twigs and soil off her clothes and began walking at a contemplative pace to where her chariot was stationed. Upon sighting her, Ballabh and his men hurriedly rose and reached for their grazing mounts.

The Nagarvadhu had only just mounted the chariot when her ears caught a strange jangling noise. The source of the sound she could not fathom, but whatever it was, she could tell by the increasing intensity of the noise that it was heading towards them. Also discernible was an accompanying racket, a cheer of sorts that seemed to be emanating from a bunch of tumultuous and enthusiastic kids. Gripped by curiosity, by a sway of her hand she instructed the charioteer to remain till the noise-source presented itself.

Soon enough a bunch of about ten to twelve youngsters emerged, running and cheering wildly. At the head of the group was another boy, slightly older than the others, about fourteen or fifteen years of age, whom the others appeared to be chasing. The boy had a strange expression on his face—a mix of shock, dread and panic—as he sporadically turned back to glance at the reason for his discomfort, not the bunch of kids chasing him but something else that was trailing behind. Amrapali followed one of his fleeting looks through the rope dangling from his waist to its other end where pieces of scrap metal were fastened.

It was the noise from these metal pieces grinding against each other or against the road surface that was responsible for startling the boy. As he tried to outrun them by increasing his speed, they clashed even more ferociously, resulting in a much louder noise that was greeted by fervent cheers from those in his pursuit. He was a differently-abled child, one with restricted mental faculties, Amrapali guessed, and the other children were deriving perverse pleasure from his plight. Perhaps it was one of them who had fastened the rope to his waist, creating an object of amusement out of a living, breathing human being.

'Ballabh, stop them,' she nearly screamed, and Ballabh, already atop his horse, dug his heels and pulled on the reins to give the beast an immediate start. The sight of a galloping warrior, a strange looking one at that, galloping towards them proved much for the other kids and they fled instantly leaving behind the lone boy even more baffled than he had been. As Ballabh halted his horse a few paces ahead of him, the boy cringed and shuffling his eyes between the man and the beast, withdrew a few paces. But his steps once again ruffled the stationary metal pieces and the rattle forced him to trace his steps back towards Ballabh. It was a funny sight alright, but only for the unkind, insensitive and cold-hearted.

Not meaning to ruffle the boy any further Ballabh stood his ground, unmoving and waiting for Amrapali's approaching chariot to reach them. The boy too stood motionless, recoiled slightly, but his intense eyes focused on Ballabh, as though he were expecting the strange man to transform into an even stranger being any moment.

Even before the wheels of her chariot had stopped rotating, an eager Amrapali got down with a slight skip off the last step. Maybe it was her feminine warmth or the evident burst of compassion in her eyes, but the boy did not flinch or withdraw as she approached him. He did glance at her, but unfazed by her approaching steps, he was quick to shift his suspicious gaze back towards Ballabh. Slowly, she reached out for his head and began stroking his hair gently, signalling to Ballabh with her free hand to withdraw.

It was only when Ballabh was at a safe distance that the boy turned his eyes towards her, two deep-set pools brimming with innocence and a lifetime of unexplained suffering. The moment was overwhelming and the Nagarvadhu struggled to contain the heave of emotions threatening to tear her apart.

'What is your name, my child?' she spoke as softly as she could manage.

The boy continued looking at her, his expressions unaltered. Continuing to stroke his hair, she repeated her question again and again, till his parched lips quivered slightly.

'Kundali,' he stuttered, each syllable emerging from his lips like a precious pearl.

Amrapali pulled him closer and tenderly held him to her bosom, slowly whispering his name back. After a while, when his tense body began relaxing in her warm embrace, she resumed her enquiry.

'Where do you live? Who are your parents?'

But each time she was greeted by a vigorous shake of Kundali's head. After repeated attempts at getting him to divulge more information about himself failed, she summoned one of her guards with a wave of her hand. She would have preferred consulting Ballabh, but calling him or any of the other Xingnous near the already nervous boy seemed a perilous prospect, so she had settled for one of her local bodyguards instead.

'The boy doesn't seem to remember his father's name or the directions to his house. He is lost and we can't leave him here like this. The sun is going down rapidly and it will be night-time soon,' she said, glancing up towards the darkening sky. 'I will take him to the palace with me while you scan the adjoining areas and try locating his family. The task might prove arduous, so take another man with you and keep me informed of the developments. His name, he says, is Kundali...'

Kundali hesitatingly boarded the chariot and holding Amrapali's hand for reassurance, began his journey towards the Old Palace. The ride back was uneventful, but for the constant sound of metallic collisions which had now become a familiar background score to the city's night-time. Bladesmiths, arrowsmiths and fletchers, as they forged weapons through the night, razor-sharp and deadly, produced the cacophony of sounds that had been eluding the city of its erstwhile nocturnal stillness.

In the distance Amrapali could hear the screeching whinnies of injured horses and stifled cries of wounded soldiers or kins of those who had been less fortunate. The sounds, barely perceptible but abetted by the nightly air into spreading far, appeared to her like an opera of anguish and gloom—disquieting and gut-wrenching. She felt something turn inside her stomach which rapidly intensified into a queasy, nauseating feeling.

By the time the entourage entered the Old Palace, she was fraught and distressed. As soon as the chariot came to a standstill, she rushed down, clasping her mouth with her palms and leaving a baffled and drowsy Kundali to fend for himself. A little later, when she emerged from the washroom, she was feeling much lighter and her sickness had subsided, but her head was whirling with the only plausible reason she could think of to explain the sudden bout of nausea.

'Where is Prabha? Has she returned yet?' she checked with one of the dasis.

'Yes my lady, Devi Prabha had returned early in the evening and has already retired to her room. Do you wish for me to summon her?'

She had begun to respond, when abruptly, as if struck by a sudden thought she turned around and rushed towards the palace portico. In the courtyard she saw Kundali, scared and flinching, standing not very far from the immobile chariot he had disembarked from. He was incessantly staring at Ballabh and the group of guards who were pensively studying him from a reasonable distance. Amrapali dashed towards him, and instantly, with a flicker of recognition, the tension on his façade began to settle.

She embraced him and gently stroking his hair, gradually led him inside the palace. Hurriedly, she instructed a dasi to ready the room next to her own for the boy and serve their dinner there. Though she herself hadn't eaten since the morning, it was only after she had fed Kundali with her own hands and stroked him to sleep that she could transfer her attention towards her plate. She felt awfully tired and even the effort of picking food from the plate and depositing it in her mouth seemed daunting. But somehow she got herself to finish her meal before retiring to her own room. Within moments of collapsing on the lavish, carved oakwood bed, she was firmly in the grasp of sleep.

Later, around the last pehar of the night, the two guards returned after aborting their search. They had checked every housing cluster around the mango grove, but let alone find Kundali's house, they couldn't even locate someone who had seen or heard of a boy matching his description. They had even tracked down some of the children who had been chasing the boy, but the story they had to tell didn't prove of much help either.

Apparently the children had first seen Kundali outside a playground near the mango grove that very evening. He had been playing with a string that had scrap metal pieces strung on one end, making funny faces and noises each time he heard a metallic clatter. He had then playfully fastened the other end of the string to his waist and started running around, visibly scared of the sound following him. This was when the kids, drawn by his antics, had begun rooting and cheering, and when he began running they too followed. It had only been a short chase when their little sport had been spoiled by Ballabh's intrusion. They too, like all the others the two guards had spoken with, were completely clueless about where Kundali had come from.

The tawny glow emanating from the pair of sconce torches mounted on facing walls of the tent was doing little to brighten the prevailing mood. An intimidating silence, the kind that usually precedes a storm, supplemented the pervading gloom as the seven men seated on cushioned stools circling a small table looked for appropriate words to respond.

'Speak up, gentlemen. The highly revered and accomplished battle strategists of Magadh can't be dumbstruck by a simple question such as this, or can they? For the past eighteen weeks we have been camping here, on the shores of Vaishali, with no sight on how we will ever manage to enter the city. Thousands of our men have lost their lives, slain by the enemy, disease or nature, and we are still no closer to our goal than the day we had embarked upon this campaign. I can't bear to witness such brazen slaughter of my men and thus I seek your opinion, esteemed members of my war council, on whether we should persist with the siege of Vaishali or withdraw like gutless cowards who had foolishly undertaken an enterprise much beyond their faculties?' Ajatshatru's voice rang through the tent.

The Yuvraj was pacing up and down the rear of the tent, outside the circle of stools on which the council members were perched, his hands clasped behind his back and gait stiff. In the dim lighting, his eyes appeared crimson—red, like simmering pieces of coal ready to smoulder anything that stood in their way.

Ajatshatru was still adorning his battle gear, the domed helmet replaced by a red cloth turban and his chainmail armour jangling with each step he took. The scabbard holding his sword hung to a leather belt strapped around his waist and swayed indolently as though scouting for an unwary prey to carve. His left forearm was heavily bandaged and the dark red patches on the otherwise clean bandage suggested that the concealed wound had far from healed.

A gash, fresh and pink, could be seen running across his dimpled cheek, from just below his right eye to where his lips thinned out.

Ajatshatru had returned from the frontier to the base camp only a while back and had hastily summoned a meeting of the war council comprising principal commanders of the Magadh army. Prasenjit, through the runners deployed for ferrying information and messages across the patch of woods that separated the vanguard from the camp, had learnt of the surprise offensive, yet another blitzkrieg, by the enemy troops that had led to several casualties within their ranks.

The strategically timed raid had commenced at the precise moment when a fresh set of soldiers were heading towards the anterior to take their positions for the night and those exhausted from the day-long watch were being relieved. The bleak dusk light and the pandemonium from the change of guard had amplified the usual reaction time for their men, a failing they were made to account for dearly. The pits they had dug and cleverly covered with thorny shrubbery to prevent exactly such a charge had proven futile as the attackers had deftly snaked past or jumped over them on the backs of their sturdy stallions. Only a handful, most while affecting their rushed retreat, had taken the bait and gone crashing down into the earthly crevices, but by then the damage had been inflicted.

Ajatshatru, the warrior that he was, on sighting the sudden offensive had charged towards the approaching cavalry, shouting to draw the attention of his fellowmen who had not yet detected the threat, without waiting for his customary bodyguards to accompany him. Slashing through the frontline, like a farmer cutting through thick sugarcane stalks, he had soon entered the heart of the attacking brigade, only to find himself surrounded by enemies on all sides.

His bodyguards who were desperately trying to catch up were held back by a bunch of Vajji horsemen who had spotted the opportunity to capture an important enemy commander. Meanwhile Ajatshatru, now alert to the delicateness of his situation, was slowly carving his way out of the enemy ranks towards a nearby group of combating Magadhan soldiers. His gallantry was matchless, as, swivelling his sword with one hand and a metallic spear with the other, holding the horse reins between his teeth, the lone Prince continued to bring down his opponents, slowly drifting towards the protective presence of his own men.

His assailants, over a dozen in count, were barely able to stand their ground against him, let alone capture the valiant warrior. And with the piercing sound of a trumpet, the sign for them to retreat, they were only too glad to return to the safety of the city walls. Listening to the runner's account, Prasenjit had wondered if the attackers would have retreated just as easily had they been aware of the identity of the Magadhan warrior they had come so perilously close to claiming.

Prasenjit knew that the risk Ajatshatru had taken was an impulsive and unwise one, but it was not for him to admonish the Prince. The King, Bimbisara, had left the battlefront only about a week back to tend to certain administrative exigencies at Rajgriha, and in his absence Ajatshatru, though theoretically his equal in command, was the de facto leader.

Moreover, a seasoned warrior himself, the Senapati knew that in such circumstances it was often adrenaline and not blood that rushed through the veins of a warrior, dictating every thought and action of his. It was such spontaneous and sometimes reckless action that differentiated the bravest from the brave, and Ajatshatru was by far the most courageous young man he had had the privilege of riding alongside.

The combat, Prasenjit had learnt, had left many soldiers dead and several more gravely wounded. Ajatshatru too had taken a few injuries, nothing severe, but bloody and painful nonetheless. The Prince's aggravation, with the recent attack in particular and their collective inability to break the deadlock in general, had begun oozing with the first words he had uttered in the presence of his war council.

His question on whether to persist with the siege of Vaishali or withdraw had been a mere rhetoric and his council members knew better than to respond. Though seeds of uncertainty and doubt over the judiciousness of the campaign had begun to sprout in some of the assembled minds, under no circumstances they could bring themselves to dare voice them. Their silence meanwhile appeared to be getting under Ajatshatru's skin who had perhaps been hoping for a suggestion, a miraculous intervention maybe, which could help their forces scale the seemingly invincible walls of Vaishali.

'Your silence, gentlemen, is most unsettling for me. Should I then presume that the venerated Magadhan commanders concede to the supremacy of Vaishali's forces over our own?' Ajatshatru bellowed once again.

Prasenjit was conscious that none of the other commanders would dare talk back to the Prince given his belligerent mood and if the meeting was to be steered in a conclusive direction he needed to step in. Sifting slightly in his seat, he began, 'with your kind permission, Yuvraj, I would like to table some thoughts for the council to debate upon.'

Upon receiving a nod from Ajatshatru, he continued, 'The mistake we made was to lose the initiative of surprise. We went ahead with our plans despite the knowledge that the Lichchavis were in the know of our intentions, if not the detailed campaign outline, and would be prepared to confront us. In our haste to taste victory we did not review our strategies and went ahead with the frontal assault, an error I believe to be at the root of this undue elongation of the siege. However, now that we are here, the option of returning back is an unthinkable one. Not only is the Magadhan pride at stake here, but if we return now, we might not again, not in the near future at least, be able to accumulate such a formidable army. This is our best chance to annex Vaishali and we must not let it slip.

'There are two main hurdles we face today. First is our inability to reach the city gates without exposing our troops to enemy assault, who, with their positions atop the ramp crowning the boundary walls, have a definitive advantage. We have tried everything from charging with elephants clad in multiple armour to using the veil of darkness for our approach, but to no avail. The torrent of boulders and blazing pots brimming with smouldering oils that they shower upon us has burnt alive or crushed many men and beasts while several others have been trampled in the resulting stampede. And unless we figure a way to approach them, our weapons shall continue to be eluded of their mark. The second problem is their tactic of mounting sudden and rapid attacks on our frontline. They materialize suddenly and even before our men have had the time to react, they inflict measured damage upon us and withdraw. We have attempted various mechanisms to thwart such offensives, but none have proven effective thus far. The answers to both these problems lie in innovation,' he said, briefly pausing for effect and scanning through his audience. He had the undivided attention of all men present inside the tent, Ajatshatru included.

Satisfied, he continued, 'Our traditional weapons are not working, we need to design new ones. Weapons with such reach that they enable us to wreak havoc in the enemy ranks from our extant positions without exposing our men to danger. And weapons which can slice through raiding enemy brigades with precision and alacrity that is yet unknown to mankind.'

'You speak the truth, Senapati, but your words, I am afraid, sound more like fanciful abstractions than being attuned to reality. If indeed such weapons existed, why would we, or any other king for that matter, risk the lives of their men in battle?' Ajatshatru mocked, drawing few suppressed snickers from the audience.

'Such weapons don't currently exist, your majesty,' he replied unfazed, 'but shall soon be. You would recall when the minister, Devdutt, had paid us a visit to appraise His Majesty, the King of the state of affairs in Rajgriha. It was then that I had mentioned our predicament to him and he had offered to work with his engineers to fashion such devices like those I have just mentioned. Only today a messenger arrived from Rajgriha carrying a message from Devdutt. He claims to have come up with a few potential conceptions that could instantly alter the course of this war and that over the next few months he should be able to fabricate the prototypes and test them. Of course, after discounting for the obvious exaggeration that Devdutt is more than capable of, the developments appear reasonably promising to me.'

'Devdutt is a man of theory and though I am not entirely convinced about the impact his contraptions will have on the battlefront, they might still be worth a try. But the bigger question facing us is what do we do for the few months he says it will take to develop and test these equipments? We can't just allow the carnage to continue unabated, living in the hope that these weapons, whatever they are, will actually see the light of day and arrive in time to help us win the battle,' Ajatshatru argued.

'I don't quite have the answer to that, but we need to hold fort and keep attempting to gain an entry into the city without unduly hazarding our men. Perhaps we could look at digging a tunnel, starting somewhere in the woods and leading us to the gate or even beyond, into the city,' he suggested.

'The sandy surface around the river banks is not fit to support a tunnel. The ground will doubtlessly cave in at some point, endangering the lives of the men working inside. No, a tunnel is not a feasible option,' Ajatshatru replied.

'Also, the animals, our elephants and horses, will be unable to pass through a regular-sized tunnel. And digging one large enough to accommodate them shall be an immensely time consuming and burdensome affair,' one of the other commanders chipped in.

'Why can't we look at an overhead tunnel then? We could ship in sandstone from Patligram and make a strong structure that can withstand the enemy arrows,' Prasenjit argued.

'No, we will not be able to build a structure strong enough to withstand boulders hurled from that height. Moreover, as soon as the construction workers will breach their range of fire, rest assured, they will be greeted by a volley or spears and arrows,' Ajatshatru said, pausing ponderously before adding, 'but this does give me an idea. We could build a wall, a strong barricade, around the area near the river where our vanguard is stationed.'

A sudden glint had appeared in Ajatshatru's eyes and the excitement that seeped into his tone was palpable. 'The wall shall begin at the periphery of the jungle, allowing unrestricted access to the front from the base camp, and run parallel to Vaishali's boundary wall before curving into the river. In two strategic spots we shall allow gaps in the wall, big enough for our forces to march ahead when they need to. These openings will be heavily guarded night and day, and then if the Lichchavis attempt one of their sudden raids, it will only be at their own peril. How long do you suppose it will take us to ship sandstone from Patligram and have the battlement ready?' he shot out to no one in particular.

'We can start shipping whatever material is readily available immediately and the rest can continue to be delivered as the construction progresses. A simple wall should not take very long to build. Two weeks, three at the most, would be my best estimate,' once again it was Prasenjit who had spoken, but the hopefulness was visible on all the assembled faces. Suddenly their hushed worries had become a thing of the past and suggestions and ideas for implementing the plan were pouring in from all corners.

It was decided that one of the commanders would immediately set sail for Patligram and return with whatever building material he could lay his hands on. Construction of the Magadh battlement on enemy grounds would commence before sundown the next day.

When Ajatshatru exited the tent, Prasenjit in tow, his lips were curled in a content smile. The wounds on his arm and face were no longer hurting as much as they were just a while back. All was not lost, at least not just as yet.

7

'Don't get me wrong, your quandary does not remain hidden from me. But decisions, no matter how grave they appear, must be made when their time comes. You have nurtured this bond absorbedly and unselfishly, giving it all that you had, unflinchingly staking the very best years of your life for its sake. I know what Devi Amrapali means to you and you to her, and I would not, even in my wildest dreams, suggest anything potentially deleterious for your relationship. However, you need to understand that we will be getting married once the clouds of war shrouding Vaishali have been dispelled and then you will need to move out of the Old Palace. If you keep her in the dark about this till the very end, given your mutual affection and reliance upon each other, the information will prove that much more disturbing for Devi Amrapali. Hence, it is also with her interest in mind that I advocate that you break the news without any further delay,' Suraj Mal counselled Prabha.

The second pehar of the day had just begun and the sun, no longer as scorching as the weeks gone by, was still agreeable and pleasing. The month of Chaitra was at its fag end, and trees, having shed their prior covering, were being draped afresh by the Vasant Ritu. Sprouting leaves and shoots in assorted shades of green were lending an air of hope and promise to the surroundings—a near perfect weather for souls soaking in the elixir of love.

The two, Prabha and Suraj, were perched on the broad marble stairway of the Vasini temple, not far from the Old Palace of Vaishali, and engaged in deliberations on a matter that had been consuming a considerable share of their time over past few days. Their love, nurtured by the tides of time and longing, had blossomed into a mellow and mature bond. So, it hadn't come as a surprise when Suraj had informed Prabha about his dialogue with his parents and their accordance to the conjugal union.

Prabha had been ecstatic, soaring like a little bird on its first flight, and instinctively wanted to rush back to the palace and break the news to Amrapali. It was then that Suraj had raised the highly pertinent question of her leaving the palace and parting with the only friend she ever had, and her rush of excitement had come crashing down. If Suraj was the dream of her future, Amrapali was the foundation from her past. If he was her desire, she, her need, and the thought of parting with either was simply unthinkable. Though, with time, and aided profoundly by Suraj's persistent persuasion she had come to terms with the inevitability of her departure from the Old Palace, the debate on when she should break the news to Amrapali was still far from reaching a conclusion.

'Not now, not when she needs me by her side the most. Any day now her child will be born, the child whose father she has not set eyes on for over eight months. I can only imagine the inner turmoil and trauma she has silently endured over all these days. So often I see her gazing at the sky, lost in a world of her own, and I can feel the waves of tension seeping out from every pore of her body. And yet when I make an attempt to talk to her—not meaning to burden me with her sorrows, she smiles and steers the conversation clear of the subject. No Suraj, I cannot bring myself to abandon her at this delicate juncture of her life. I will need more time, at least till her child is born, before I can break the news to her,' Prabha argued, her eyes turning moist as she spoke.

The logic was sound and Suraj found neither the courage nor the inclination to offer a counter. The siege of Vaishali by the Magadh troops was still underway and he was not even sure as to how long it would take for the war to end and their wedding to materialize. Prabha had agreed to have a word with Amrapali and he could draw comfort from the fact that she had now put a definitive timeline to it. All he needed to do was to wait for the child to be born, and once Prabha managed to have a word with Amrapali, the last traces of uncertainty in the path of their impending union would stand cleared.

Suraj nodded in agreement and reached out to wipe the solitary tear that had escaped her eye and was snaking down her cheek, but Prabha withdrew, using an end of her dupatta to dab her eyes instead. The discussion had wiped away, albeit temporarily, any remnants of the romance that Suraj's company and the agreeable weather had kindled within her. Feeling a sudden need for solitude, she got up and wiping nonexistent specks of dirt from her dhoti, readied herself to leave. Suraj did not make any attempts to stop her as she climbed down the staircase and headed towards the tree to which her horse was tethered.

They rode silently, Suraj deliberately maintaining a few paces between their trotting mounts, till the large gates of the Old Palace came visible. 'I shall see you tomorrow,' he said, as Prabha halted her horse to look back at him. This was their customary parting point. Every time they went out into the city, Suraj insisted on riding back with her and at precisely this point, from where he could see her entering the secure premises of the palace, he stopped to bid her farewell.

She nodded her head, meeting his gaze briefly before turning back and patting the horse on the side of its neck, a signal for the beast to resume walking. Suraj too turned around and, without waiting to watch her enter the gate, kicked his mount into a gallop.

Their meeting today hadn't ended on its usual romantic high and he, for once, didn't feel the urge to steal those additional moments of looking at her before she was consumed by the vastness of the palace.

Upon sighting Prabha, the guards were quick to part the flanks of the iron gate and permit her to ride in. She had barely crossed the threshold when her eyes caught the shape of a man and a sudden spark of recognition emerged in her eyes. The man, old and skeletal with apricot-like wrinkles on his face, was standing near the entrance, flanked by two guards. The asperities of age and possibly sickness had reduced him to a gaunt, frail structure, only a shadow of his former self, but the deep-set eyes, spilling with worldly wisdom and sagacity were unmistakable. The man was indeed Acharya Narhari.

'Pranam Acharya,' she said, disembarking from the horse and reaching out for the old man's feet to seek his blessings. 'Prabha isn't it?' he said, frowning to focus his ageing eyes as he dabbed the back of her head.

Acharya Narhari, in his better days, had been the Pradhanacharya of Rajkul—the most revered gurukul of Vaishali. Impressed by little Amrapali's virtuosity and innocence, he had taken her under his aegis and tutored her within the confines of her home. Though Prabha, a resident of the same neighbourhood, had seen the Acharya during his visits to Amrapali's house, it was only much later that she actually got the privilege of meeting him.

Prabha had been accompanying Amrapali when—after her appointment as the Nagarvadhu and being pushed to the brink by the then king's explicit overtures—she had visited the Acharya to seek his guidance. It was the Acharya whose words of encouragement had given her the audacity to embark upon a journey that was to alter the political landscape of the kingdom.

Prabha couldn't help but admire the old man for being able to recollect her name from the solitary meeting many years ago.

The guards standing on either side of the old man were already fidgeting and when Prabha enquired the reason behind his visit, one of them broke into a dialogue even before the Acharya could open his mouth. 'Devi, he is here to visit Devi Amrapali and since we were unable to recognize him we had sent a guard to seek her permission before admitting him. Of course, we shall immediately show him to the audience chamber now. Forgive our indiscretion, Devi... Please forgive us, Acharya.'

'That won't be necessary now,' she said, waving the guard away, but not before she, by way of a quick glare, had expressed her displeasure at the treatment meted out to the elderly guest. She then escorted the teacher through the large carved-stone courtyard to the audience chamber—the expansive room where the Nagarvadhu of Vaishali entertained her personal guests. Narhari had barely occupied one of the velvet-cushioned, silver chairs when the door to the chamber opened again and Amrapali stepped in. There were two attendants supporting her and Kundali, absorbed in the bunch of little pearls dangling from the corner of her dupatta, was trailing along.

She looked different. The massive baby bump of a woman in the last leg of her pregnancy was clearly discernible despite the clever attempt to camouflage it with her drapery. Her face appeared fuller and cheeks smoothened, but the most glaring change was the murky luminescence bathing her skin—a divine radiance known only to expectant mothers.

The news of her pregnancy had come as a shock to Amrapali and initially she had been apprehensive about the very idea of giving birth to a child without the consent, or knowledge even, of its father. She had remained clueless about the whereabouts of Bindusen as her thoughts about him had acquired even more anxious hues. 'Where and how is he? Is he even alive? How will he react to the news? Will he be willing to give the child his name or would he rather let it struggle with the dreadful tag of illegitimacy for the rest of its wretched life?'

But the nervousness proved temporary and with each passing day, as the realization of another life form shaping within her began to settle, she was usurped by a wave of motherly affection and alacrity. She imagined what the baby would look like, a faultless combination of Bindusen's handsome features—still vivid on the canvas of her mind—and her own. She longed for the day when she would hold the little one in her arms, nursing and cradling it to sleep, and her heart would begin to leap and prance carelessly like a playful rabbit.

She still experienced intermittent bouts of anxiety, flared by pregnancy induced hormonal shifts, but the bundle of joy contained within lent her the patience and resilience to tide over them. And when she found herself unable to emerge from her musings, Kundali, with his zealous antics and guileless craving for her attention helped wrench her away from her thoughts.

Kundali's ingress into her life had come as a blessing and in tending to him and his most basic needs Amrapali felt a strange sense of satisfaction, one that made her feel complete as a woman. Now that her baby had begun making its own presence felt—twisting, turning and kicking inside the womb—she saw not one, but two eager beneficiaries of her motherly warmth and affection.

Since his arrival at the palace, Amrapali had felt a special bond between Kundali and herself. Throughout the day the boy would follow her like a shadow and at night-time it was only her lullabies that put him to sleep. In the little time he had spent at the palace, he had become an inseparable part of her life, never ceasing to charm her with the naïvety of his actions and the purity of his uncorrupted soul.

Narhari glanced over Prabha's shoulder and at the sight of his favourite pupil, a barrage of emotions fleeted across his face. Smiling, Amrapali paced up to him, trying to bend down and touch his feet, but Narhari held her by the shoulders. 'No beti, in such a state you should not be bending down,' he said.

'Acharya, this is such a pleasant surprise. It has been so long and…and…you look so different. Why, please sit down and make yourself comfortable,' she greeted him enthusiastically.

'I heard the news of your pregnancy and since I was passing by this part of the city I thought I must stop by to check on you,' he replied. The warmth in his tone was palpable, but the old man had suddenly begun fidgeting, overwhelmed perhaps by the sight of his disciple in her expectant bloom.

'I can't stay for long and must get going at once, but my best wishes shall always remain with you and the little one. May God shower the baby with his grace and blessings and may the child usher into your life a wave of joy that has eluded you for long,' he said, closing his eyes in a silent prayer before dabbing her forehead with his palm.

'No, Acharya, I can't let you leave like this. There is so much that I need to speak with you about, so many things I need your advice on. You will have to join me for dinner and spend rest of the night here at the palace. In the morning, at whatever time you wish, my chariot will stand ready to take you back to the ashram,' she insisted. But the old man remained unmoved. Fully aware that even if a fraction of the resolute Acharya Narhari of the past remained in his current decrepit frame, it would be impossible for her to get him to change his mind, she tried all that she could— appeal, plead and reason—but expectedly, to no avail.

Instead the old man said, 'The Sakya Muni, I hear, has set up camp in the city, not far from where my ashram is. It would be nice if you pay him a visit and seek his blessings for your unborn child. Blessings of the Buddha will prove a precious influence for the little one when he is born. And if you do happen to be visiting the Sakya Muni, do drop by at the ashram and see me as well. I have there a thing from your past life, a thing that I have preserved through many years and which I wish to hand over to you now.'

Nodding her head in accordance, Amrapali, with a heavy heart, escorted the old man to the courtyard where her chariot was waiting to ride him back to his ashram.

'Remember my words Amrapali—you have led, albeit not by choice, a life with many shades and of much adventure. Look around you and weed out, with utmost care, any elements from your past that might prove to be an untoward influence on your child,' were his last words before embarking on the chariot.

Amrapali stood in the courtyard, quiet and poignant, watching the chariot steer out of the gate, drawn by the four stallions pulling it. She was repeating Narhari's words to herself, attempting to infuse perspective into the ramblings. The Acharya, she knew, was not one to make meaningless statements. There had to be something of significance in those words that she was failing to latch on to. What was it that the Acharya had been implying? And what was 'the thing' from her past life that he wanted to give her? Despite straining hard she could not come up with any plausible answers to the questions her old teacher had left behind.

'Look, look what I got,' she was startled by a voice. It was Kundali and he was holding a red rose he had pulled out from one of the nearby vases. 'Now smile,' he said, stuttering, as he handed over the flower to her. She couldn't help but heed to his words. Kundali had perhaps noticed the anguish on her face and done what he could think of to assuage it. The look of innocence on his face was endearing and impulsively Amrapali pulled him to her bosom and planted a kiss on his forehead.

'Maybe the old Acharya was only rambling. Maybe I am reading too much into his words and they actually are just what they appeared to be—words of care and concern from an elderly well-wisher to an expecting mother,' she thought as the two ambled back inside.

'About eleven thousand men, two and half thousand horses and over four hundred war elephants,' the man read from a list in his hand before retiring to the chair he had risen from. His audience remained contemplative, pensively absorbing the numbers he had hurled at them.

'That is indeed severe,' Yudhveer uttered, addressing no one in particular.

The scene was unfolding in a meeting room at the King's Palace (New Palace) in Vaishali where members of the Vajji council had congregated to take stock of the war and deliberate on the future course of action. At the Senapati's behest one of his subordinates had just apprised the gathering of the battle casualties, an alarming revelation for most of the assembled council members.

'Of course, and unless we do something drastic urgently, the losses will continue to mount. As I had informed you Maharaj, enemy fortifications across the gate are complete now. Safety of the large stone walls they have erected has made our surprise attacks, a ploy that had served us well thus far, redundant. By building the wall they have seized the initiative and our forces are left with no option but to wait for them to mount an offensive and hope that we are prepared and able to thwart it every time. The situation is undeniably worrisome,' Chetak, the senapati, elaborated.

Outside, the sun was exiting the horizon, leaving behind a scarlet splash, like a sword gradually slicing open an enemy heart. Torches and diyas were fluttering in various nooks of the chamber, but their combined radiance, comfortably overshadowed by the fading light of dusk, seemed shackled and confined. The air within the room, much like the prevailing mood, was weighed down by tense apprehension.

'We can't just sit back and allow the losses to mount, can we? The port and the city gates have remained off bounds for traders for over several months now and the citizens are surviving only on the most basic rations that are available to them. Markets have run out of spices, nuts, oils and several such commodities for which we are reliant on imports and now, within most households, meals have begun to constitute of meager servings of rice and lentils only. Vegetables and dairy products have become so scarce and expensive that only the affluent are able to afford them. And with the approaching winter, I suspect, the shortage of woolen garments might spiral into a crisis of sorts too. If this siege continues unabated, we are heading for definite disaster. Tell me, Senapati, what should be done for us to stay clear of this looming catastrophe?' the King spoke once again, his distressed words well-directed this time.

'Maharaj, the invaders, judging by the resources they have spent in fortifying their frontline, do not seem to be in a hurry to leave. They are receiving constant reinforcements, of men and material, through the waterway and we are not in a position to obstruct their supplies. Unless we take a bold step and shake them from their zone of comfort, they can continue camping outside the city gates for years together.'

'So, what is this "bold step" we must take?' Yudhveer interjected, snapping at the Senapati's unwarranted rhetoric.

'One single forceful attack that can uproot them from their positions,' Chetak replied.

'What are we waiting for then, why haven't we begun planning for the assault already?' the King retorted.

'It is because they outnumber our forces two to one. And given their recent fortifications, any unplanned advance will be akin to leading our men straight into the jaws of death,' the Senapati began.

'We have already summoned all men and beasts we could from the Khandas and the cordoning of the city means that we can't even approach other nearby kingdoms for assistance. Moreover I have serious reservations about the willingness of any of these rulers to take on the might of Bimbisara without any direct provocation. Therefore the only option we are left with is to bore into our reserves and create a force mighty enough to face and vanquish the enemy,' he explained.

'What reserves are you referring to? Didn't you just say that we have summoned all the men we could?' one of the council members shot out.

'I did, but the troops we have called upon comprise men who were already in the employ of their respective Rajas. These are soldiers from military units that are maintained by individual Rajas for the purpose of protection and policing within their own Khandas. And true, we have inducted all such men into the main army of Vaishali. However, the reserve I refer to remains untouched—the common citizens of Vaishali.'

A series of gasps rallied across the room, some out of disbelief and others from incomprehension. 'What? Are you suggesting that we induct civilians into the army?' the King eventually voiced the common concern.

'Why not Maharaj? With all the pride we take in being the only democratically governed kingdom in the whole of Aryavart, why would the people hesitate in picking up arms when the very foundation of this belief is under threat? I realize it would not be an easy task to rally the men together and train them for battle, but if the honourable council members pass a verdict mandating it for every healthy man in the city to join the army for a limited period, it might just work,' Chetak responded.

'You mean everyone, the Brahmins, the Vaishyas?' another council member spoke.

The social fabric of Vaishali, like most of Aryavart was stratified on the lines of four Varnas. The Brahmins or descendants of those believed to have been cast from the mouth of Brahma—the creator of the universe—occupied the highest pedestal in this hierarchy. They were considered to be the custodians of knowledge and were usually engaged as teachers or temple priests. The Kshatriyas or the warrior race, cast from Brahma's arms as per the Rigveda, comprised land owners, soldiers and rulers. All the eight clans to which the 7,707 Rajas of the confederacy belonged were of the Kshatriya race.

The two remaining castes were Vaishyas—traders and merchants whose ancestors had been shaped from the Creator's thighs and the Shudras or the workers and peasants, believed to have been cast from Brahma's feet. The occupational boundaries segregating the four Varnas were well defined, leaving no scope for ambiguity. Battlefront was a domain of the Kshatriyas only. Brahmins, Vaishyas and Shudras were not only devoid of any battle training but even their participation in active combat was completely unheard of.

The Senapati's suggestion, though budding out of sound logic, had left the King and other ministers bewildered. They were not sure how members of other non-warrior communities would react to such a dictate. The ramifications could be grave, so much so that even an uprising against the present regime could not be ruled out. And given the drawings of war, the state was inadequately equipped to deal with any such internal unrest.

Deliberations followed. Alternatives that the rulers of Vaishali were left with were the first to be weighed, but in no time the hopelessness of their situation was evident to all. In the absence of any external allies to aid them, resources they could garner internally remained their only hope to take on the enemy. They could of course have opted to defer the decision and allow status quo to prevail at the front, but that would have been a certain recipe for disaster. Situation within the city walls would have expectedly deteriorated and then it would only be a matter of time before they would be compelled to open the city gates to the enemy.

'But what makes you think that the pundits, traders and peasants will not object to such a ruling from the council?' Yudhveer said, steering the discussion back to the Senapati's suggestion.

'Maharaj, we will need to play to their sense of patriotism, their love for Vaishali. The declaration we release will need to be opaque, revealing the enormity of the disaster that looms ahead of us. Its language will need to be inclusive, such that it appears more like an appeal and less of an order. We will simultaneously engage the key opinion makers from other Varnas so as to dispel any possibilities of an organized backlash. And once the majority heeds to the dictate, others, those who harbour reservations against it, will be compelled to follow,' Chetak responded.

'Suppose it works and we are able to enlist thousands of commoners into the army, how much of an advantage would it actually translate into? Do we have sufficient weapons to arm them? A bunch of novices, untrained in warfare and never exposed to the drudgeries of battle, how much of a chance do they stand against the practised Magadhan warriors?' the prime minister was the next to voice his concerns.

'Our weapon-makers have been working day and night since the war began and in the time we would take to enlist the men into the army and impart a basic training, they should be able to forge enough armaments to meet our requirement. As for the aptitude of these men, I am afraid, Minister, I have to concede to your argument. Despite the fundamental training in warfare we give them, these men will be no match for the Magadhan infantry, and that's a reality we must live with.'

'Most battles, as you would know, are won and lost in the mind. It is not always the dexterity or even valour of the men staking out at the front that determines the outcome of wars. These men, with their sheer numbers, will help us generate fear and panic in the enemy ranks and it will be our regular soldiers who will use the ensuing fissures to win the battle for us,' Chetak explained.

'But doesn't that mean that many of them run the risk of losing their lives?' the minister shot back.

'They do. But then, aren't the soldiers battling at the front staking their own lives for the sake of these people today? My men, thousands of them, have already lost their lives in defending these very men and their families, in protecting their freedom. Who is answerable for those lost lives? I agree, there will be a price to pay and some civilians might not return home, but those who do will go back to their families and lives while my men shall continue to wager their existence for the sake of their security. If we hesitate today, who will be accountable for the many more men, women and children who will be butchered once the enemy troops march into the city?' the exasperation in the Senapati's tone was palpable.

But quickly checking his impulsive imprudence, he continued, 'However, one assurance I can give you is that we will try and limit the damage to the best we can. The civilians will be stationed at the heart of the unit, flanked on all sides by our regular troops. We will attempt to limit their exposure to the enemy ranks and God willing, most of them will manage to return to their families unscathed and victorious.'

'How long will you take to induct these men into the army and plan the concluding assault?' Yudhveer enquired.

Chetak could feel the tides turning in his favour. The Vajji council, though under severe duress from the absence of viable alternatives, was on the verge of making a landmark pronouncement—a decision that would provide Chetak with the impetus to expel the supercilious Magadhans from his land.

'About two weeks, Maharaj,' he replied.

8

It was a pleasant morning, the cool mist hanging in the air giving it a surreal, almost dreamlike semblance. Amrapali had woken up from her slumber a while back, but unable to resist the temptations of indolence, lay lounging on her bed. Her eyes, still puffy and yet wistful were peering out of the ajar balcony doors, affixed on something distant, slicing through the hazy curtain of mist. She had spent a better part of the previous night twisting and turning on the soft muslin bed sheet, her unrestrained thoughts darting across disparate spheres. She imagined herself nursing her unborn child, she thought about its absent father and she reflected upon the ostensibly unrelenting battle that had claimed the serenity of her beloved city. But the one predominant thought she found herself preoccupied with was that of Acharya Narhari, her elderly teacher who had paid her a visit only a few days back. Since then, his words, 'Seek the Sakya Muni's blessings for your unborn child … I have something from your past life that I wish to give you,' had persistently echoed in her ears.

Despite the predominantly wakeful night she had risen with a smile, brimming with cheerfulness, delight and an enthusiasm she had not encountered in a while. 'Mood swings, one of the many hazards of pregnancy! Well, I had been cautioned and in this particular instance I am not even complaining,' she mused, her lips curling in a slender smile.

'Oh, you are up already?' It was Prabha. Amrapali had failed to notice Prabha's entry into the room or the few steps she would have taken to reach the foot of her bed. Turning to face her friend, she responded with a beaming smile, and with a pat of the hand motioned for her to sit alongside her.

'You are looking much better today,' she responded, marching towards the silver framed polished metal mirror that ornamented one of the bedroom walls. Below the mirror was a silver inlaid rustic-wood table on which Amrapali's shringar peti or box of adornments was placed. Gently lifting the lid, she took out a leaf shaped ivory container and dabbed her finger into its contents, before placing it back in the box. Walking up to Amrapali she lifted her finger—now smeared with kohl—and left a black mark on her forehead. 'May God ward off the evil eye and protect you.'

'Yes indeed, I feel well,' Amrapali replied, her lips stretching further to broaden her smile. 'You know, I was thinking of what the Acharya had said and I was wondering if we could pay him a visit today. From his ashram we could proceed to the Sakya Muni's encampment and pay our obeisance to the sage as well,' she suggested.

'Even I am curious to know about what he wanted to give you,' Prabha replied, 'And it might not be a bad idea to visit him, but do you think you will be able to handle the travel. The road leading up to the ashram might be rough and potholed.'

Prabha's concern wasn't completely unfounded. A few ghatis later, once the mist had lifted, and when their chariot, surrounded by the usual detachment of bodyguards was headed towards the ashram, Amrapali was forced to consider if she had made the right decision. The road, visibly neglected for a long time, was peppered with bumps and craters, and had overgrown branches hanging dangerously at regular intervals. Each time the wheels hit a bump and creaked, she would feel something churn within her belly.

But well aware that if she chose to return, she might not get another chance to visit her guru anytime soon, she endured the adversity, occasionally clasping her mouth to prevent what she thought to be her guts from spilling out.

All through the ride Prabha's hand was gently resting against her bulging belly, a gesture she found deeply comforting and helpful. She had been desirous of bringing Kundali along too, but the boy, in his trademark obstinate fashion had refused to partake in the journey. In the hindsight she was glad that he had done so, for the arduousness of the ride might have proven tough and challenging for him. Lost in her thoughts she leaned towards Prabha and slipping her head on her shoulder, shut her eyes.

'We are there,' she heard a soft whisper and felt Prabha's hand gently brush her hair. Gradually she opened her eyes and looked around. They had indeed arrived at their destination—a solitary hut standing in the zone where the Mahavana thinned out to dissolve into the city's periphery. The scene wasn't very different from what she could recall from her last visit many years ago. Only the shrubbery had taken over most of the portico that she remembered once existed and there were discernible traces of wear and tear marking the edifice of the dwelling. 'Perhaps age has been preventing him from engaging in regular upkeep of the property,' she thought, getting down from the chariot, holding Ballabh's hand for support.

She called out for the Acharya, gently at first and raising her pitch each subsequent time till she was virtually shouting, but she heard nothing, not a sound of reciprocation from inside the dwelling. Praying that her host had not ventured out into the city rendering her laborious expedition useless, she ambled towards the hut's entrance with Prabha close on her heels.

The door, an uneven panel arranged by binding together ill-fitting wooden planks, and clearly inept of fulfilling its purpose of keeping intruders at bay, was slightly ajar giving the impression that the hut wasn't actually deserted. Filled with a glimmer of hope, Amrapali pushed it gently, opening it with a mild creak. And instantly she was forced to step back, recoil almost, barely managing to stop from bumping into Prabha.

An unbearable stench, a dank smell of musty air tinted with the putrid odour of mortal decay had gushed from within the hut to crash against her nostrils and sending her staggering back. Prabha, who had stepped alongside her and could now experience first-hand the reason behind her friend's stumble, had instinctively pulled one end of her dupatta to cover the lower half of her face. The ladies looked at each other, holding the gaze for a fraction, apprehension and dread looming in both pairs of eyes.

Time appeared to have frozen to icicles as they tried to regain control of their senses, allowing themselves a few moments of quiet contemplation and mentally preparing to face the sight that lay awaiting them.

'Come,' Amrapali eventually uttered—her faltering voice almost unintelligible. By now, witnessing their quandary, Ballabh had walked up to them and his sheer presence did wonders in bolstering their faltering courage. But signalling for him to remain, Amrapali once again reached out for the door—her legs shaking with a mixture of fear and nervousness—and battling the excruciating stench, stepped inside the hut. Within a few moments she heard Prabha step in too.

Despite the sun liberally dispensing its illumination, the area within the enclosure was relatively dark with the lone window on the rear wall partially covered with creepers and unkempt weeds. Having just stepped inside, it took them several blinks to accustom their vision to the new surroundings, but the origin of the stench, the shadowy lump from which an incessant buzz was emanating, did not escape their notice.

Taking measured steps, plastering their dupattas over their nose and mouth, they approached the figure, fearing the worst. But despite the forewarning and mental preparations, the sight that greeted them made their steps freeze midway. An involuntary shriek emerged from Prabha's mouth, but was muted at source by the firm casing of her dupatta.

A bulbous mass of cartilage and bone that had formerly been the revered Acharya Narhari stared back at them from the floor. His guts and intestines lay spilled adjacent to a hollow stomach revealing the white of his ribs. Bare patches of bone were visible everywhere—his legs, his torso and his face—and where the coating of flesh remained, it was putrid and decaying with swarms of black and purple flies hovering over it. His startled and lifeless eyes, as though suddenly surprised by death itself, still contained a look of disbelief and horror.

Horror it was—a sight capable of freezing the sturdiest of hearts and the sanest of minds. Gulping to moisten her parched throat, Amrapali stepped back, her sandals making tearing sounds with each step she took on the pool of congealed blood surrounding the body, and shouted out for Ballabh. Prabha was frozen still, her eyelids having forgotten even the act of blinking.

Ballabh was quick to step inside the hut and after sparing a quick glance to check for the well-being of the ladies, busied himself in examining the scene. After surveying the body and the immediate surroundings, he came to face Amrapali. 'He has been dead for over a day, but not more than three. The assailants have sliced open his stomach with a sharp object, possibly a sword,' he said.

Ballabh had spoken in his native language, the tongue of the Xingnou that Amrapali was proficient with but Prabha could not comprehend. 'These wounds,' he continued, pointing to other parts of the body where flesh was missing and bones were showing, 'are from after his death, inflicted perhaps by wolves or dogs who would have been drawn in by the smell of blood.'

Teetering on the verge of tears, Amrapali listened to Ballabh's analysis, unable to pose questions or seek explanations. Her words, like her other senses seemed to have deserted her momentarily. It was not as though death had been alien to her. Through her life she had witnessed death at perilously close quarters, but never a manifestation so grotesque and heart wrenching. She was dumbstruck.

'Why him? What could a frail old man like him have done to harm anyone? And such ruthlessness! How can one human display such cruelty towards another?' Then, realizing the futility of her mutterings she checked herself and glanced at Prabha, who remained still, staring into oblivion.

Stepping closer, Amrapali wrapped her arms around Prabha and gently led her out of the hut. Instructing Ballabh to stay back and carry out the last rites for the deceased, they mounted the chariot and embarked upon the return journey to the palace. Their fragile state of mind and the shock that they had suffered led them to forgo their intended visit to the Sakya Muni.

The more Amrapali tried to emerge from the gathering gloom, the more ubiquitous its presence seemed to become. Every sound she heard—the rumble of her chariot's wheels, the creaking of wood, the jingling of harnesses and the rhythmic thudding of hooves—sounded like a desperate moan, a helpless cry for escape. She saw the faces of men and women on the roadsides, bowing courteously to her passing entourage and a veil of despair and misery was all that she registered. The trees, the clouds, the houses, every object she crossed appeared to be bound in an inevitable rut of monotony and crying for their release.

Just then she saw a group of men, all dressed in white, carrying a bier, chanting the unmistakable hymn of death. '*Ram*

Naam Satya Hai,' the boy in lead, carrying a dripping earthen pot on his shoulder, head clean-shaven, would bellow—*Ram Naam Satya Hai*—and others would follow. As her chariot passed the procession, she glimpsed at the bier supported by four able shoulders and saw a middle-aged man, not more that forty years of life behind him, lying peacefully on it. His body was wrapped in a white cotton cloth, but his face, nostrils plugged with balls of cotton, adorned a garb of tranquility that was absent from all the living and breathing faces escorting him.

'A victim of war perhaps,' she thought, 'but he was lucky to have found his end with all his organs intact and without any notable distortion to his appearance.' Impulsively her thoughts darted back to the lifeless remains of her guru and she flinched.

When she tried to wrench her mind away from the ghastly scene, it caught on to the thread she had just deviated from. 'The war! Just what purpose does it solve? Men killing hundreds of their own kind each day, not to mention the equal number of Satis who burn themselves alive on the smouldering pyres of their husbands. All this for the lust of power and control, when they are well aware that it is all but transitory! Their end too, like that of those they slaughter mercilessly, is certain, why then do they engage in such inhuman and barbaric acts?'

She understood that life and death were meagre cogs in the larger wheel of existence, but it was the meaning of the former, given the certainly of the latter that was confusing her. Suddenly everything around her appeared inconsequential, worthless even, and she found herself questioning the very tenets she had imbibed in her growing years and preserved since then. She was disgusted with the ability of mankind to stoop to depressing levels of animalism and wondered whether it was right for her to introduce the pure, sinless lifeform shaping within her womb into the corrupt world she lived in. Suddenly the wheels of the chariot came to a grinding halt, breaking the chain of her thoughts. They had arrived at the Old Palace and the gates were instantaneously flung open to allow the Nagarvadhu's entourage in.

'Devi, Suraj Ji is here to see you. He has been waiting since the afternoon,' an attendant walked up and informed Prabha just as they alighted from the chariot.

Amrapali glanced towards the sky and saw a few scattered stars lining the horizon. The sun had set and darkness was spreading rapidly. It was odd for Suraj to be waiting to meet Prabha for so long, she thought, and glanced towards her friend. She noticed a similar look of anxious concern fleet across Prabha's face.

'You go ahead and meet Suraj. I feel the need for some rest, so I shall head to my room,' she said, holding Prabha's arm as though meaning to steer her towards her waiting lover.

'I shall escort you till your chamber first,' Prabha responded.

'No, go and see what the matter is. It sounds urgent. The attendants can usher me to my room, don't worry,' she said, tightening her grip on Prabha momentarily. There was a sense of finality to her tone that forbade any further debate, and leaving her in the care of the attendants, Prabha headed towards the audience chamber, her heart thumping like a beating drum.

'Where is Kundali? Did he behave himself through the day? Has he eaten his dinner?' Amrapali shot out at one of her escorts as soon as Prabha was out of her sight.

'Oh dear, where have you been? You look disturbed and exhausted,' Suraj's concerned voice greeted her as soon as she entered the chamber. He had been examining a parchment in the yellow luminescence of the candelabras and torches lighting up the room. But on the sound of Prabha's footsteps, he was quick to roll and resign the document to the folds of the garment wrapped around his waist.

Instinctively, she glanced down at her dress and brushing the loose strands of hair dangling on her forehead with the back of her hand, she approached him. If not a complete mess, her appearance certainly left a lot to be desired. But it had indeed been a taxing day and she hadn't exactly been expecting him to be waiting for her.

Suraj Mal greeted her with a warm embrace, the question still lingering in his eyes. Occupying the gilded seat next to his, she began narrating the events of the day as they had unfolded—right from their arduous journey to the discovery of Acharya Narhari's mangled remains.

As she broached the subject, images—morbid and daunting— came streaming back and she began to cry, silently at first, then aloud, convulsing sobs welling up from the pit of her stomach. It was perhaps Suraj's reassuring presence that permitted her to liberate the emotions she had bottled within, and once they began oozing out, there was no holding back. It wasn't just the Acharya she was crying for, but also the grotesqueness she had witnessed and the shiver she had felt crawling up and down her spine ever since.

Aware that it was in her best interest to flush out the distress and pain along with her tears, Suraj assumed the role of a spectator, lending only a consoling hand intermittently. It was only when the intensity of her convulsions subsided, and having exhausted the tear reserves her eyes dried out, that he pulled her closer to him. Gently brushing his hand over her head he whispered soothing nothings into her ears so as to pacify her jangled nerves. If the revelation of the Acharya's sudden and tragic end had unsettled him, he did not allow it to show.

'But what is it that you wished to speak to me about?' she eventually asked, pulling herself away from him and dabbing her bloodshot eyes with her dupatta.

'Oh, yes! I had completely forgotten about that,' he said with a smile, reaching out to retrieve the parchment. Despite Suraj's relaxed deportment Prabha could not shake a feeling that there was more to the document he had just handed over to her than he was making it out to be. As she unfolded it, the first thing to catch her eye was the royal emblem and it made her heart leap.

'For the past several months Vaishali has been at war and your brave brothers, members of our defence forces have, albeit at the cost of some of their lives, managed to thwart every offensive of the enemy, ensuring the safety of our families and loved ones,' the letter that was addressed to Suraj Mal began.

Further, the letter went on to quantify the losses—of men and material—that the war had inflicted and elucidate its effect on the citizenry—emotional and commercial. It spoke of the grave circumstances they were facing with respect to the supply of essential commodities and how it was crucial for Vaishali's sake for them to uproot the enemy force and put an end to the siege. 'It is no longer just a matter of pride and vanity. It is now a matter of our survival—do or die,' it read.

Prabha could feel goosebumps forming up and down her arms and the hair on the nape of her neck stand up. Overcome by a patriotic fervour, she read along, 'and to make this a reality, on behalf of the King and members of the Vajji council I invite you to join the royal army on a short term attachment,' the letter continued. By now a frown had emerged on Prabha's face which only deepened as she read the last paragraph which contained detailed instructions on where, when and how Suraj was expected to report for his induction and training. His training was to begin the very next morning.

The letter had been signed by the local magistrate on behalf of the King of Vaishali. 'So, what do you intend to do?' she asked, handing the parchment back to him. Already a duel was ensuing within her—between her affection and concern for her beloved and the surge of patriotic passion she felt towards her motherland.

'It doesn't leave me with a choice, does it?' he responded nonchalantly, hint of a smile still affixed on his face.

'But how can they? You are not a soldier... How can you just pick up a sword and march at the enemy? Wouldn't that be suicidal?' The tussle within her had reached an early conclusion and a clear winner between the warring sentiments seemed to be emerging.

'They have mentioned that they will impart extensive training, spread over three days, before dispatching us to the front. They have also stated that additional manpower is needed for patrolling and other ancillary activities to support the warring regiments. So, for all you know we might not even get a glimpse of the real action,' he said, continuing to sound calm—a manifestation that had begun to irk Prabha now.

'This is senseless! Being present at the border during wartime is a risk in itself, irrespective of the tasks you are engaged in. An enemy arrow or spear does not differentiate one man from another basis their position or battle expertise. I have a terrible feeling about this. I think you should refuse to go,' she said, traces of annoyance seeping into her voice.

'You read the letter! It is an order from the Governing Council and not a request. I will need to go,' he responded.

'I will get Amrapali to have a word with the King on this. The order can be retracted.'

'You don't understand. All the men in my circle, all my friends have received similar summons and they are all going to join the army tomorrow. I can't use your or Devi Amrapali's influence to selfishly worm out of this and live with the sobriquet of a coward for the rest of my life,' he replied. His tone had now acquired a certain degree of seriousness and Prabha suddenly found herself tongue-tied.

His quandary was evident. The disgrace of not rising to the call of his motherland, the shame of using unscrupulous means to gain an exemption for his own self while his cohorts remained in the lurch—possibly some of them were even putting on heroic public façades given the inescapable certainty of the order—were simply unthinkable for him. It occurred to her that the decision had already been made and his desire to meet her stemmed not from the need to deliberate, but to bid farewell before he embarked on his chosen path.

'Don't worry, nothing will happen to me,' he said, reaching out and holding her hands.

Just then a loud knock on the door startled them both. Hurriedly pulling her hands away, Prabha instructed the intruder to come in. It wasn't normal for anyone to infringe when the audience chamber was occupied and especially when its doors were shut. 'What other unpleasantness does the day have in store,' Prabha thought to herself as the door came ajar.

One of Amrapali's attendants, still panting, rushed in. 'Devi Amrapali…Devi Amrapali is in pain… She is asking for you… It appears as though the labour has set in,' she stuttered, still gasping for breath.

'Oh!'

'I will have to go,' she said, turning towards Suraj. 'You take care of yourself and come back soon,' she added, her eyes boring into his.

He simply nodded, uttering not a word, but letting his eyes do the talking. In that brief moment they conveyed to her what a thousand words could not and she reciprocated in a muted tongue of intimacy spoken only between two throbbing hearts.

Then, almost abruptly, she turned on her heels and walked out of the room, the attendant close behind. She didn't pause to look back, perhaps to avoid the tear drops that had escaped her eyes and were now running down her cheeks from being noticed.

'*Aum trayambakam yajamahe...*' the maha mrityunjaya mantra dedicated to Lord Rudra was ringing within the walls of the room. Three Brahmins had been taking turns all through the night to ensure continuity of the chanting, an action meant to invoke the highest consciousness for enabling healthy and uncomplicated delivery at the destined hour and to assuage the ailing mother-to-be in the meantime.

Prabha, upon learning that Amrapali's labour pain had begun, had rushed to her side, shouting instructions for waiting women to summon the midwife and the Brahmins immediately. She had instantly fuelled the entire machinery into action and the Old Palace had begun buzzing with eager anticipation, waiting for its newest resident to arrive. Amrapali had been in excruciating pain and Prabha had remained by her bedside, constantly holding her hand and wiping her forehead with wet cloth.

The contraction induced pain—spasmodic and intermittent— would materialize suddenly sending her into agonizing, barely bearable, fits before abruptly subsiding. While it lasted though, Amrapali would lose all sense of control, wailing and screaming like a banshee, and tightly holding on to anything she could lay her hands on. By now Prabha had several scratch marks on her hands and wrists to speak for her friend's agony.

It hadn't been long that Amrapali had shut her eyes when once again she got up screaming. The midwife rushed to examine her and the attendants, well-rehearsed in their roles by now, quickly drew up a makeshift curtain by forming a human chain around the bed, holding cotton sheets in their upstretched arms. Prabha remained outside the enclosure, nervously fiddling with the thin string of fine pearls dangling from her neck.

'The dilation is near complete. The baby should be arriving any moment now,' the midwife, sticking her head out of the slit between two sheets and screaming to make herself heard over Amrapali's resounding cries, announced. The cries continued, only mounting in intensity, as Prabha paced up and down the room nervously, her anxiety too managing to scale its pinnacle.

And then it happened. A frail but magical cry rang from within the cloth enclosure and spread across the chamber, silencing every other sound—the chants of the Brahmins as well as Amrapali's cries. Every eye in the room was turned towards the bed as the midwife emerged, holding in her hands a delicate, minute being, wrapped in spotless muslin and wailing with a surprising display of strength.

'It is a son,' the midwife said, handing the baby over to Prabha. 'The Nagarvadhu is fine too. She has just passed out with the distress of delivery, but shall be up very soon,' she added.

As Prabha held the little one, his tiny body gently pressed against her bosom, she felt all her worries and sorrows rapidly begin to drain. It was a feeling not like any she had ever experienced—unparalleled and heavenly—and the baby too, as though reciprocating her warmth, had stopped crying straight away.

Pulling out the pearl necklace from her neck she dropped it in the midwife's hands and looked around. The mood within the room had suddenly transformed to a celebratory one and each of the occupants was rejoicing in their own peculiar manner, desperately trying to control their volumes so as to not disturb Amrapali. The waiting women were laughing and hugging each other—some, with tears of joy rolling down their eyes—while the Brahmins showered the baby with generous blessings.

Another witness to the celebrations was a slouched figure lurking behind the large wooden doors of the chamber. The petite frame of Kundali, clinging to the partially open panel of the door, was carefully monitoring the happenings, a mysterious frown affixed on his face. His anxious eyes revealed a wide array of emotions—concern, jealousy, suspicion and bewilderment—but the most obvious feelings of joy and elation were distinctly amiss from the lineup.

9

The night was slipping into its second pehar, a time when even the most vigilant sentries find themselves battling the enticement of sleep, when to the astonishment of Magadh soldiers manning the forward posts, the humongous gates of Vaishali flung open. With shock-widened eyes they watched as a sea of people—mounted and barefoot—came streaming out, swallowing everything that came in their way, like the angry waters of a dam breaking from its containment.

Senapati Chetak's initiative had yielded rich dividends and the citizenry of Vaishali had descended in generous numbers to register themselves for battle on the designated day. A stringent selection process had followed. Those found wanting in strength, stature or stamina to endure the adversities of battle were graciously sent back, still leaving a sizeable count of civilians willing to take up arms for the sake of their motherland.

Those who knew how to ride a horse and possessed a mount of their own (the royal stables were not left with many beasts to spare) were separated from the rest and sent for an intensive cavalry training while the others were groomed as foot soldiers over the following week. A week's time was barely enough to get complete novices—those who had spent better part of their lives manning cash tills or tilling the soil—ready for battle. But will and determination, when married with the right motivation is capable of seducing even the severest of adversities, and this case was no different.

Suraj Mal, after having spent the past few days in the company of patriots who ate, slept and walked the yearning to preserve the modesty of their motherland, was no longer the chance recruit whose enlistment had been inspired by societal pressure or a parchment commanding him to do so. Somewhere along the line he had transformed into a true soldier, one whose paramount emotion was the love for his country. In the cerebral seclusion of the night, on his bed in the tent he shared with nine other men, his thoughts did meander towards the other love of his life—Prabha—but even then he would mostly imagine her face gloating with pride when he, having successfully deracinated the enemy, would return to her.

That morning the Senapati had visited their camp and addressed the trainees. His talk, though brief, had been stimulating. He had touched upon the damages the war had inflicted, both material and human, and sincerely thanked the volunteers for rising to the occasion. 'By calling upon you to ride alongside our regular soldiers, we have exercised the last resort we had and this is going to be our only chance to uproot the enemy from our soil. We are over a hundred thousand strong now, and looking at your commitment I have little doubt about our success. You might be called into battle any day, any time now, and the one thought I wish to leave you with is that battles are won not by sacrificing lives but by claiming them. Therefore, do not hesitate even for a fraction in bringing down your sword when you spot the slightest opportunity to draw enemy blood. Jai Vaishali… Victory shall be ours!' he had said.

The same night, sometime after his exhausted body was consumed by sleep, his dream, where he was being welcomed by Prabha, enemy blood still dripping from the sword in his hand, was abruptly interrupted by the sound of a blaring trumpet. He had opened his eyes to find his other mates hurriedly getting out of bed and reaching out for their battle fatigues. He had followed suit, and in little time they were all gathered in the designated assembly area.

The Senapati, flanked by two other high-ranking commanders had once again materialized in their midst. Only, this time the senior officials including Senapati Chetak were replete in their complete battle gear—chain mail armour covering their bodices, scabbards dangling from their waistbands and sturdy metal helmets on their heads—a sight thrilling enough to give Suraj goosebumps. 'The time has come,' the Senapati declared, eliciting gasps and murmurs of anticipation from the crowd.

With the help of a large map, held in place by two tall soldiers, he went on to indicate the precise spots where, between the city gates and the Magadh encampment, the enemy ditches and trenches were situated. 'This is only for your information. The soldiers and platoon commanders who will be leading you are well versed with the locations of these obstructions and you need to only ensure that you follow them without diverging,' he added. One of the commanders then took over and briefed them about the strategy for the assault. Once the briefing was done, they were given two ghatis to get ready and reassemble, this time in formations they had been painstakingly taught over the past week.

The experience was unlike any that Suraj had even imagined. As he galloped out of Vaishali's gate, enveloped by thousands and thousands of men bound by the singularity of their purpose, he felt a gush of blood rush through his veins. He was strangely thrilled at being there, at being presented with the opportunity to play a part, no matter how miniscule, in shaping the history of Vaishali.

The distance they needed to cover wasn't much, but in steering past the ditches several men failed to negotiate them despite the forewarning. They fell, swallowed by the ravenous crevices, their cries of protests subdued by the deafening rumble of the colossal contingent on the move. The offensive, meanwhile, continued unabated, vanquishing enemy outposts and annihilating any forms of life they encountered in their stride. However, by the time the agressors began nearing the Magadhan fortifications, the enemy troops had already taken up defensive positions atop the newly built wall. They began showering the Vajji army with volleys of arrows and spears, forcibly checking their rapid advancement.

This was when the right flank of the invading army detached itself from main body and began to proceed further rightwards. The move was a part of their strategy to take the enemy by surprise. The attacking troops would make a rush for the two gates dotting the wall and when the enemy, assuming that they intended to force their way in, would have deployed majority of their troops around the gates, a section would break away and head towards the right end of the wall where the gap between the structure and the riverbank would allow them to pierce into the fortifications.

Ducking showers of arrows from atop the wall, the detachment rode hard and soon they could see the point where the structure curved away from them, towards the waters, before abruptly ending. Suraj was somewhere in the middle of the brigade, his vision restrained by the riders in front, but the surge of excited cries from ahead telling him that they were fast approaching their destination.

He was making good ground when suddenly the horse ahead of him pushed back and bumped against his own, startling him momentarily. He had to tighten the grip of his legs on the beast to prevent himself from falling, but he could not stop the animal from retreating a few paces and crashing against the one behind.

It was as though some massive force had collided against their frontline to shove them back, and the inertia induced ripples were now sailing through the body of the unit.

The scene had instantly transformed from that of an orderly advancement to one of utter confusion and chaos. The inexperience of men and beasts showed as shocked by the sudden jolt they began scampering hither and thither in a state of complete disarray. And then a sudden uproar, unlike the earlier cries of a charging brigade, as though multiple sounds had been mashed into one—of metal clanking against metal, of metal tearing into human flesh and bones, gut-wrenching cries of anguish and thuds from falling bodies hitting the ground—rose through the horizon, intensifying with each passing moment.

It was apparent that their ploy had failed to deceive the enemy and that they were not going to be allowed an easy passage. In a bid to emerge from the commotion surrounding him, Suraj steered his horse haphazardly through any fissure he could find amidst the sea of men. And before he could realize where he was heading, he found himself in the thick of action, encircled by battling soldiers, swishing swords and flying spears. Strewn around him were mutilated bodies—that of his comrades and the enemy's men, but humans all the same—being trampled to pulp under beating hooves and charging steps. The sight was gruesome, enough to curdle the blood in his veins, and he was desperately trying to prevent his intestines from popping out of his mouth when a desperate yell made him turn sideways.

An enemy trooper was dashing towards him, galloping at breakneck speed, a pointed spear in his hand, its base buried within his armpit for support, and one of his own men, a foot soldier, realizing that Suraj was oblivious to the assault, called out to draw his attention. Consumed by an instant surge of hormones, Suraj kicked his own horse forward, heading straight for the attacker. It appeared as if their mounts were going to collide head-on, but at the very last moment, barely a fraction before the enemy's spear would have found him, Suraj slipped to one side of his saddle and wielded his sword violently. It caught the man at the back of his head and with a deafening shreik, he fell face first to the ground.

Suraj turned around meaning to thank his saviour, but only in time to watch the soldier's headless body slump to the ground. His severed head had beaten the body in the race and was lying still after rolling a few paces. The body too, after wriggling momentarily, like he had seen detached tails of house lizards do, fell silent. His slayer, a Magadh foot soldier, was walking away, the sword in his hand soaked in the dead man's blood.

Consumed by an overwhelming fury, Suraj turned his horse towards the man and approached him from behind, flashing hard with his sword. He had intended to strike at his neck and decapitate him—an eye for an eye and a head for a head—but he missed his mark and caught the shoulder instead. The man collapsed nonetheless, letting out an agonizing scream, while Suraj, without waiting to watch him die, had already identified his next target and was darting forward to engage him.

In this little time Suraj had become immune to the gore splattered across the combat zone and was moving like a seasoned warrior, butchering enemy soldiers as if he were harvesting a sugarcane crop. He had caught a few gashes on his arms and legs, but nothing that could deter him from fighting on.

The enemy resistance turned out to be much more formidable than the Vajji commanders had imagined and the conflict continued through the night, more and more enemy troops pouring out of the opening they had intended to exploit and standing in the way of their advancement.

The scene was no different around the site of the original confrontation. The two doors along the wall were still intact as, in the absence of war elephants, who had been left behind for the sake of the attacking brigade's agility, there was no other way to smash past them. With the warring troops maintaining their ground—the Magadh soldiers showering arrows from atop the wall and the Vajji archers retaliating from their points of vantage along the ground—a wearisome stalemate had ensued.

By the time the sun, after reinstating itself on the horizon, had begun its steady ascent, the warring soldiers were visibly worn out and seemed to be drawing on final remnants of their energy reserves. Chetak too had realized by now that the attack had failed to achieve its objective and that continuing the engagement any further would only lead to further losses. Shaking his head in frustration, he drew the conch shell from his waistband and blew hard into it. The sound of the shankha, the signal established for the men to retreat, reverberated through the air and was greeted with sighs of relief from men on both sides.

Suraj had fought like a man possessed, losing all track of time, unmindful of his parched throat, the soreness in his arms from incessantly manoeuvring the horse and wielding his sword, and the dizziness he felt due to the gaping wounds that were decorating his body. He had not realized when the faint white light of the moon he had adjusted his sight to for identifying his preys or escaping an assailant, had given way to the bluish luminescence of breaking dawn, followed by the significantly brighter rays of the sun.

Not that he was keeping count, but he would have brought down over a dozen Magadh soldiers—both mounted and on foot—and escaped at least four life threatening assaults. It was no less a miracle that a man with minimal military training had been able to endure the night, let alone accomplish what he did. It wasn't just valour but also his maniacal blunt obsession—for in wartime it is often a mistimed blink that proves fatal—that had helped him sail through. He was sizing up his next adversary, a young enemy cavalryman when the shrilling echo of the shankha diverted his attention.

His conscious, suddenly aware that the ordeal was nearing its end, began to recognize other sensations that it had been deliberately ignoring all this while—the aching limbs, the flaming abrasions and the fatigue that threatened to consume him. Using his heels and the reins he was holding, he got his horse to halt. His adversary followed suit. He then made the beast retreat a couple of steps. Once again his opponent did the same. Next, Suraj turned around and galloped behind his retreating comrades without looking back. This, the only mistake he had made all night, proved to be his undoing.

His horse would have covered not more than a few dands when a dagger, tearing the air behind him with a hiss, landed on his back, just below the left shoulder, right where his heart was. He slumped forward, losing his grip on the reins. He desperately tried to grab the horse's neck for support, his feet held in place by the stirrups, but he felt his hands flailing and a curtain of darkness descending before his eyes. The sharp stab he had felt when the dagger had lodged itself on his back was no longer there, there was no pain, no fear, not even any memories of the night gone by. He did have memories though, and they were streaming past his eyes at a rapid pace—the first time he had seen her, the first time they had held hands, their arguments, their love and their abruptly interrupted farewell. He tried to speak out her name, but his lips failed him and he remained slumped on the horseback, eyes open and staring into oblivion where he could see a face— Prabha's smiling face, unblemished and radiant, just the way she had always appeared in his dreams.

The disciplined horse continued heading in the direction it had been shown, its gallop now reduced to a trot, carrying the burden of its master's body. Just before it could enter the city gates, the horse caught a passing rider's eye. Seeing a man precariously slouched on the horse, a dagger hilt protruding from his back, he steered himself close and grabbing Suraj's unresponsive hand, pulled him atop his own mount in one swift motion. He did not disturb the dagger to prevent any further blood loss, but in his heart he knew that the cold hands he had held could not belong to a living man.

The days following the baby's birth were a hazy, obscure reality for Amrapali as she slipped in and out of sleep, just as the little one did, recuperating and nursing her exhausted body. Each time she opened her eyes two constants were waiting to greet her: the baby suckling on her breast and the comforting form of Prabha stationed at her bedside.

With Suraj having left for his military training, Prabha had once again found her calling by her friend's side. She had taken over the task of nursing the newborn and his mother, leaving the attendants to take care of only the peripheral chores. Twice a day, she would wipe the child clean, delicately—wary of holding the tiny frame in her unschooled hands—before wrapping him in fresh muslin.

She would hold the glass of turmeric blended milk to Amrapali's mouth for her to drink, and she would gently rub her palms and forehead when she saw her face contort with sporadic bursts of pain. It was only on the third day of the delivery that Amrapali managed to take to her feet unaided. Though still ambling, she was able to walk till the door and back, and the pace of her recovery gained a sudden momentum thereafter.

Though her body had begun to heal rapidly, the childbirth had unsettled Amrapali from within. Her emotions as well as her conduct had become extremely erratic. Sometimes she would become highly poignant, holding the baby to her chest and uncontrollably shedding tears, and sometimes she would be cold as an icicle, sitting in the balcony and staring into oblivion for long stretches, leaving the baby in Prabha's custody. Worried, Prabha consulted the midwife, only to be informed that it was normal for some mothers to experience feelings of depression or anxiety following childbirth and that in due course the Nagarvadhu would return to being her normal self. But despite the reassurances Prabha knew that there was something deep-rooted and much graver that was burrowing into her friend's mind. And her presumption wasn't entirely unfounded.

The handsome child was now a living, breathing reality and the anticipation and excitement that had been driving Amrapali until his arrival had now abated. Instead she was consumed by an overbearing concern for his well-being and his acceptance within the society. He was after all a fatherless child—a bastard—in the eyes of the world, and a mere contemplation of the insults and ridicule he would have to endure, for an act that he was merely an outcome of, was enough to send a shudder of guilt racing down her spine.

But was it really a mistake? A child, so fine-looking and angelic: could his very essence be explained as an imprudence resulting out of an unrestrained surge of passion? Will he too, like his mother, be denied admission into the patronizing gurukuls of Vaishali? And even if she exercised her influence to push him through one, what hell would the other children make him endure? After all, at such an age sensitivity towards others was at its lowest and disparagement and mockery were the favoured indulgences.

The longer she sat brooding, the more apprehensions kept sprouting, spiralling her deeper and deeper into a maze she had not yet learnt to emerge from. Why should her little one be the one to suffer? For what fault of his? This was not a life she had chosen for herself. It had been thrust upon her, against her will, by the competent and powerful men who ruled the kingdom. Why then should the enforced restraint on her marriage cast aspersions on the life of her child? Or by appointing her the Nadarvadhu, had they willed for her to not only sacrifice her desires and wants in this life, but also mercilessly snap the thread of continuity for her lineage? If anyone deserved to bear the brunt of this, it was them and not her innocent child.

This was when the weight on her soul would become unbearable and she would cry incessantly holding her baby in her arms. She would apologize to him for bringing him in this world, she would pray to the gods for their mercy and she would curse all those who she thought to be responsible for her son's predicament, including the little boy's absent father.

Today morning, she had woken up feeling the same jangle of nerves that she was fast becoming accustomed to. The baby had not allowed her a single peaceful stretch of sleep, breaking into a wail the very instant she managed to shut her eyes. Between Prabha and herself, they had remained singing lullabies and taking turns in cradling him to sleep for better part of the night. It had been a busy night and the annoyance was reflecting in her sombre mood.

Suddenly one of the attendants barged into Amrapali's room looking for Prabha. She looked flustered. Amrapali redirected her to Prabha's room—where she had gone to freshen up—without bothering to enquire about the reason behind her troubled look. 'Must be some domestic issue: the cook has called in sick today, or other such,' she assumed. Ever since her pregnancy was on its last leg Prabha had taken on the mantle of handling such trivialities, which, to her utter amazement, had a way of acquiring cataclysmic proportions in the eyes of the attendants, and Amrapali was only happy to let the status quo remain.

The baby, who had been asleep till then, suddenly summoned her with a sharp wail and she rushed to attend to him. She tried breastfeeding him, but perhaps he had other designs, for he simply refused to open his mouth. So, she picked him up and was heading towards the balcony when a strange sound reached her ears. It appeared as if a group of people were howling at the top of their voices. Intrigued, she allowed her steps to follow the sound, holding the baby in her arms, and found herself heading towards the audience chamber. As she neared the chamber, the pace of her steps accelerated and a look of concern appeared on her face, she could distinctly make out Prabha's chords amidst the chorus of distraught voices. Her heart was pounding away furiously, an unknown fear gripping her from within. Shoving the door open, she barged in, only to be greeted by a peculiar sight. A middle aged man and a woman, presumably husband and wife, both clad in white cotton garments were howling inconsolably, and Prabha, tightly embracing the woman, was matching their vocals with her own. Before Amrapali could make sense of the scene, the baby, not meaning to be left behind, had begun pitching in as well.

She signalled for one of the nearby attendants to carry the child out of the room, but by then Prabha had sensed her presence, and leaving the woman she was clinging to, she rushed towards Amrapali. It was then that a flicker of recognition struck her. The man in white facing them was Parimal, the trader. While her mind processed the information to draw inferences, her heart had already proclaimed the worst. And Prabha, holding her in an embrace now, was quick to confirm her fears. 'Suraj…' was the only coherent word she could utter before her voice dissolved into her sobs once again.

Prabha's cries instantly brought back memories from a different lifetime altogether—the pleasant morning of the day she was to get married, the nervous excitement and eager anticipation she had felt, and her father's sombre voice as he had informed her of Pushp's demise. For her, it was like reliving one of the most horrific moments of her own life through Prabha, and as she stroked her friend's hair in a gesture of consolation, she felt a stream of tears rushing down her own eyes.

'My son, Devi… He had been summoned by the council to join the army, and yesterday…yesterday afternoon, some officials from the government came home to return his lifeless body… They said he had fought valiantly, but had fallen prey to an enemy knife while retreating. My son was a trader, a businessman, and we had told him not to go, but…We knew that he wished to get married to Prabha, so we thought we must personally come to break the news and invite both of you for his funeral,' Parimal, partly regaining his senses at the sight of the Nagarvadhu, said.

He was unusually cheerful today, and with good reason. He had been pulled out of the bed much before his usual time due to the unexpected and untimely arrival of a messenger from King Bimbisara himself. Somewhat perplexed, Devdutt had rushed through his morning rituals to give the man an audience. The man, much to his delight, had informed him about Bimbisara's keenness to know the progress he had made with his machines and that the King would be visiting his workshop the very afternoon to inspect them.

Devdutt had toiled over several months to come up with the six strange-looking structures that stood in the field behind his makeshift workshop, and he was convinced that these instruments were capable of not only altering the course of this war, but history itself. He had been delighted when, during his visit to the battlefront, Senapati Prasenjit had sought his help to come up with something that could break the near stalemate in the battlefield. His delight came from two reasons. Firstly, he was finally getting a chance to make an active contribution to the war and play a part in the downfall of Vaishali—the city that had murdered his father, and secondly, this was the first time that the Senapati, a man used to looking down upon him, had displayed any kind of appreciation for his aptitude and knowledge.

Upon his return he buried himself in thinking of weapons or machines that could aid their men scale the formidable walls of Vaishali. He thought about various alternatives—large bird-like contraptions that could ferry soldiers aerially into the city, a humongous ram that could raze not only the walls, but the entire city—but these were mostly manifestations of his yearning to see the complete annihilation of Vaishali. His ideas proved nothing more than mere fantasies with little practical standing and he ended up spending a considerable amount of time attempting to design them.

Frustrated at being failed by the one attribute he considered his greatest asset—his ability to think his way through a maze of complexities—he was purposelessly meandering through the streets of Rajgriha one evening when a stray stone pellet struck him on his forehead. The pain was piercing, the abrupt nature of the strike adding to its sting, and holding his head in his hand, he peered around to find a group of young boys, now at a fair distance, fleeing away from the scene. They were perhaps trying to bring down the green fruit from nearby mango trees and their catapult shot had found him instead. And then, like a flash, one that he would thank the deities for, the thought stuck him. A massive catapult: yes. This was the answer to his dilemma. A tried and tested apparatus that needed only to be blown up in proportions to be ready for use!

He rushed back to the workshop to put the idea to paper. And once his brain cells began ticking, they started to hurl idea upon novel idea at him. He held on to another one—a chariot covered with spikes, hedgehog like, that could tear its way and wreak havoc deep into the enemy ranks—an inspired thought that could transform into a fearsome weapon. There was a challenge though: the beasts drawing the chariot would remain exposed to enemy weapons, and as soon as they went down, the vehicle would come to a standstill. But he found his answer within the problem itself. It had to be a horseless carriage, a self-propelled one.

The catapult was easy to design, but the second blueprint took time as he had to come up with an elaborate mechanism to use the momentum of the chariot itself, through a complex maze of rods originating from the wheel's circumference and converging at its axis, to fuel its further propulsion. But this time around his mind was siding with him and he managed to design, in theory at least, a self-propelled carriage that could, following an initial shove, continue to run for several kosas. Pleased with himself, he had immediately dispatched a messenger to inform the Senapati of his progress and got down to gathering the material required to come up with prototypes of the two blueprints.

He had summoned the best craftsmen in the city—ironsmiths, carpenters and engineers—and after placing them on oath for complete secrecy, had started the task of giving concrete shape to his designs. He hadn't expected the task to be simple and when he got down to doing it, it didn't disappoint him. Logic which had appeared flawless on paper, continued to fail him in reality.

On numerous occasions he was forced to go back to the drawing board, tweaking and reworking the blueprints, but he remained persistent, never leaving the thread of optimism.

It was the seemingly simple catapult design that presented him his biggest challenge. Originally he had planned to use a supple bamboo shoot for its body, secured to a mobile trolley on one end and affixed with a metal pan that would hold rocks and pots of burning coal to be hurled at the enemy on the other. The free end holding the pan could be pulled down by a couple of strong hands and released swiftly to fling the desired merchandise in the designated direction. The first contrivance had been extremely easy to put together and had worked fine too, but it was after a few days when the bamboo had dried in the sun that the problem surfaced. The bamboo no longer remained as supple as it had been, and on the very first attempt to pull it to the required level, it snapped into two.

The device he had come up with had a life term of barely a few days, a failing that would render it useless in the battle zone. He had spent the next three days locked in his room, without any food or sleep, thinking of a more durable alternative, and in the end his determination had paid off. He got the ironsmiths to beat a long metal rod into spirals, giving it the shape of a spring. The rationale of the catapult remained the same, but now, instead of depending on the flexibility of bamboo shoots to power the projectile, the task had been entrusted upon the spring's recoil—a much sturdier alternative that not only made the weapon more accurate, but also expanded its reach dramatically.

Thus, overcoming unexpected hurdles, the first prototypes were eventually readied and Devdutt's team got down to replicating them. They had put together four more structures, two of each of the designs, leaving the final assembly and finishing touches for the end, when the unexpected message from the King had got him racing down to the workshop.

Rousing some of the workers who were asleep in the workshop shed, he got them to clean and grease the original prototypes and prepare the ground on which they stood to enable him to put up the most spectacular show he could, the paucity of time. He checked the weapons himself the weapons to ensure that they were in working condition, and he had a stack of hay placed at the precise spot where the test projectile had landed. The messenger's unexpected visit had left him a changed man—energetic, confident and purposeful—unlike his previous solemn and brooding self.

Bimbisara, though aware of the project Devdutt had been pursuing, had never even courteously enquired about it, let alone show interest in the progress he was making. In fact sometimes he got the distinct feeling that the King wasn't particularly convinced about his ability to deliver an object of significance or utility at the front, perhaps due to his lack of experience in matters of the brawn. But things appeared to be changing with Bimbisara's keenness in his project, and he was not going to let this opportunity to showcase his worth pass.

The King arrived with the minimal protective paraphernalia he could afford. He appeared to be in a hurry, and after a quick exchange of pleasantries proceeded straight to the point. 'You must have heard about the Vajji attack on our campsite last night?'

Hesitantly, Devdutt nodded his head in the affirmative. No, he hadn't heard about any such attack, but obviously he could not admit his ignorance to the Emperor.

'We have suffered considerable losses in the night-long skirmish, and Narsinh Dev and I will be heading to the base camp later today to take stock of the situation. The Senapati is highly expectant of the contraptions you have been working on and I thought I must see for myself if they are worth basing our future strategies on,' Bimbisara said.

Meekly nodding, Devdutt led him to the ground where his weapons were displayed. He hadn't missed the King's condescending tone and though he instantly had a series of clever replies buzzing within his head, he, as always, found himself unable to voice them. But today was going to be different. Today he had something to stand up and speak for him—his work.

Very briefly he explained to the King what the two weapons were capable of delivering before signalling his helpers to bring the pot of burning coal he had asked them to keep handy. He had refrained from elaborating upon the mechanics at play behind the apparatuses, for he nursed his own reservations about Bimbisara's ability to grasp them. Upon his signal two men pulled the wooden plank over the metallic spring and, pulling a latch to hold it in place, placed the pot in its pan-shaped head.

'You must watch the haystack over there,' Devdutt said before stepping forward. In a flash he released the latch, the spring's recoil propelling the plank forward till it hit a smaller plank ahead, to send the pot flying high in the air. Within moments, the pot landed right in the center of the haystack setting it ablaze. The King burst out in an instant applause. 'Marvellous,' he said, unable to take his eyes off the fire in the distance.

Immediately Devdutt asked his men to push the second weapon, Rath Musala, as he had named it, towards the burning heap. The chariot rapidly progressed towards its target, retaining its initial momentum along the way, its spikes spinning dangerously like a predator on the prowl. Bimbisara watched in amazement as the ram tore through whatever remained of the hay heap, slicing to bits everything that came in its way, before hitting a padded stone wall ahead.

'You are a true genius Devdutt and your weapons will not only help us conquer Vaishali, but also help spread the Magadh Empire across the breadth of land. Tell me, how long it will take for you to have these ready and shipped to the front?' he enquired, gesturing towards the four semi-finished structures in the background.

'Anything between a week to ten days Maharaj,' he replied, the smile once again returning to his face.

'Give it all your attention, and if you need anything just send a word to the royal treasurer. He will have my instructions to fulfill any demand you might have. Get these weapons ready and ship them to the front as soon as you can,' Bimbisara instructed before turning on his heels. When he emerged from Devdutt's workshop, there already was a triumphant glint in the King's eyes.

10

'Had it not been for the wall protecting the campsite, the damages could have been monumental,' Prasenjit said, concluding his report about the skirmish of the previous night.

Bimbisara had arrived at the base camp late that evening and had immediately summoned the Yuvraj, the Senapati and the principal commanders for an emergency meeting. All, barring the two commanders who were manning the frontier, had immediately convened inside the large tent. The Senapati had initiated the proceedings by recounting the losses they had incurred from the last enemy assault, leaving Bimbisara in a pensive frame.

'And what is the estimate for the losses the enemy might have suffered? What was the strength of their attacking party?' Bimbisara further enquired. The Senapati, who had his statistics handy, was quick to offer a precise response.

'A hundred thousand men!' Bimbisara exclaimed. 'But isn't that significantly higher than our initial estimates? With over nine months of relentless battling, and with no means to garner outside support, the count of their soldiers should have depleated. How then did they manage to put together such a formidable force all of a sudden?'

'Yes Maharaj, that is something which continues to baffle us,' the Senapati said, dropping his gaze to the ground between his feet. 'Maharaj, but it is probable that we had underestimated their strength to begin with,' Ajatshatru interjected, rising to the defence of his co-commander.

'That is an extremely remote possibility. We, Narsinh Dev and I,' he began, raising his palm towards the prime minister, 'had obtained the estimates from highly placed sources within Vaishali's government and revalidated them during our clandestine visits to the city. The credibility of our sources remains unquestionable. Something is certainly transpiring beyond those walls that we are not in the know of.'

After another contemplative pause, Bimbisara spoke, 'Anyway, the good news I bring to you is that before coming here I managed a visit to Devdutt's workshop and saw for myself the weapons he has designed—the Agni Varshak and the Rath Musala. These weapons, between them, are capable of turning any unfavourable situation in the battlefield on its head. They, once deployed alongside our men, will help us vanquish Vaishali in no time. Devdutt has assured me that within ten days he will send us some ready-to-use samples for both these machines.'

The news was greeted with a flurry of excited questions about the weapons, whether prompted by its heartening nature or the sheer stature of the news-bearer, one couldn't tell. Bimbisara went on to explain in detail the working of these remarkable inventions, and leaving a buoyant bunch of people behind, exited the tent.

Later that night a second meeting was called with a much smaller list of attendees, comprising Ajatshatru, Prasenjit, Narsinh Dev and the King himself. 'As I see it, our failure to make headway in this battle stems from two facts,' Bimbisara began without a prelude, as soon as the other three had arrived and were duly seated. 'First, the lack of adequate information pertaining to the enemy's plans and tactics—a deficiency brought to the fore by the fact that we remained oblivious to their massive build-up of troops as well as the source for their reinforcements. Second, we have not been able to insulate ourselves against infiltration by their spies—we should have been alarmed when Amanverma, Bhadresh and Ramdev were executed, but in our vanity we chose to ignore the development. As a result, today we can't be sure about the layers of our defences that they have already managed to penetrate.'

It wasn't by chance that Bimbisara had risen to become one of the most revered rulers of Aryavart. His diagnosis of the problems plaguing their campaign was irrefutable. It was indeed intelligence, or the lack of it, and not courage and might that had dictated the terms on the battlefield thus far, and his generals could only nod in acquiescence.

Pausing briefly to survey the three faces, Bimbisara resumed, 'It is this error that we need to rectify urgently. Also it is important that by the time Devdutt's weapons arrive, we have with us exact locations of the military installations and camps on the other side of the wall. This will help us target the Agni Varshaks so as to inflict maximum damage with each fired shot. Hence, I intend to sneak into Vaishali, with the prime minister for company of course, and gather the required information in the time we have on our hands. Another crucial objective of this venture will be to try and find out the source of the leak that exposed Amanverma and our other supporters.'

Bimbisara's plan sounded preposterous on more counts than one and Ajatshatru was the first to voice his concerns. 'Maharaj, but how will you manage to enter the city? The gates have remained shut ever since the war began,' he said.

'There is another way in, a small crevice in the wall, along the Mahavana, at about a day's travel from here. It opens up near a village on the outskirts of Vaishali and is mainly used by the village folk to enter the forest in search of firewood and herbs. We had stumbled upon it accidentally during one of our reconnaissance visits to the city,' he said looking at Narsinh Dev to remind him of their discovery. The prime minister nodded in return.

'But if there was a way to get into the city and you knew about it, why didn't you tell us beforehand? We could have sent our men into Vaishali using that route,' Ajatshatru questioned, exercising a liberty that only he could take with Bimbisara.

'The gap as well as its approach trail is suitable for one or two people to travel, but not a brigade of soldiers. Moreover, the passage opens in a section of the settlement where it would be impossible to escape the prying eyes of the villagers. Given that it is war time, they would not hesitate in raising alarm if a bunch of strangers were to emerge from the passage. As for us, they know us as a Vaidya and his helper from the city. We will carry some herbs with us on our way in and they will have no reasons to suspect us,' he explained.

'Maharaj, as you said, it is wartime and the risk of you entering enemy territory, unprotected, is not worth taking. We might as well send a couple of our spies and hope that they get into Vaishali undetected through the passage. However, if by a stroke of ill-fate they do get caught, our loss will still remain bearable,' Prasenjit said, joining the discussion.

'That, Senapati, would be akin to sending those men into the jaws of death. Moreover, we have contacts in Vaishali that have been cultivated over a period of time, something the spies cannot even dream of matching. They will not have access to anyone senior enough in the Vajji hierarchy who could possibly reveal the source of their information about Amanverma's deflection. If we need to obtain the kind of information that will help us turn the fortunes of battle in quick time, this risk will need to be taken. I have spared enough thought to this and before the break of dawn Narsinh Dev and I shall embark on our journey,' there was a sense of finality to Bimbisara's tone that prevented any further discussions on the matter.

Still not convinced about the King's decision and somewhat perplexed at his unusually obstinate behavior, Prasenjit and Ajatshatru stepped out of the tent. If either of them had known about the other pressing motive behind Bimbisara's decision, his conduct would have ceased to appear so outlandish to them.

In Prabha's eyes Amrapali could see the questions she had once grappled with herself. She could appreciate the pain, the agony behind every word she spoke, every step she took and every breath she breathed, and her heart went out to Prabha. If this was destiny it was indeed a cruel and pitiless thing.

Amrapali did not know Suraj Mal all that well, but she knew that he was responsible for the sudden glow she had noticed on Prabha's face. When she had seen his lifeless body wrapped in white, nostrils plugged by cotton, and face scarred by a recent slash, she had felt a bond with him that she had never experienced during his lifetime. It seemed as though she had once again lost a member of her family, one of her own. She had cried, not the hysterical wailing of Prabha and his ill-fated parents, but a controlled, measured flow of tears that did little to alleviate the pain within.

It was Amrapali's turn to play the anchor now and she had done well to take over complete charge of her baby and the mundane housekeeping chores from Prabha, allowing her the necessary space and time to grieve in peace. She had resisted the urge to talk to her about the loss, about how she was coping with it, aware that in such times she would be best left alone. From experience she knew that answering ridiculous questions about her own well-being on having suffered an irreparable loss of such proportions could only further aggravate her wounds.

A heart's weight, defying conventional wisdom, increases considerably when it splits into two, and Prabha's had shattered into a million pieces. She could feel its shards piercing and boring deeper where they had lodged in her chest with each passing moment. The reality that Suraj would no longer be there to ride with her, to hold her hands, to tie beads of fragrant flowers to her hair, and to finally take her home as his bride one day, had turned her life into a purposeless cavity. Every waking moment she would be lost in his thoughts, and he would not leave her even within the confines of her dreams.

She was furious from within, at all those who were responsible for Suraj's death—at those who had ordered him into battle, at him for obeying their orders, and most of all at those who were responsible for inflicting painful wounds on his body. In her heart she prayed to come to face the coward who had flung his dagger at a retreating man and she had no doubts that if ever her prayers were answered, she would tear him apart with her bare hands. She would tremble, attempting to contain the intensity of her anger, aware that her prayers would not be answered and that Suraj would never come back, and she would try to escape into the sea of her cherished memories of him.

In her present state, the only people she could feel one with were Suraj's parents. To her, they were her only partners in misery who could understand the depths of her indignation and anguish. Therefore she had begun to ritualistically visit them every morning, staying back for as long as she could, cooking for them, eating with them, and listening to their reminiscences or stories from their son's childhood. It was as if in their company she were rediscovering Suraj all over again, falling in love one more time with a side of his she had never known. Spending time with the old couple—behaving as she would have, had she come into the house as their son's bride—had become an escape from reality for her, a distraction she could not do without. Moreover, wouldn't Suraj have expected the same of her—taking care of his elderly parents in his absence?

Today morning, too, she came to see Amrapali, as she always did, kissed the sleeping baby on his forehead, and wordlessly set out to spend another day in the house she had desired to spend her lifetime. Since then, the little one had hollered out of his sleep and, satiated after consuming the desired measure of milk, was now idling in his mother's lap. Amrapali was humming some long forgotten melody, words involuntarily streaming from the crevices of her memory when an attendant barged in. The dasi had an unusual spring to her steps, and with what Amrapali thought to be a blush she said, 'Devi, Bindusen Ji is here.'

She did not believe her ears at once. It was very likely that her own subconscious had conjured the words and the dasi had never actually uttered them. 'What?' she shot back, seeking reaffirmation.

'Devi... Bindusen Ji... He is here, waiting for you in the audience chamber,' the attendant repeated. The dasi, like other residents of the Old Palace—from the hushed whispers that ceaselessly went around—knew that Bindusen was the father of her mistress's son, the man whose glimpse Amrapali's eyes had been longing for since very long. And now, when she was breaking the much anticipated news of his arrival, even she felt her voice trembling with excitement.

She had heard it right. The dasi had undeniably announced Bindusen's arrival. The moment she had been waiting for, the one she had played out on the stage of her mind umpteen times had finally arrived, and yet her own reactions were puzzling her. The exhilaration she should have felt was missing and she did not feel the urge to rush out and see him. In fact she was suddenly not sure what to do or how to react.

Every extreme emotion when experienced over a sustained period dissolves into a phase of apathetic indifference, just like the pain that loses its sting when endured for long. It was this zone of indifference that Amrapali's mind had slipped into. Wiping the beads of cold sweat that had broken on her brow, she handed the child to the attendant, and somewhat embarrassed that her excitement had not managed to match even that of the dasi, she stepped out of the room.

Cagey, she pushed open the doors to the chamber, and there he was, tranquilly seated, as though he had always been there waiting for her. Their eyes met and she froze mid-step. At that precise moment she wanted to melt into the ground and disappear through a sewer grate like a puddle of hot wax. He walked up to her, touched her face with the open of his hand, and she felt a new spirit filling her body, like water being poured into an empty cup.

A desperate heart usually manages to have its way with the mind, and she was no different. Her pain, her endurance, her longing for him, in a flash they were all reduced to a hazy mist from the past and the only reality that remained was the man she loved— Bindusen, looking at her with eyes just as dreamy as she remembered. Gently holding her arm, he led her to one of the velvet cushioned chairs. Then, bending low on his knees and taking her hand in his, he said, 'How have you been, my love?'

The words brought her drifting back into reality and she responded by nodding her head vigorously, tears beginning to drip from her eyes.

'I missed you,' he said, lifting her hands to dab his eyes before pressing them against his lips.

'Then why did you go away?' she complained, surprised that the cooing voice had been her own. Gently getting up to occupy the adjacent chair, still continuing to hold her hand, he said, 'Work, my darling! Work! It makes one do all sorts of things that the heart might not always agree with. I meant to return much earlier, but the circumstances did not allow me to.'

'I hear that the Magadh troops are still camped outside the city gates. How then did you manage to find your way in now?'

'Being resourceful is a prerequisite in my line of work. Finding our way through fortifications and unfriendly frontiers becomes a necessity if we are to transfer our merchandise from one corner of the earth to another,' he said with a crafty smile, hinting at the obvious use of unscrupulous means, a hefty bribe perhaps, to secure his entry into the city. 'I came to the city late last night and since then I have been waiting for the day to break so that I could come and see you. And now that I am here, with you by my side, everything else seems so inconsequential… Tell me my love, tell me about all that I missed by being away from you—tell me about your anger, your sadness and your longing. I wish to hear it all.'

Then the thought struck her like a bolt of lightning. Clearly Bindusen was not aware of the most significant development to have taken place since his previous visit—the birth of their son. Seizing the opportunity to surprise him, she beckoned one of her dasis by pulling a satin string dangling nearby, a chime sounding in the distance, and whispered something in her ear. The Nagarvadhu had a mischievous sparkle in her eyes as a bewildered Bindusen looked on.

Shortly there was another knock on the door, a couple of restrained taps, and Amrapali stepped out, the baffling smirk still pasted on her face. She returned immediately, clutching a bundle in her arms, cleverly concealed beneath her dupatta. Approaching Bindusen, she gently placed the bundle in his arms and said, 'I was busy preparing this gift for you while you were away. I hope you like it.'

As the veil of her dupatta lifted and the baby's face came in view, Bindusen remained staring in utter disbelief. 'Our…son…' he eventually murmured, and Amrapali nodded. For a long time he remained staring at the baby, holding him to his chest, opening his clasped fingers and slipping his own between them to be held, making funny sounds, and engaging in antics of an overwhelmed father holding his newborn for the first time. Amrapali watched on, a sense of satisfaction at the unrestrained display of paternal affection warming her from within. The tears welling up in Bindusen's eyes were not hidden from her either, and she felt a wet stream racing down her cheeks as well.

'This…this is simply incredible… Our son, the souvenir of our love… Your gift, my dear, is more precious than all the treasures on land and heaven put together,' he said, slowly emerging from his reverie. 'What have you named him?'

'Well, he wouldn't allow me to give him a name. He has been insistent that we wait for his father to arrive and do the honours,' she replied teasingly.

'Pure and dazzling as he is, we shall call him Vimal Kondana,' Bindusen proclaimed after a brief contemplation.

'Vimal Kondana, he shall be,' she said, picking up the baby from Bindusen's lap, who by now had opened his eyes and begun wailing, perhaps meaning to register his displeasure at sighting the unfamiliar face. She stepped out of the room once again and leaving the baby in the care of the waiting attendant, walked back to where Bindusen was seated. But to her utter dismay, in just this little time, Bindusen's expressions had changed from that of blissful contentment to an awfully grave one. Alarmed, she looked at him questioningly, urging him to voice his thoughts.

'There is something I have been meaning to tell you, a fact that I can no longer bear to conceal. I am not who you think I am,' he began. She remained silent, her eyes transfixed on his face. He continued, 'I know this might come to you as a surprise, a terrible shock even, but you must allow me to explain the situation I was faced with and I will be willing to accept any punishment that you deem suitable thereafter.' Amrapali remained silent, though intently absorbed in his words.

'I am not Bindusen, the trader I said I was. I am the King of Magadh, Bimbisara,' he said. The revelation elicited no immediate reaction from Amrapali, but for the slight frown on her forehead and the magnified intensity of her gaze. 'I was in Vaishali establishing my network of informants and supporters, and when I heard about your divine beauty, I could not assuage the pressing urge to see you in person. I came to pay you a visit, and back then, the only introduction I could offer you was of the identity I had painstakingly established for myself among the people of Vaishali—Bindusen, the trader.

'I had planned for it to be my only visit, assuming that once my curiosity was allayed there would be no reason for me to visit the Old Palace again, but I was wrong. You left such an impression on my mind that I could not stop myself from dreaming about you ever since I left here. An invisible thread was drawing me to you, and unable to resist it, I sought your company whenever my engagements allowed me to. I was scared of shattering the bond that I had experienced between us, strengthening with each subsequent visit, and hence I chose not to interfere with the path our destinies had ordained for us.'

Amrapali remained dumbstruck, incessantly staring at him. And then, suddenly, something snapped within her and she said,

'So Maharaj, you mean my son… He is not only a *bastard*, but also a *bastard* Prince?' Her voice was dripping with scorn and contempt and her eyes were suddenly blazing red.

'Don't say that, Devi! Our son is a Prince and he, like you, shall get his due. I urge you to accompany me to Rajgriha where we shall bind our love with the auspices of marriage. You and Vimal will live in the Raj Mahal, with me, as the rightful Queen and Prince of Magadh.'

'You forget, Maharaj, that I am already wedded. As the Nagarvadhu of Vaishali, I am married to the city and its people, and I cannot desert them till my last living breath.' Bimbisara's revelation had already created a fissure which had erased the intimacy of addressing each other by first names. Her flaring eyes concealing the layer of pain, Amrapali continued, 'You claim to love me and yet you not only deceived me, but also took away the lives of thousands of my people for your own selfish motives. Let me be the one to show you the mirror Maharaj Bimbisara—you are not only incapable of loving anyone, but in truth, you are a loathsome blotch on the entire human race.'

Her outburst was justified and Bimbisara continued to humour her with the hope that it will do good to assuage her anger and make her accept his proposal. Driven by his aching heart, he continued to explain, debate, and ask for her forgiveness, but Amrapali remained unyielding. His arguments had somewhat settled the fervour of her fury and managed to blunt the razor-sharp edges of her words, but she remained unwavering on her decision to remain in Vaishali.

'And if there is anything you can do for me, for the relationship we once shared, I urge you to withdraw your troops from the soil of Vaishali. There has been enough bloodshed already. Mothers have lost their sons, children, their fathers, and women, the men they had devoted their entire lives to…' she said, Suraj's face dancing before eyes for a split second, the distraction making her words tail.

'But this is my destiny, Devi. As a king, entrusted with the right to rule, it is my duty to expand my empire for my people, for the heirs to my throne. This isn't something new, it is a tradition that has been around from time immemorial,' Bimbisara argued.

'Who are these men you refer to, Maharaj? Those who are camped outside, living each moment fearing the sword or the spear that will snap the threads of their lives or those who wait for them in your kingdom, spending their nights turning on beds and mornings, praying for the safety of their loved ones? Have you ever spoken with these people to figure out if this is what they really want…? And this destiny of yours you refer to, who is the author of this density? Which of the Granthas say that a king who dedicates himself to the welfare of his existing subjects, instead of obsessively pursuing expansion of his empire, is not a worthy one?'

The only emotion that has the wherewithal to supersede ambition is love, and finding this to be the only opportunity to profess his love to her through his actions, Bimbisara agreed to retract his troops. But his accord came with certain degree of reluctance and a pre-condition.

'Okay, I will do as you say and withdraw my troops immediately, but there is something you will have to do for me in turn. I need to know the names of the people who were responsible for leaking the identities of my supporters here in Vaishali to your people. I seek this information guided not by the need of vengeance, but to ensure the safety of my reign and my kingdom. Those people who, by way of some or the other form of corruption, can be motivated for such acts of treason, can be coerced into doing just about anything. And considering that the information was closely guarded and not known even to many of my top aides, the source of the leak is bound to be from my innermost circles, making it essential for me to identify him. Given that King Yudhveer owes not only his throne to you, but also regards you very highly, if there is any one person in the whole of Vaishali who can get this information for me, it is you,' he reasoned.

'Okay, I will do this. Not because I am concerned about your reign or your kingdom, but because this will help bring the war to an end and save more lives from being lost,' she said. What she refrained from stating was that this was the first time that the man she had loved so dearly had sought something from her, and perhaps the last time too, and there was no way she could bring herself to refuse this wish of his.

Bimbisara left the palace with a promise to visit her soon. Amrapali remained seated for a long time, on the chair that he had left her sitting on, brooding over the thread of uncertainties we call 'Life'. Had it not been for the need to feed Vimal, there was no telling how much longer her self-imposed isolation would have lasted, but a little after the sun had begun its descent she emerged, looking rather composed for the ordeal she had undergone. Summoning one of the guards she instructed him to send a message to King Yudhveer that she was desirous of seeing him and would visit his palace the next morning, she proceeded towards her chamber to tend to her son.

When Prabha returned from Suraj's house that evening, she was informed by an enthusiastic attendant about Bindusen's unexpected visit earlier in the day. Elated, she rushed to Amrapali's room, meaning to partake in her friend's moment of joy. She had been expecting to see a jubilant Amrapali, but shockingly, the image of the figure sprawled on the bed presented a sharp contrast.

'I heard that Bindusen has finally returned. Shouldn't you be celebrating instead of painting this picture of gloom and despair?' she said, motioning towards Amrapali's face. Getting up from the bed, Amrapali smiled at her, but the effort she had had to make for it was clearly visible. Prabha remained unmoving, demanding an explanation with the look in her eyes.

'Yes indeed, my son's father did visit us today. But he wasn't Bindusen.'

'What?' Prabha exclaimed.

'That man we knew as Bindusen...' she said, bitter sarcasm seeping into her voice, 'is actually Bimbisara, the Emperor of Magadh.' The hues on Prabha's face changed a hundred times as she tried to soak in the words.

'Bimbisara? He was here? Why did you allow him to leave then? Why didn't you get Ballabh and the other guards to apprehend him?' she finally said, her voice rising with rage.

'Apprehend him, for what?'

'Don't you know "for what"? He is the supreme commander of the army that has been stationed outside our city for months now. We are at war, remember? He is the man responsible for spilling the blood of so many innocent people, and yet you ask why you should have detained him?' Prabha shot back.

'Prabha, I understand your sentiments. But for once put aside your personal loss and think objectively. What would we achieve by having him arrested? His men, his sons, would only find in this a compelling reason to persist with the siege. Instead, he has given me his word that he would withdraw his troops and end the war.'

'How can you be so naïve? You still believe his words, after all that he has done to you?' The resentment in Prabha's tone was palpable and she made no attempts to conceal it.

'No, I don't trust him any longer; in fact I have even severed all my ties with him. But on this one subject he has offered me a deal. I need to get him the names of the people in his camp who betrayed him and in turn he will end the offensive. If I am able to live up to my side of the bargain, I am confident that he will do what he has promised,' Amrapali replied.

'Oh, so now you are going about making deals with the enemy. This is simply fantastic!' she said, lifting her hands in exasperation. After a brief pause she spoke again, dramatically switching her tone to a pleading one. 'Pali, why don't you understand? This man, he is our enemy. He has killed so many of our people, including my Suraj. If indeed he is expecting to receive some information from you, it means he is still hiding somewhere within the city. This might be our only chance. When he comes to collect the information, let us have him arrested. It will be the least we can do for those who have lost their lives in the war.'

'Prabha, you are thinking from your heart and not your mind. Go, sleep over this and we shall talk tomorrow. What you propose is a certain recipe for disaster. If anything, it will only intensify the war and claim more innocent lives, for which there will be no one but us to blame. For once lets assume that I do trick him into getting arrested, an act that my conscience will anyway not permit, but then, will you be able to live with the guilt of allowing the battle to prolong when we had the opportunity to bring it to an end without any further bloodshed?' Amrapali argued.

Prabha stomped out of the room without bothering to reply. The discussion was heading nowhere and there was no point persisting with it at this point. Amrapali was hoping that once Prabha was able to review the situation without her personal loss clouding her thoughts, possibly in the seclusion of the night, she would see the merit behind her stand rather than the reckless action that she was proposing. Prabha meanwhile had retired to her own room and was lost in deep thoughts. Her clenched fists and tautened jaws painting a picture very different from one that Amrapali had been anticipating.

11

Her day held its breath till she had safely eased Vimal into its arms—feeding, bathing and dressing the little one, to take on yet another day of his life and the vagaries that lay within its folds. Last night she was unable to inform Prabha about the meeting she had already scheduled with King Yudhveer. She had originally hoped to get Prabha to delay her ritualistic visit to Suraj's house till she returned and to take care of Vimal in the interim, but Prabha had been absconding since their altercation the previous night. Amrapali hadn't caught even a glimpse of her all morning.

A part of her wanted to rush to her friend's chamber and check on her, see if her fury had somewhat abated through the night. But Amrapali held herself back. If Prabha had found reason in her arguments, she would have paid her a visit by now. And if she still felt that the best alternative they had was to get Bimbisara arrested, it would be a daunting task trying to explain to her the purpose behind her sudden tryst with Yudhveer. So, leaving her friend's anger to be assuaged by time, and her son in the custody of her attendants, Amrapali boarded her chariot and emerged from the Old Palace. In tow was a minimal detachment of her bodyguards, comprising only Ballabh and his five comrades.

It was time for the advent of the scorching summer season, and the sun, shedding its languor of the past months, had made an early appearance to occupy its place in the horizon. Consequently, the morning breeze too had lost its pleasantness and felt like an invisible screen of heat as it brushed past her. Recoiling slightly to bring her legs in the shade of the chariot-canopy, Amrapali eyed the surroundings. There was a flavour of mutiny about everything she saw—the fluttering flag on the mast of her chariot, the angrily swaying branches and bustling leaves of the trees she passed, and the grim pallor of humans that went by. Or perhaps, it was only Prabha's reaction that was still playing on her mind, making her see a conjured gloom in just about everything.

However, despite all the pessimism surrounding her, Amrapali was relishing the momentary escape that the ride offered from the humdrum her life had slipped into. Since Vimal's arrival she had ceded the reins of her mind and body to the wayward whims of the baby—trying to decode his cryptic requests which were almost always made by way of a whimper or wail, and tending to them subsequently. She thought about the bliss of solitude that the ride was permitting her, and almost instantaneously she pushed aside the thought. It was an extremely self-centred one. She couldn't blame little Vimal for her woes, he was her own flesh and blood. If anything, he had come into her life like a fresh breeze and given her a reason to live.

It was when her chariot veered through the large metal gates of the royal palace that she emerged from her reverie to spare a thought for the task at hand. Despite the equation she shared with Yudhveer and the absence of any pressing reasons for him to question her intent, she needed to tread carefully while trying to extract the required information. One wrong stroke or a word spoken out of place could prove her undoing.

The guards, bowing in deference, were quick to usher her inside the palace, into the special chamber meant exclusively for notable dignitaries like the Nagarvadhu. The room, with its gold inlaid furniture and richly brocaded upholstery stood testimony to the opulence of the kingdom of Vaishali. Candelabras—intricately crafted in solid gold, vases—embedded with deep reddish purple amethysts, pink lustrous beryls, and other precious gems and imposing artifacts were scattered across the room, as if someone had dumped a treasure there and forgotten to retrieve it later. If the purpose of the lavishly done up chamber was to intimidate its guests, it certainly lived up to the task.

'Devi, it is an honour that you decided to pay this humble servant of yours a visit,' the King entered the chamber with folded hands and greeted her.

'Maharaj, it is your magnanimity that you found time within your demanding schedule to see me at such short notice,' she replied, but with a joshing smile that transcended the barriers of formality their verbal exchange seemed to be erecting.

Yudhveer returned her smile. Occupying the chair facing her, the one that rose marginally above the rest and had ferocious looking lion-faces carved on its hand-rest, he said, 'Truly, the times have been trying, especially with the war dragging along for almost a year now. But it is imperative that one finds time for their friends and well-wishers even in such times. Isn't it? Tell me Devi, what brings you here? What can I do for you?'

'I have been hearing disturbing accounts of the war, about how we inducted civilians into the army to mount a decisive offensive which failed and the ever-mounting losses we are incurring on an everyday basis. Therefore, I thought I must speak with you and check if there is anything I can do to help. I have my contingent of guards at the palace, who, though not too many, are skilled in warfare and can fight alongside our regular troops,' she offered graciously.

'That is extremely kind of you, Devi. I shall inform the Senapati of your proposition and tell him to summon your men as and when required,' the King replied.

'But tell me, how long is the siege expected to last? Wouldn't their men be exhausted too? And the conditions within their camp, aren't they bound to deteriorate once the rains begin?' she enquired for the sake of continuing the conversation.

The King, a man comprehensively overshadowed by his Senapati on matters pertaining to war, was quick to latch on to the opportunity of exhibiting his battle-prowess, albeit more for the sake of soothing his own bruised ego. 'They have been receiving constant reinforcements through the river route and are even free to approach their allies and friends for raising more troops. Whereas, given the blockading, we are solely reliant on men and beasts we can find within the kingdom. I don't know for how long they intend to, or will manage to continue with the siege, but one thing is for sure, if it doesn't end soon enough, we will be left with no option but to surrender.'

The words were not his. He had simply lifted them from his recent conversations with Chetak and presented them as his own. But there was no way for the Nagarvadhu to discover the harmless sleight he had pulled off. Amrapali, meanwhile, continued to play along, listening attentively to his discourse, as a novice would to an expert, massaging his bruised ego whenever such an opportunity arose.

'What?' she would exclaim, and 'Really?' she would feign surprise as Yudhveer went about elaborating the predicament he was faced with in his capacity as the ruler of the state under siege.

'So, is there no way out for us then? I mean, we could ask our spies within their ranks to murder their king or something. They could attack him within his camp at an opportune time when his security cover is at its minimum,' she said, her voice mixed with exasperation and the passionate desperation of an amateur.

'I wish it were that simple, Devi,' Yudhveer replied with a coy smile, one of a teacher addressing senseless queries from the more enthusiastic among his pupils. 'The King you refer to is Bimbisara, the mighty ruler of one of the largest kingdoms of Aryavart. His security cordon, even within his own camp, will be so robust that even a fly intending him harm will not be able to pierce through, let alone a man. Also, we don't exactly have our men scattered across their encampment.'

Amused, Amrapali thought about Yudhveer's reaction if ever he were to learn that the 'mighty ruler' he was alluding to was masquerading about in his city as a common businessman even as they spoke. Perception, she mused, doesn't allow a man to look beyond its boundaries. It was the perception Yudhveer carried of Bimbisara, one of a formidable and colossal ruler, which prevented him from even harbouring thoughts about his susceptibility. And it was this perception, one that Bimbisara had tediously built over time, which provided him with another layer of protection during his perilous jaunts. If Yudhveer couldn't imagine him without his cordon of security within his own camp, there was no chance for anyone to even suspect that Bimbisara could be roaming the streets of Vaishali, sans any protection, at that very moment.

Deliberately checking her thoughts and ensuring that the expressions on her face remained sombre, she said, 'What do you mean when you say that we don't have our men amidst them? We must be having our spies embedded within their ranks. Isn't that a usual fare? Besides, how else could we learn about Raja Amanverma's betrayal?'

'You are right, moles and spies can prove an invaluable asset, especially in times like these, but their roles and presence, as common people know them, are largely exaggerated and shrouded in fantastical imagery. If we had our spies in every enemy order, life would have been so much simpler,' he began, pulling up his brows and letting out sigh of resignation for effect.

'As for Amanverma and the other two traitors, it was by sheer chance that we came to learn of their plans. Had it not been for this timely discovery, the Magadh army would have marched into Vaishali long back,' he went on, without realizing that he was now on the verge of breaching the boundaries of confidentiality.

Amrapali could feel a churn of excitement within her belly. She was worryingly close to obtaining the desired information and one wrong step now could negate the progress she had made thus far.

'Oh really? Thank God for it! But I am sure such vital piece of information would have been meticulously guarded by the Magadhans, how then did you stumble upon it by chance?' Her words carried the curios urgency of a child wanting to know the climax of a fascinating fairytale in advance.

Yudhveer contemplated her question and getting up from his chair, made decisively towards the door. A barrage of unnerving thoughts suddenly swarmed through Amrapali's mind and her heart nearly skipped a bit. He stopped near the side table where a patterned gilt-silver jar was placed adjacent to six upturned glasses. 'Can I get you some?' he asked, glancing at Amrapali from the corner of his eye, as he poured himself a glass of water. Much to her respite, he returned to his seat, holding the glass in his hand.

'Vihalla Kumar, Bimbisara's son. He was the one to betray the defectors to Senapati Chetak,' Yudhveer said. His melodramatic tone notwithstanding, the revelation was a truly shocking one.

'Vihalla Kumar! But why would he do that? I mean, tell on his people and betray his own father, what reasons could he have to do such a thing?'

'Well, whatever reasons he had, they must have been compelling enough, and thankfully so. He didn't share his compulsions with us, but what mattered in the end was that the information he provided turned out to be true,' Yudhveer replied.

In the recess of her mind Amrapali heaved a sigh of relief. Her job was done. She was now equipped with the information that Bindusen (she was yet to come to terms with his newly revealed identity) required, and she would ensure that the bloody war soon came to its end. She remained in conversation with Yudhveer for a while longer, lest her departure came across as abrupt and suspicious. And finally, reiterating her pledge to send her private troops to fight alongside the Vajji army, a need, she knew, was not likely to arise in the near future, she departed from the royal palace. The sun's rays were now sterner and punitive, but Amrapali's mind, lost in a chain of its own thoughts, barely noticed them.

It had been a difficult night for Prabha. She had turned on the bed, pulled up her sheet to cover her body, pulled it further to cover her head as well, before eventually jerking it away, and then, turned and turned again. Sleep was evasive, and even if it did make an attempt to permeate her senses, it would only have encountered a disconcerting degree of tension and strain. She hadn't come to terms with Suraj's death yet, and just when she had begun to reconcile with the fact that her pent up fury would remain unvented, an unexpected fissure, a ray of hope amid the bleakness within her heart, had surfaced from nowhere. The man responsible for his death, although circuitously, was within her grasp. The opportunity for vengeance had presented itself and even if she was unable to put to use the horrific devices of retribution she had mused over for several long stretches—spilling the man's guts with her bare hands, bathing her hair in his blood, serving his carcass to the ravens for devouring, and other such— she could at least turn him in and assuage her troubled heart.

However, she had hit the most unexpected and shocking roadblock with Amrapali's refusal to side with her. The friend she had stuck with through thick and thin and the one best equipped to appreciate her condition, given that she had suffered a similar blow of destiny in the form of Pushp's death, had refused to entertain the idea of having Bimbisara arrested. She had felt betrayed, and unable to contain her frustrations, she had stormed out of the conversation with Amrapali. Through the night she had struggled to release the burden of her friend's inexplicable stance that had deposited itself on her heart, but to no avail.

She was conscious of the relationship Amrapali had once shared with Bimbisara and that they had together sired Vimal, but wasn't that entire episode the most blatant example of the man's treachery and deceit? Wasn't it Bindusen and not Bimbisara that Amrapali had fallen in love with? Shouldn't Amrapali have been feeling the same abhorrence for all the mendacities that the man stood for? Why then was she still trying to protect him instead of siding with her?

Or, was it something else? Was it her own relationship with Amrapali that had been the culprit? Had they somehow, unintentionally and undetected, drifted so far apart that her friend could no longer empathize with her angst? There might have been some merit in the rationalities Amrapali had put forth, but in times such as these—her irreparable loss and the ever so rare opportunity to avenge it—was it wise to permit logic to prevail over the obstinate demands of her heart? Had her friend deserted her and was she now the lone crusader for delivery of justice to Suraj's forlorn and ageing parents?

The questions were many and the time too little. She was still struggling with the answers when tell-tale signs of the Old Palace waking up to another day began to emerge—maids scurrying about the corridors, unmistakable sounds of water being pulled up from the well and being distributed to various corners of the palace, and the whiff of assorted spices initiated into pans with sizzling oils within the kitchen walls. The night had ended, but Prabha's quandary had not.

She heard sounds emerging from the direction of Amrapali's chamber. Perhaps little Vimal was up too, she thought. And just then, as if to endorse her assumption, a high-pitched cry reached her ears. This was the time she would usually head to Amrapali's room and give her a hand with Vimal, before getting ready herself and leaving for Suraj's house. But today was different. Even the thought of facing Amrapali seemed somewhat discomforting, and unsure, she remained sprawled on the bed, her wide open eyes transfixed on some obscure spot of the tall ceiling.

It was later, when from her window she saw Amrapali embark upon her chariot and leave the premises that she found the courage to emerge from her room. Plagued by habit and partly driven by curiosity about her friend's unusual behavior, she headed to the chamber where two attendants were dutifully engaged in the baby's care—one making chuckling sounds with her tongue and the other dangling a hay-filled cloth doll over him. The baby, smiling engrossedly, was yet to discover the one missing face among those around and appeared to be relishing all the attention.

'Where has his mother gone?' Prabha asked one of the dasis. She had nonchalantly walked up to the baby and the deliberate attempt to make her question sound unvarnished was unmistakable. One of the women looked back at her, faintly puzzled. It wasn't usually that she addressed Amrapali as 'his mother'—a cold and impersonal label—and the attendant had been quick to take note.

'Devi, she departed from the palace on her chariot just a little while back,' one of them replied. 'I know that, you moron,' she wanted to scream, 'I saw her leave the palace. But where is she headed?'

'And did she say where she was going or when she would return?' she said instead. Expectedly, the attendants were not aware of Amrapali's destination or her itinerary. Prabha turned to leave, but felt a slight tug on her dupatta. Vimal, attracted by the shiny beads embellishing the garment she had been wearing, was holding one of its corners and smiling expectantly at her. She could not muster the heart to disappoint the baby and picked him up lovingly.

Prabha remained with Vimal for better part of the morning, assuming, at her own accord, the duties that Amrapali had intended to entrust upon her. It was obvious that Amrapali had been disturbed by their spat too, and Prabha supposed that she had probably gone to the temple seeking divine intervention for allaying her disturbed mind. 'I must visit the temple too. Maybe the gods will be able to guide me through this impasse,' she thought.

Her subconscious had been hoping that when Amrapali returned she would have had a change of heart and their discord would have resolved itself in her favour. But one ghati became two and two became four, and still no word came from Amrapali. Her hope had turned to concern and it was further mounting to impatience now. Her edginess, with each passing moment spent in the impassive wait, had been escalating too. She knew that the window of opportunity for avenging Suraj was slight and if she failed to arrive at a decision or to act at the precise moment, it would be gone forever.

Resolutely, she handed Vimal back to the attendants and headed towards her room. She had no time to waste. She needed to visit Suraj's parents and there was also the all-important stopover she had to make along the way.

✦

Amrapali had just alighted from her chariot and was climbing the stairs of the courtyard when once again the gates of the Old Palace opened behind her and a lone rider passed through.

She was eager to get to Vimal and to nurse him. Her meeting with the King, though fruitful, had taken up more time than she had anticipated and she knew that the baby would be hungry by now. But the intuitive backward glance at the unexpected visitor made her freeze mid-step. The rider was none other than Bimbisara, the man she had once known as Bindusen and loved.

Skillfully dislodging himself from the mount, he clasped his palms together in greeting. 'Pranam, Devi,' he said.

'Pranam, Maha… Bindusen Ji,' she said, hurriedly checking herself. There were guards and dasis in the vicinity and any out of place word was certain to arouse their curiosity. 'I wasn't expecting to see you so soon,' she added.

'Well, I thought you might have some information for me by now, so I decided to come by. I hope my visit is not the cause for any inconvenience,' he said.

'No, certainly not,' she said. 'But if you don't mind waiting for a little while, I need to nurse my son. I shall return soon.'

Bimbisara nodded meekly. Amrapali's emphasis on the words 'my son' had not escaped him and he felt incapable of dodging their excruciating sting. It was true, he wanted to unravel the identity of the traitor who had betrayed Magadh, but there also was the tacit desire to see Amrapali and Vimal, and the hopefulness that a miracle of some sort would make her agree to accompany him back to Rajgriha. He was wishing that the ambers of their once-burgeoning relationship had not completely extinguished and that they would ignite again to resurrect the love-twines that had bound them together.

He wouldn't speak it aloud, ever, but it was the desire to see Amrapali that had made him brave the perils of battle and sneak into enemy territory. He had indeed intended to reveal his true identity to her and persuade her to come with him, but one sight of Vimal, his youngest son whose existence he had remained oblivious to, had left him shaken out of his wits. Still, he had told her all that he had intended to, but under the altered circumstances, his revelation had come across more as an afterthought than a well-intended disclosure.

Amrapali had instantly recoiled, plugging all fissures from where her pent up emotions had begun to ooze upon his arrival, and refused to leave Vaishali. He could empathize with her. She had every right to feel betrayed. And thus, he had reasoned with her, explaining how her decision would impact not only the future course of her own life, but that of their son. He had pleaded, begged and argued, but Amrapali had remained unyielding.

As the attendant, upon the Nagarvadhu's instructions, led him to the private audience chamber, he could not shake away the sinking feeling of having lost the most crucial battle of his life. Amrapali's deportment had not been cold—an indication of hurt and angst from unmet expectations, not leaving any room for him to defend himself and hope for a possible resolution. She had been indifferent and detached. She had even referred to their child as 'my son', brutally and callously ejecting his existence from her life. The implications were obvious and his optimism waged a losing battle with reality as he sat waiting for her to return.

Amrapali meanwhile was engulfed in an intense internal tussle of her own. She had allowed her mind to guide her and she knew that the decision to call off her relationship with Bimbisara had been the right one, but some part of her was still waging a protest. It hadn't been an easy decision to make. Letting go of something that one has truly loved is never easy. She was struggling with a sense of unease which only grew as she looked at the innocent and blithe frame of the baby, who was gleefully suckling away at her breast. Was she right in depriving him the name of his father? Did she have any right to allow her values and tenets to dictate a decision that would steer his life away from the veneration and privileges he was entitled to by virtue of his lineage?

She checked with one of the dasis about Prabha and was informed that she, having spent a considerable part of the morning with Vimal, had gone out of the palace some time back. To meet Suraj's parents, Amrapali assumed.

But how did Bimbisara turn up just when she was returning from her meeting with the King? Was it an act of pure chance? If it was, it was certainly an incredibly timed one. Was it possible that Bimbisara's men had been keeping a watch on her movements and it was through them that he had come aware of her visit to the royal palace?

The thought of being under the constant vigil of enemy snoops sent a shiver down her spine, but despite herself she could not place the contemptible act beyond Bimbisara's faculties. After all had the man not concealed his true identity from her even as she had gone about professing her love for him? The thought made her cringe. She felt like a worn garment—used and discarded—and it was anything but a pleasant sensation.

She glanced at Vimal, who, upon having downed his desired quota of milk, was now playfully tugging at a loose thread of her embroidered blouse. At once she knew that the time had come for her to act and that she could no longer delay the inevitable.

Once again, leaving the baby in the custody of the attendants, she emerged from the chamber to pensively plod towards the room where Bimbisara waited for her. She wasn't completely sure of her stance as yet, but siding with her instincts, had decided to persist with it nevertheless. Strangely though, she felt a weighty nervousness shackling her steps. Was this going to be the last time that she would be setting her eyes on Bindusen, the man who had rekindled the longings of love in her otherwise insipid life? Was she destined to lead a lifetime marred with unfulfilled love and everlasting yearnings?

She had taken one of the blind turns of the winding corridor when a rushing frame suddenly materialized ahead, stopping barely in time to prevent a head on collision. Amrapali was startled. 'S-s-sorry didi,' Kundali murmured. His voice sounded different, deep, with a recently acquired baritone. An impulsive rush of guilt paced through her. The boy had been transforming, slowly and surely, but she had failed to take notice. Had she been selfishly ignoring him? She couldn't recall the last time she had spoken with him at length, as she had done during his initial days at the palace.

She eyed him. He stood there, shuffling nervously, allowing the satchel in his hand to slap against his hip, making a succession of unpleasing thuds. He looked uncertain, as though the interruption had made him forget the cause behind his purposeful dash. 'It is okay,' she said, lovingly patting his head and letting her hand slip on his shoulder. 'How have you been Kundali? I am sorry that I haven't been able to spend much time with you lately, but I promise to make amends. How about coming with me to the temple tomorrow morning?'

She had insentiently resumed walking towards the private chamber, her hand still resting on Kundali's shoulder, while he attempted to match her steps. He consented with a shake of his head. 'What's in this bag? And where were you rushing?' she reflectively added, pointing to the cloth-bag that was now dangling on his side and brushing against his leg with every step he took.

'Nothing, just my catapult and a few other things… I was going to the orchard with the other boys,' he murmured. It was that time of the year when mango trees in the region were laden with little green fruits and the children made sport of bringing them down with their catapults and slingshots. Amrapali had seen Kundali in the company of other boys his age—sons of her employees and domestics—and she was glad that he had managed to find his footing among them.

'Fine, but don't forget about tomorrow. We shall go to the temple in the morning,' she said, rummaging through her troubled interiors to extract a warm smile for Kundali. Then, turning towards the door ahead, she pushed it open and stepped through the sill. Bimbisara, who had been occupying one of the chairs on the far end, immediately rose to greet her.

'Maharaj, I have the information you seek, but let me caution you, the name of the man who betrayed you might come as a rude shock. One that you might not be prepared for,' she came to the point without opting for any verbal distractions. Bimbisara remained quiet, his silence providing the assurance she was looking for.

'Rajkumar Vihalla Kumar! The traitor you look for Maharaj is none but your own son.'

'What?' Bimbisara exclaimed. 'This can't be. Why would the Rajkumar betray his people, his motherland and his own father? And moreover, he is not even involved in such matters of the state which makes it highly improbable for him to even have access to such information. Surely Devi, someone has fed you with a fabricated story.'

'It is not for me to judge the reliability of the information Maharaj, but I see no likely motive for my source to try and deceptively incriminate anyone. After all, he, even in his wildest dreams, can't imagine that through me the traitor's name will find its way to your ears,' Amrapali replied. Bimbisara's reluctance to believe her words showed, and upon his insistence she recounted her meeting with the King of Vaishali to the minutest detail. And gradually—as her words began to find their mark—she saw a mix of pain, fury and distress emerge on his face.

When Bimbisara finally emerged from the seat, he was very different from the man who had got up to greet Amrapali just a while back. He looked frail and feeble, not even a shadow of the mighty Emperor Bimbisara. It seemed as though he had aged by a few decades over the conversation that had lasted for barely a ghati or two. Amrapali felt sad for him as she saw him trudging towards the door.

'Can I see Vimal once before I leave, please?' he said, pausing to look at her. His tone was almost pleading and in his eyes she saw the desperation of a father on the path of separation from not one, but two of his sons.

'He would be asleep right now,' she replied coldly, regretting the words as soon as they reached her ears. The words didn't sound to her like her own. She couldn't, under the direst of circumstances, deprive a father the chance to see his son perhaps for the last time ever. But the damage had been done and there was no assuaging it.

Maybe it was a way for her subconscious to share her pains with the man who had been at their root, or perhaps she was not prepared to elongate the sequence of her separation with the man she had once loved. After all, it was with tremendous effort that she had been retaining her composure thus far and even a tiny fissure was capable of undoing it all.

'And about your promise?' she enquired meekly, the burden of guilt still weighing down on her words. Bimbisara glanced at her, his forehead creased in a frown and then suddenly, as if struck by a sudden recollection, nodded in acceptance. 'Yes Devi, I shall live up to my part of the bargain. As promised, my forces shall soon evacuate the shores of Vaishali,' he said, before turning to walk down the steps of the veranda, towards his waiting mount.

As she watched the father of her son ride away from her sight, she was overcome by an odd feeling of emptiness and mild dread. Her guilt at having prevented him from meeting Vimal had momentarily abated, but little did she know that it remained lurking in the shadows, waiting for an opportune moment to exalt itself in a more formidable avatar.

Just as Bimbisara's horse rode out of the Old Palace gates, elsewhere in Vaishali a chariot emerged from another palatial dwelling. The heavily guarded house belonged to Senapati Chetak, the formidable commander of Vaishali's army who, some claimed, overshadowed even the King in the corridors of power and influence.

'Towards Suraj's house,' Prabha instructed the charioteer amidst the sound of beating hooves and gravel being crushed under the creaking, wooden wheels of the vehicle. Her face carried a brooding look, but superseding it was a veil of satisfaction and contentment which came with the decisiveness of action following a bout of uncertainty and confusion.

Her meeting with the Senapati had not been an impulsive step. She had mulled over it for long. In fact initially she had planned to see Yudhveer instead. She was better acquainted with the King and given the circumstances he would have proven far more approachable than the Senapati, but in the end her wisdom had guided her to Chetak. She was aware of the rapport the King and Amrapali shared, and if anything, she could not risk her conversation finding its way back to her friend's ears.

Such eventuality would not only have exposed her plan but also jeopardized her relationship with Amrapali, an upshot she intended to avoid at all costs.

A part of her had hoped that she would be able to take this step with Amrapali's consent. She had even waited on her, wishfully expecting a dramatic shift in her position when she returned to the palace, but eventually her patience had worn out, and given the need for urgent action, she had decided to act on her own. There had been no news of Amrapali even as she left the Old Palace to embark on this decisive jaunt.

To her delight, the Senapati had agreed to see her and after a brief wait, she had been led by a pair of menacing-looking guards into his private chamber. 'Devi Prabha, welcome. Tell me, what this humble man can do for the Nagarvadhu's dearest companion?' he had said for a greeting. There was a dash of contempt in his voice which Prabha opted to ignore.

'Pranam Senapati,' she responded, folding her hands and bowing faintly out of courtesy. 'My sincere apologies for this sudden visit, and thank you for granting me audience despite your many pressing preoccupations. I have come to you with a vital piece of information. However, before I share with you what I know, I would need your personal assurance that under no circumstances this information would be used against the Nagarvadhu or me.'

'Pardon me, Devi, but until I know what this information you allude to is all about, I am incapable of giving you any such assurances,' he responded. There was a sense of finality to his tone which jarred her from within. This was his turf and if ever a negotiation was to be shaped here it would happen only on his terms, he appeared to be establishing. Prabha had not pre-empted this hostility and it took some effort for her to cling on to the thread of determination that had brought her to him.

'Sure, if that is what you wish,' she began, resuming her composure and applying an additional coating of confidence to her demeanour. 'The information I have is capable of altering the course of the battle with Magadh. I can lead you to the enemy Emperor Bimbisara and that too at a place where he will not be protected by his usual contingent of guards. You could arrest him without as much as a skirmish if you so wished.'

'What? How can you lead me to Bimbisara? And just where do you suppose he will venture out without his bodyguards for us to apprehend him?' Chetak shot back. His tone had scaled up a few notches and his voice shook with a blend of apprehension and excitement. At once Prabha realized that she had hit the nail on its head.

'I intend to address all your concerns Senapati, but not before you give me the requisite assurance,' she replied, an assured smile emerging on her lips.

'For your sake, I pray you know what you are talking about. Because if this is some sort of a joke, I am not amused to the slightest,' he said, an obvious threat looming in his voice. Ordinarily his words would have left Prabha trembling, but now she knew that the conversation was tilting in her favour and she had the Senapati exactly where she intended him to be. Without uttering a word, she returned his gaze, the smile still affixed on her face.

'Fine, you have my word. No harm shall come your way or Devi Amrapali's. Now please share with me the information you possess,' he eventually surrendered.

Prabha then went on to tell him about Bimbisara's assumed identity and how he had frequented the Old Palace to meet Amrapali before the break of war. An astonished Chetak listened, his eyes unblinking and lips ajar in amazement, as she revealed that it was Bimbisara who had fathered Amrapali's child. She informed him of the Emperor's last visit to the Old Palace whereby he had revealed his identity to Amrapali and also the deal that the Nagarvadhu had struck with him.

'He is still hiding somewhere in Vaishali. But if you do anything hasty like intensifying the vigil within the city or mounting a combing operation, it might scare him and he might escape. The best bet you have is to lay a trap around the Old Palace and arrest him when he visits next to obtain the information he has requested from Amrapali,' she said.

Chetak nodded ponderingly. Before his eyes were the glories that would befall him once he managed to capture the mighty Bimbisara. A glimmer of hope had emerged, piercing the dark poignant clouds surrounding Vaishali, and he had every intention of making the opportunity count.

'And one more thing. I would urge you to keep this conversation between just the two of us. No one, not even the Nagarvadhu should learn of my visit and our dialogue,' Prabha added.

'Oh, so it isn't Amrapali who has sent you here?' Chetak rhetorically remarked.

The meeting with the Senapati had gone well and Prabha was pleased with herself. There was a slight remorse she felt for failing her friend and going against Amrapali's wishes, but her vengeance-seeking eyes were prohibiting her from seeing beyond the obvious. Bimbisara, to her, was also Amrapali's culprit. After all, wasn't he the one who had tricked her into bearing his child, only to leave her alone to negotiate the agonies of childbirth? And he had the nerve to suggest that she and the child leave Vaishali and go to Rajgriha with him. What arrogance and conceit!

Prabha was convinced that she was doing Amrapali a favour, only, of a nature that she herself was too naïve to comprehend. She knew that Amrapali would be furious if ever she were to discover her little manoeuvre, but she had Chetak's discretion to bank upon. Bimbisara would be apprehended trying to approach the Old Palace and no one, not even Amrapali, would know if this had happened due to his sheer misfortune or as a result of a crafty manoeuver.

Prabha had managed to justify her actions to herself, but a part of her still lacked the courage to face Amrapali. Therefore, later that evening, when she returned from Suraj's house, she quietly made for her own room, silently praying against a chance confrontation with her friend. The trap had been laid and all she needed to do was to wait. The prey was sure to be drawn by the bait's lure sooner or later. Or so she thought.

12

It was a gloomy morning. The usual early morning breeze was missing and the moisture-laden air felt fetid and heavy. Clouds, a bunch of nomadic ones, had congregated on the horizon and were ensuring that the sun's brilliance remained at bay. It wasn't long before Prabha's temperament had begun aligning itself with the surliness of the surroundings, and as she sat brooding on her chariot-seat, her exuberance from just a while back seemed like a thing from the distant past. She had slept peacefully last night, a welcome anomaly to the disturbed nights she was gradually becoming accustomed to. It was perhaps a result of her release from the encumbrance of retribution, but she had got out of bed feeling calm and content. Impulsively she scurried towards Amrapali's chamber, only to check her steps mid-corridor and retreat to her own room just as hastily. Her sensations from the previous evening, when she had returned to the palace, had suddenly come rushing back—her guilt at having acted against Amrapali's wish and her reluctance to come to face her.

Her hesitation, she knew, was temporary and once Bimbisara was arrested and the dust around the episode settled, it would subside on its own. But the challenge was the present. The guilt within her made her shudder at the thought of looking into Amrapali's eyes and behaving as if nothing had happened. The two had known each other since childhood and even if a shard of ambiguity remained in her bearing, Amrapali was likely to latch on to it.

Thus, deciding to persist with her ploy of circumvention in the interim, she had summoned her chariot and set out. Her destination once again was Suraj's house. His old parents were slowly emerging from their loss, and her visits, she realized, had become a comforting habit to them. Though she had refrained from telling them about Bimbisara or the pact she had made with Senapati Chetak as yet, she knew that the news, as and when it broke, would further help in alleviating their pain.

She was carrying with her a bag full of raw meat which she had got one of the dasis to bring her from the palace kitchen. Spicy meat and potato curry was among Parimal's favourite dishes and she had intended to cook it for him, but the weather appeared determined to play spoilsport. Humidity levels in the air had suddenly spiked exceptionally and beads of perspiration were already forming on her forehead. It was simply too hot to spend the entire morning sitting across a flaming chulha, to cook a dish that wasn't designed to be relished in such weather.

She was cursing the weather and its vagaries, her chariot lumbering along the gravel arterial path linking the Old Palace to the main street, when the sound of approaching hoof-beats drilled through the quiet. She was alarmed. The only object of significance along the narrow road, before it eased into the dense foliage of the Mahavana was the Old Palace and whoever the intruders were—at least a few of dozen of them, judging by the clatter of their galloping horses—their destination could only be one.

The guests of the Old Palace, even the most distinguished ones, seldom rode with such a sizeable guard-unit, and to that effect the approaching brigade further added to Prabha's curiosity. A blind curve kept them from her view, but the sudden slackening of the pitter-patter meant that they were checking their pace. They were now alive to her approach, and this knowledge only made her even more anxious. 'These can't be Senapati Chetak's men,' she thought, 'he would undoubtably have opted for a more discreet approach for the fear of scaring Bimbisara away.'

Her contemplation was however cut short as her chariot, steering past the turn, came to face the intruders. Her estimate had turned out to be way off the mark. They were over a hundred men, a complete battalion of the Vajji army, with the royal flag fluttering haughtily atop the chariot-dome emerging in their midst. And then she saw the flag move forward, carving a path among the sea of horsemen, to approach her. Hundreds of ominous thoughts fleeted through her mind as she waited for the outer layer of the formation to tear and the encased chariot to emerge.

When it eventually appeared, the sight of its occupant sent her into yet another frenzy of contemplations. The daunting form of Senapati Chetak peered at her from under the chariot-dome, his hands spread wide to clutch the wooden banister commandingly. 'Pranam Senapati,' she greeted him meekly, her questioning eyes showering him with a volley of unspoken questions.

'Pranam,' he responded emotionlessly. 'And if I may, where is it that you are headed?'

Prabha was further perplexed. First, the unsociable response to her salutation, and now this, an undisguised attempt to invade her privacy! Something untoward had surely transpired since she had last met the Senapati. Keeping her emotions at bay, she cordially replied, 'I was going to tend to some personal matters, but if it is me that the Senapati has travelled this far to meet, I will be happy to escort him back to the Old Palace.'

'No, it isn't you, but your mistress, the traitor Amrapali that we seek. She is still at the palace and hasn't eloped as yet, I assume?' he shot back. Suddenly Prabha felt the hard of her knees turn to jelly. Reaching out to the handrail for support, she babbled, 'Amrapali…a traitor? What are you saying Senapati? You know that this is not true. I had told you the entire story, had I not? And you had promised not to hold the information against either Amrapali or me. How can you go back on your words now?' She was furious from within, but the awareness that only a reasoned dialogue could dissuade Chetak from his intentions made her bite each word as she articulated it.

But the Senapati remained unwavering, the crimson of his face deepening portentously as he spoke. 'Either you are genuinely naïve and have no idea about the engagements of your mistress or you are extremely crafty and are still trying to shield her. But that is all inconsequential now. I have enough evidence of her chicanery and it is about time she was made to pay for her sins.'

'Trust me Senapati Ji; I have no inkling of what you allude to. As soon as I became aware of Bindusen's true identity, I rushed to share the information with you. I am a victim of Bimbisara's covetous ambitions myself. Suraj, the only man I have ever loved, lost his life to Bimbisara's men and there is no length I shall not scale for an opportunity to avenge him. As you are well aware, any hasty action might deprive us of the only opportunity to capture Bimbisara. So pray tell me Senapati, what is it that you claim to have learnt, and I shall corroborate the information to the best of my knowledge. And if the information turns out to be untrue, you could avoid your march to the Palace and prevent alarming Bimbisara,' she reasoned in a near pleading tone.

'The information, you said, Bimbisara had sought from Amrapali, she has already passed it on to him,' he revealed after a thoughtful pause. Prabha was stunned. His words rang like a bell within her ears. 'How can that be?' she questioned herself.

'I was informed of this by someone who was privy to their meeting and there is no reason for me to doubt the credibility of my source. Moreover, I have also had a word with Maharaj Yudhveer and he confimed that Amrapali had paid him a visit yesterday. The sly wretch steered the conversation in such manner that the King trustingly took the insidious bait and revealed the identity of our informer to her.'

Pausing briefly to appraisingly eye Prabha, he continued, 'The Nagarvadhu, through her actions, has not only disregarded the adulation and respect of the people of Vaishali, but also committed an unpardonable felony. She is a traitor and she shall be dealt with in accordance with the laws of the land. You, my lady, by virtue of your endeavour to help the state in nailing one of its most dangerous foes, are not being construed as an accomplice to this act of treason. However, if you stand in my path or make any attempts to forewarn Amrapali, I will not think twice before relegating you to the state dungeons as well.'

Chetak's voice was determined and Prabha had no doubts that he meant every word that he spoke. 'Therefore, I suggest that,' he continued, 'you carry on to wherever you were heading and not harbour any clever thoughts about interfering with the course of justice.'

She nodded meekly, her eyes blinking under the weight of the profound anguish that had precipitated upon her, before gesturing to her charioteer. Retreating was the only sensible step for her to take. Chetak's men, like a python wiggling to ingest its prey, allowed her chariot to tear through their collective frame and emerge behind them. As she passed the heavily armed men, stiffly postured on their mounts like starched garments on a clothes line, she could feel their glances surveying her intently.

'Steer the chariot to the left,' she instructed her charioteer when the hind of Chetak's unit had taken the turn to plunge off her line of vision. The man holding the reins turned to look at her quizzically. Towards his left he saw only a dense assemblage of trees and shrubbery. 'Yes, in there, quick! Release the sturdiest horse from the chariot and wait for me right here. Remember, no passersby should see you or the chariot till I return. Hurry now!'

In no time Prabha's chariot and the three remaining horses had been swallowed by the forest, while the fourth one dashed through thorny shrubs and vines, carving a path of its own in the seldom-trodden terrain. Prabha's legs were tightly clasped around its shaft, the reins dangling from one hand as she used the other to pat the beast into continuous acceleration. There was a look of ferocious determination on her face and the hurt from riding an unsaddled horse seemed not to matter at all.

She was aware of the punishment Vaishali meted out to its traitors and unless she reached the Old Palace before Chetak, Amrapali's life-thread was bound to be mercilessly sliced, hanging from a flailing noose, or worse still, trampled under the feet of an enraged battle-tusker. Of course she had the advantages of knowing the terrain well enough to carve a shorter route for her return and the size-induced mobility restrain that plagued the Senapati's troops, but time was still of utmost importance. If there was anyone who could dispel the certain doom inching towards the unsuspecting Amrapali, it was her, and this was one battle she could not afford to lose. After all, wasn't she the one to have selfishly led her friend into the clutches of this crisis in the first place?

The heavy wooden door flung open, banging with a thud against the sandstone wall, and a harried Prabha burst in. Amrapali was startled and so was Vimal, who instantly began curving his lips to cry and record his displeasure at the sudden intrusion. But Prabha looked a woman possessed. Beads of perspiration were lining her forehead and her face, pale and sapped, appeared as if a puckish ghost had stopped by to gaily greet her.

She marched up to Amrapali and snatching the wailing baby from her arms, instructed her to follow her. 'Hurry, we don't have much time,' she said, turning on her heels and making for the door.

'Will you at least tell me what happened? What is this rush all about?' Amrapali quizzed, scampering to keep pace. She had barely managed to slip on her sandals when Prabha, clutching little Vimal, had already crossed the doorsill. There was a sense of desperation in Prabha's actions which made Amrapali abide with her directions, but the curiosity within her remained to be addressed.

'We don't have the time now. I shall explain everything, but first we need to safely get out of here. Just trust me,' she said, speaking over her shoulder without compromising on the pace of her strides.

If there was any one person that Amrapali could blindly trust it was Prabha, and pursing her lips, she once again got down to keeping pace with her friend as they headed towards the courtyard through the winding corridors of the palace. Ballabh and two of his comrades who were stationed outside the Nagarvadhu's chambers had also joined them and were walking briskly, flanking the two ladies. The baby, perhaps amused by the flurry of activity surrounding him, had stopped crying and was happily clinging on to Prabha's chest now.

The small entourage, with Prabha at its helm, had just cleared the maze of corridors to emerge in the veranda when their rapid progression was brought to a screeching halt by the scene they came to face. A man, legs slightly ajar in a ready-to-tackle stance, brandishing a sword in each hand, stood blocking their path. The sun, having momentarily emerged from the cloud cover, as though especially to witness this spectacle, had its rays reflecting portentously from the sharp blades of the swords.

'Not another step, anyone,' he roared, brandishing his swords threateningly. No one moved, not even the mighty Ballabh. It wasn't intimidation or the threat, but the identity of the challenger that had them frozen stiff.

'Kundali…' the name escaped Amrapali's lips like a whisper of disbelief. There was hardly any resemblance between the differently abled boy she had been sheltering and tending to for several months and the Kundali standing in her path now. In fact Kundali appeared more like a young warrior ready for battle, of course in complete command of his mental faculties.

'Kundali—oh, how I hate that name. I am glad that finally the time has come for me to discard both the name and the exasperating persona that came with it,' he said dramatically, his lips curving into a shrewd smile as the last set of words left them.

'Kundali, or whoever you are, we do not have the time for your theatrics right now. Whatever your grievances, you can take them up with her at a more opportune time. But for now, please move out of our way,' Prabha intervened. Kundali's transformed avatar was a shock to her too, but she knew better than to permit such indulgences to stall their escape.

'Oh, is that so Devi Prabha? But I thought we, you and I, were bound by the singularity of our motives. After all, weren't you the one to inform Senapati Chetak of Bindusen's true identity?'

Amrapali, still unsure of the spectacle unfolding in front of her eyes, glanced towards her friend. Prabha's face had turned ashen. It appeared as though Kundali's words had been a shower of grime and soot that had deposited itself over the original texture of her skin. Gaping at him with widened eyes, she stuttered, 'Who are you?' Her words had suddenly lost the confidence they had previously been bearing.

'Now, that is a relevant question. And I see no harm in assuaging your curiosity...and hers...' he said, tilting the tip of one of his swords towards Amrapali, 'now that she is left with very little time to rue her deeds of the past. I am Mukul Deva, son of the erstwhile king of Vaishali, Manudeva.' Turning to bore his eyes into Amrapali's, he added, 'Does the name ring a bell, Devi Amrapali?'

Manudeva's was a name Amrapali would never forget, not in this lifetime at least. It was his mad obsession that had turned her life on its head, and instead of a sedentary existence in the arms of the man she loved, she had found herself tending to the carnal desires of the entire city. It was Manudeva, who, leveraging an antiquated law had shoved her onto the pedestal of the Nagarvadhu, brutally crushing all her dreams and desires.

The scene from many years back was still vivid in her memory, when after the council elections she had been pensively sitting in the palace garden. The coup she had meticulously planned and shaped had come through, and Yudhveer, her candidate for the King's throne, had emerged victorious, ending Manudeva's long drawn authoritarian regime. Her reverie had been interrupted by a messenger who had arrived bearing a letter for her from Yudhveer. The letter, an invite from the newly appointed King to attend his coronation ceremony had also carried the information that Manudeva, devastated by his unexpected defeat in the elections, had ended his life by hanging himself.

Amrapali had felt a barrage of emotions surge through her then, as she did now. With the end of her tormentor, she had been overcome by a sense of relief and finality, and tears had involuntarily begun to trickle down her eyes. She had felt that the story of her life had finally taken a full circle to find its conclusion, but she couldn't have been further from the truth. A fragment from her past life still remained, and emerging from the least expected quarters, it was threatening to consume her all over again.

What troubled her even more was that her adversary now had a face she had come to love, to treat like one of her own. First Bimbisara and then Kundali, had she become so emotionally frail that anyone could simply walk into her life and stake claim to a plinth of significance? Had her affection become so trivial a substance that she had taken to squandering it indiscreetly?

'But I got you here, tended to you like my own child…' she mumbled. She had not completely emerged from her thoughts yet and the words were mere fragments of the feelings jostling within her.

'Oh no, don't flatter yourself. You did nothing that I didn't want you to do. You got me here because I wanted you to do so and you loved me only because I wanted you to love me. It was all preordained, part of a broader scheme I have been putting in place for better part of my life. The sight of my father's lifeless body, staring into oblivion so desperately that it was a miracle his eyes remained in their sockets, perhaps trying to look beyond the boundaries of time to the day when his son would avenge his death, remains etched in my memory till this day,' he said, ambers of hatred spewing from his eyes.

'I was a small child then, too young to think or reason, but the one name that kept appearing in my mother's agonizing wails night after desolate night, reminding me of the requite I owed my dead father, was yours Devi Amrapali. And today is merely the culmination of the curse that befell upon you the day you orchestrated my father's brutal assassination. It is nothing but your own sins that stand in your path today.

What was my father's fault anyway, that he fell in love with you? But for that mistake he was willing to marry you, to make you the Queen of Vaishali, but no, you had other designs. One man was never enough for you, was it? You wanted every man in Vaishali to drool at your feet, to be a helpless hostage of your beauty, and so you chose the option that suited you most—eliminating the one who truly loved you. Isn't that true Nagarvadhu Amrapali?'

Amrapali remained speechless while Prabha nervously shifted her weight from one leg to the other. Time was ebbing and Mukul Deva's rhetoric didn't seem even remotely close to its culmination.

'I took up the identity of Kundali only to gain your pity and a window of accessibility for later, but my performance must have been profound, for you ended up bringing me back here with you. Since then I have had some opportunities of payback, of causing you pain—poisoning one of your favorite mounts or hurting this bastard son of yours, accidently of course—but none excruciating enough to lessen the anguish of my revenge. I was patiently waiting for the right opportunity when that old Acharya turned up out of nowhere. He was a good man, an erudite scholar, who, upon my father's insistence had once coached me briefly, even though he had retired from active teaching.

The old man had recognized me instantly and for once I thought that my game was over. It wouldn't have taken much for him to deduce the purpose of my presence in your vicinity. But I guess it is true that a man's courage only wanes with age, leaving him feeble and fragile. My incessant gaze frightened him into keeping my identity under wraps, but not until he left you with a curiously worded invite to visit him. The old man must have thought that I was still the little gullible boy he could persuade to memorize his lessons with the promise of a little sweet, but he was wrong. And that proved to be the last mistake he ever made, in this lifetime at least.'

'You… It was you who killed Acharya Narhari?' Amrapali cut through his oration with a shrill that had been hitherto amiss from her voice. Her fists were clenched now and hands trembling slightly.

'Collateral damage Devi. Futile but unavoidable,' he sneered.

'The Acharya was a man of God. You shouldn't have done what you did,' Amrapali retorted. Her voice had suddenly acquired a chilling composure. She had been scared of Mukul Deva, not for his might, but for the love she had felt for his alter persona of Kundali. She had herself known the angst of losing a dear one due to the deeds of another, and a part of her could relate with the boy's need for retribution. Her fear had been that her love would prevent her from opposing him in the steadfast manner that was needed, but that was before Mukul Deva had apprised her of his inhuman deeds. She would never have associated the Acharya's violent desecration with Kundali, not after learning of his true identity even. She couldn't imagine that the boy would even be capable of such viciousness, but now that he had himself confessed to the act, she could feel her love for him metamorphosing into intense hatred, slowly releasing her from all its bindings.

'Oh, don't worry. You shall soon get to see him, up there,' he said, twisting a sword for its tip to lift upwards. 'I have completed the task your friend had begun. Prabha had informed Senapati Chetak about Bimbisara's identity, but I have also told him all about your little pact and the confidential information you have passed on to him. You do know that what you have done amounts to treason against the state, don't you? It is only when you are condemned, stripped of all your privileges and eventually shown the noose that my revenge shall be complete,' he said heaving a sigh.

'Nothing of that sort will happen,' Prabha screamed, charging at him, still clutching on to little Vimal with one hand. Amrapali shrieked. Kundali darted ahead too, the sword in his right hand ready to come down on her. Suddenly Amrapali felt something move to her right. It was Ballabh. He had remained in the backdrop till the need for his intervention arose, and when it did, there was no stopping him.

The impact of his flashing sword was concealed from Amrapali by Ballabh's flowing cape, and when the fabric gently settled, she saw Mukul Deva dropping to the ground, blood oozing viciously from a stump where his right hand had once been. His hand, still clutching the weapon, was squirming at a distance, and Ballabh, thick droplets of blood dripping from the blade of his sword, stood eyeing his collapsing adversary. Mukul Deva let out a gut wrenching cry as his body met the ground with a thud. Vimal, who surprisingly had been holding on thus far, uttered a loud scream too, but his feeble voice losing itself to the violent cries of the amputated man.

'Finish him,' Amrapali said, pausing to give the boy one last look of compassion, before stepping in the direction Prabha was already heading. Behind her she heard the slushing sound of a sharp weapon slicing through human body, the abdomen perhaps, and Mukul Deva's cries, after hitting a crescendo, fell silent. She didn't look back even as she heard Ballabh's steps break into a run to catch up with them.

They would have advanced for not more than a dozen steps when once again they were jolted mid-stride, this time by the sounds of an approaching battalion—an orchestra of beating hooves, shuffling steps and clink-clank of metal brushing against metal. Not a word was spoken, they were all aware that the noise source was perilously close to the palace gates and they could no longer use it for a clandestine exit, so, when Prabha decisively took a sideward turn, others unhesitatingly followed.

She was heading towards a small gateway on the farther end of the peripheral wall which had remained unused for at least as long as Amrapali had been possessor of the property. The opening was slight, inadequate to allow passage for their horses, but it was closer to the forest, which meant that they could still hope to make good their escape on foot. Chetak's men were sure to encounter some resistance from the Nagarvadhu's guards, and when they did eventually manage to enter the palace, it would take them time to trace her escape path. And by then, God willing, they would be far from the Senapati's reach. However, the most crucial consideration for shaping their decision in favour of the alternate exit was that this was the only alternative they happened to be left with.

His hatred for the Nagarvadhu notwithstanding, Amrapali's arrest at the hands of the Senapati spelt certain doom for her. She had no clue about where she would go once the escape was made, but for now it was crucial that she got away. The abrupt nature of developments had not allowed her sufficient time to chart out a plan, but once the looming danger had been steered clear of she would have ample time to assess her options. She could seek refuge in any one of the Khandas ruled by Rajas that had once been her patrons and seek Yudhveer's intervention in bailing her out, or perhaps she could even try to establish contact with Bimbisara and head to Rajgriha with him. But for now she had to remain focused on the task at hand.

It took one swing of Ballabh's sword and the metal chain binding the door-latch released itself and fell to the ground. They paused, ears alert to any odd sound that might follow the jangle of the restraint being breached. None emerged.

Ballabh took the first stride forward, turning to glance at his two comrades who were vigilantly positioned behind the ladies, before gently pushing the metal door ajar and stepping out. A moment of silence followed, and then, with a sudden crash, he came staggering back, scraping against the door-frame to land close to his mistress's feet. Blood oozed from where his hands pressed hard on his abdomen, spreading in a dark wet patch to soak his jersey. His lips were curled inside the mouth, perhaps to prevent a scream from leaking out, and his face was contorted with the agonizing pain he was enduring.

Even before Amrapali could bend down to inspect Ballabh's injury, the metal door once again burst open and a battery of armed soldiers began pouring in. The two remaining Xingnous charged, violently swerving their swords, but Amrapali had realized that the battle was already lost. If the tumult outside, from where the soldiers were ceaselessly pouring in, was any indication, there were enough of them out there to tire her two guards without even putting up a serious fight. 'Stop,' she screamed, hoping to assuage as many lives as she could, both of her own guards and the many soldiers they would have undoubtedly brought down before they themselves fell.

But in passing the instruction she missed accounting for the fact that while the Xingnou guards were bound by her orders, Chetak's men were not. This little slip proved fatal for the two men, who, upon her command, had pulled down their swords and were backing off when a bunch of soldiers buckled upon them like a swarm of nectar-craved bees. Amrapali remained screaming, pleading for them to cease their barbarity, but it was only upon reducing the two breathing humans into heaps of battered remains did they concede.

Amrapali turned to look away. She was disgusted, not at the brutal manner in which her men had met their end, nor even the celebratory cheers from the soldiers that followed, but with the realization that it was she who was actually responsible for their death. Had she not commanded them to back off, or had she prevented them from following her in the first place…

From the corner of her eye she looked in the direction where Ballabh's body lay sprawled. He had departed too, the trampling feet of invaders having reduced his body to a barely identifiable pulp. She could not believe that the years of selfless service, idol-like worship and unfailing loyalty that Ballabh and his men had bestowed upon her had met an end so abrupt and ghastly. The men were true warriors and they deserved at least a chance to fight their last battle, whether fair or not, but the cruel designs of fate had chosen to deprive them of even that honour. The loss was extremely personal and Amrapali felt a moist track forming from her eyes down her cheeks.

'Take her into custody,' Chetak's authoritative voice rang through the air. The main entrance to the palace had been breached too, and the Senapati, at the helm of his raiding troops, had arrived at the site.

A soldier pulled out a metal chain from somewhere and fastened it around Amrapali's wrists. The Nagarvadhu did not offer any resistance. 'You chose to ignore my advice, but I shall nevertheless honour my word and spare you. However, this is the first and last time that you are being allowed to get away with your indiscretions. If you think of meddling with the affairs of the state ever again, I will be on to you before you can bat an eyelid,' he looked at Prabha and added. Prabha stood still, too shocked to react, tears streaming down her eyes uncontrollably.

'Take good care of him,' Amrapali said to her, as the soldiers led her to a waiting horse and helped her mount it. Prabha stood there, clutching little Vimal, vigorously nodding her head and snivelling, even as she watched her friend being led to the main gate and then through it to a world that waited, with who knew what all horrors in its embrace, to greet her.

The populace of Vaishali had remained deprived of Amrapali's influence in their lives for many months now. Their enchantress, who had grown into an obsession for most, and her companionship an addiction, had suddenly been snatched away by the callings of war. Initially they had jostled restlessly, like an opium addict craving for his next pellet, but the anxiety had soon settled and other exigencies had drawn away their attention. They had gradually emerged from the stupor that her divine beauty had propelled them into, but she still remained within their hearts as a pleasing and cherishable memory.

Vaishali had not forgotten its Nagarvadhu and when the news of her arrest came, it spread like a seismic tremor, relaying from ear to eager ear with an alarming alacrity. People who heard the story in any of the several forms it had acquired during its transmission were left aghast, unable to believe that Amrapali, their Amrapali, had actually turned out to be a traitor. There was concern, panic, empathy and disbelief in their voices, but the sense of passion which on another day would have brought them spilling on the streets to stand alongside their Nagarvadhu in her hour of need, was conspicuously amiss. The tides of time had done well to soothe the surge of emotions that the men of Vaishali had once felt at the mere mention of Amrapali's name.

The room was simple, sparsely furnished, and the man lying on the charpai appeared lost in deep thought. Suddenly the door burst open and another man, much older in age, barged in. 'Oh, it is you,' the younger man said, pulling away his hand from under the headrest, to where it had darted impulsively following the abrupt intrusion. His posture, on having ascertained the identity of the intruder, had immediately slipped back to its erstwhile bearing—relaxed and composed.

'Maharaj, I bring some terrible news for you,' Narsinh Dev whispered hurriedly. 'What is it, Amatya? Have they somehow got wind of our escape route and managed to block it?' Bimbisara replied, his tone measured, but without a hint of strain as yet.

The scene was unfolding at a caravanserai on the outskirts of Vaishali where the Emperor of Magadh and his principal minister had spent the night disguised as common medicine men. Bimbisara still had accomplices within Vaishali that he could turn to for housing him, but after the debacle with Amanverma, he had opted for the anonymity of the caravanserai instead. The obscurity worked well for him too, since lesser the number of people in the know of his pursuits, lower the chances of the information dribbling over to an unwarranted ear.

As per their original plan they were to leave Vaishali the previous day itself, but Bimbisara had only managed to return from his meeting with Amrapali by the evening. Two medicine men venturing out into the jungle in search of herbs post sundown would have appeared suspicious to any onlooker, so they had decided in favour of staying back for the night. Moreover, Bimbisara had appeared distressed, visibly unready for the strenuous journey ahead, and despite the minister's persistent quizzing he had not divulged the reasons for his concerned state.

Though the anxiousness had remained, Bimbisara appeared to be in much better stead today, prompting Narsinh Dev to leave the inn for conducting a reconnaissance of the surroundings before the King emerged from hiding. The elderly minister had been gone for a while, allowing Bimbisara the solitude to brood over the many disturbing facts he had come to face lately, only to return with what he had just termed 'terrible news'.

'No Maharaj, our escape route remains unhindered, but Devi Amrapali…I heard from some people in the marketplace that Senapati Chetak has arrested her on charges of treason. Upon further enquiry, discreetly of course, I learnt that the news was indeed true and her arrest has been made on account of some confidential piece of information that she has allegedly passed on to you. She is in grave danger Maharaj, we must do something,' he explained, a look of concern affixed on his face.

Narsinh Dev had accompanied Bimbisara when he had initially visited the Old Palace in the guise of Bindusen, the trader. Though the two had never explicitly spoken about Amrapali, the old minister's practised eyes had witnessed the King's feelings for her alter from plain curiosity to unbridled love and longing. He had felt himself as an uninvited but inseparable accessory to their saga, and when Bimbisara had invited him to accompany him on this dangerous jaunt over the other younger and sturdier generals from his army, he had felt a sense of affinity, inexplicable in words, towards their relationship in general and Amrapali in particular. It was the kinship one feels when made privy to an extremely personal and crucial development by someone. And now, as he narrated what he knew of Amrapali's plight, his disquiet showed.

'We can be of little use to her by remaining in Vaishali,' Bimbisara spoke after pondering over the information for a while. 'We must get going at once. It is only once we are amongst our own men that we can even think of doing something for her. Till then, the only thing left for us to do is pray for her well-being and hope that she is able to weather this storm too, like the many she has weathered through her life.'

13

'The reason I have summoned only you and not the entire war council is the unsettling nature of information I wish to share,' Bimbisara said. He was back in his tent within the Magadh encampment and in his audience were Yuvraj Ajatshatru and Mahamatya Narsinh Dev. The mood within the enclosure was sombre, borrowing its hues from the Emperor's visage.

After a slight pause, he continued, 'As you know, one of the principal objectives behind my visit to Vaishali was to ascertain the identity of the traitor who betrayed the allies we had cultivated within their ranks. My sources did provide me with a name, but I was as shocked to hear it as I am sure you will be.' Ajatshatru continued staring curiously.

'The man who gave Amanverma, Bhadresh and Ramdev away was none other than your half-brother, Vihalla Kumar.'

'What? No Maharaj, this can't be. There has to be some gross error of judgment. Why would the Rajkumar betray his own blood? Moreover, Vihalla Kumar has not even been involved in planning and strategizing for the war. How would he have access to information that the Senapati or even I were not in the know of? Surely Maharaj, someone is trying to misguide you by deliberately feeding you with fabricated information,' Ajatshatru retorted in disbelief.

'I understand your anguish my son, but I can only wish that your brother shared the same devotion for our clan and the people of Magadh as you. The source of my information is highly credible and though my heart would want to believe otherwise, I am convinced of its authenticity. How he managed to access this piece of information or what were his motives behind sharing it with the enemy remains to be discovered, but the one thing that is certain is that Vihalla Kumar is the traitor in our midst.

It hasn't been easy for me, the discovery that my blood, my own son, could stoop to an act so heinous and disgusting, but then truth does eventually find a way to establish itself. The human mind and its myriad motivations are mysteries beyond comprehension and there must be some or the other convoluted rationale behind his actions that remains veiled from us presently. It is to discern these beliefs and motives of your half-brother that I have summoned you here today, for if allowed to foster unabated, they might pose a threat to our dynasty as well as your future reign.

You must depart for Rajgriha immediately and have a word with Vihalla Kumar. Spare no efforts in revalidating the information and in understanding the motivations that drove him to take such a step. A great ruler is not one who manages to suppress the issue at hand, but the one who is able to identify and address the cause of it. But once certain that it was indeed your brother who betrayed our men, do not hesitate in doling out the punishment his actions deserve. Remember, blood, when it stands in the path of our duty, must be spilled, even if it happens to be of the same shade as the one flowing through our own veins.'

Ajatshatru sat listening intently to Bimbisara's words and nodding his head intermittently. 'As you wish father. I shall leave for Rajgriha at once,' he said, bowing his head slightly. He was himself surprised at having addressed Bimbisara as 'Father', a salutation he failed to recall when he had last used. It had been 'Maharaj' for as long as he could remember, especially when the conversation pertained to matters of the state. Perhaps the realization that one of their own might have betrayed them had momentarily sensitized him to the blood-bond he shared with the King, one which often found itself subdued by the etiquettes and sacraments of their official relationship.

'And Maharaj, is there something you could find out about their battle strategies or the important military installations that you would want to share? A messenger has arrived from Rajgriha yesterday bearing Devdutt's message. He says that the contraptions the minister had been working on are ready and can be shipped to the front whenever we wish to deploy them,' he added as an afterthought.

'We did manage a fair idea about their military strengths, but let us discuss that at a more appropriate time. First go and settle the issue at hand and ask Devdutt to hold on to his devices for the time being.'

Bowing his head once more, Ajatshatru exited the tent, his mind a mish-mash of thoughts about all that lay ahead of him. Bimbisara took a few steps forward, following his son to the opening which served as a gate to the tent and kept staring at his frame till he took a turn and disappeared behind the maze of men, beasts and makeshift dwellings. Then, turning to catch the prime minister's eye, he said, 'Amatya, please ready a messenger to carry a message for the King of Vaishali. I will need him as soon as I am done drafting the message.'

Chetak emerged from the chair, holding the parchment in his hand with the intent of reading it aloud to the assembled members of the Vajji council. He knew that the contents of the letter were well known to every man present inside the chamber and that it had formed the subject of intense discussions amongst them ever since the Magadhan messenger's arrival, but given the gravity of the decision that the council was expected to make, it was only reasonable that he refreshed their memories one more time.

'It gives me immense grief to learn of the treatment you have meted out to Amrapali, not only because of the personal equation I share with her, but also due to the fact that her loyalty towards Vaishali remains unquestionable. I can state this with utmost conviction since I have been a party to the events that form the very basis of the allegations levelled against her. I can assure you that the only thought driving every action of hers has been the welfare of Vaishali and nothing else.

However, I see no reason for you to place your trust in me— an arch adversary of your kingdom—and I don't even intend to appeal to your benevolence or to seek your favour by pleading for her release. Just as I know of Amrapali's arrest, I am also aware of the perilous state of your defences and the deficiency of essential supplies that mars your granaries and warehouses. As much as you might wish to refute it, the fact remains that if my forces don't withdraw immediately, it will only be a matter of time before Vaishali will be forced to go down on its knees and cede itself to the Magadhan might.

So, I propose to you, honourable members of the Vajji council, an offer which will help you retain your prestige and also the sovereignty of your kingdom. Exonerate Amrapali of all charges and restore her to her erstwhile position and I shall end my siege of Vaishali instantaneously. And if by some spurt of false bravado you decide on the contrary, I promise you that within days from today the city of Vaishali shall be razed to oblivion. Not a tree shall be left standing on your lands and this is my, Bimbisara's, personal assurance to you.

You have until sundown today to accept my offer and release Amrapali, failing which the responsibility of the consequences shall rest but on your fearless shoulders.'

The Senapati could feel his hands trembling with rage as he finished reading the letter and looked probingly at his fellow council-men for their reactions. The threat in Bimbisara's words was palpable, and left to his own, Chetak would have preferred to die fighting rather than succumb to it. But the challenge ahead of them transcended personal penchants and inclinations. The decision of the council today was to shape the future of the entire kingdom and he had a plummeting feeling that they were not left with many real alternatives to consider.

Today was the second time that the council had convened in as many days. The first meeting had followed Amrapali's arrest and had been convened by the Senapati himself to apprise the council members of the developments. The question that if Bimbisara was able to breach Vaishali's frontiers and visit the Old Palace personally, how robust their fortifications had been, was raised even then, but only as a voiced concern and not the looming threat that it had presented itself as today. The council members, including the King, had been concerned about the extent to which the Magadh forces had managed to infiltrate their ranks, and today, when the messenger bearing Bimbisara's letter had arrived, their worst fears had become real.

Yudhveer was the next to get up to address the council. 'It is indeed a grave situation that we face today. What Bimbisara has mentioned in his message is not entirely untrue and if the war does not conclude soon enough, we will certainly find it difficult to hold fort. As for Amrapali, she has not spoken a word since her arrest and there is no way for us to ascertain whether the allegations of treason levelled against her are indeed true. All that Bimbisara pursues is her release and I am of the opinion that we must make good this opportunity and do what it takes for bringing the war to an end,' he said.

'But if we release her without a proper trial, will it not establish a wrong precedence? I mean, treason is a serious crime, one that warrants the harshest of punishments, and if she is simply allowed to walk away, what impression will that create of us in the eyes of the people,' one of the dignitaries said, visibly uncertain of his own argument. Yudhveer, like a few others, glanced at him, but did not offer a counter. This was no time to worry about impressions or the underlying concern that the esteemed council member had refrained from voicing—the impact an unhealthy public perception could have on the next council elections. Their priority currently was to preserve the fabric of democracy in Vaishali and only if they succeeded would the elections ever happen.

'And why should we take his word that he will indeed order his forces to retreat when he knows that victory is within his grasp?' another interjected. 'We have nothing to lose in accepting his offer. He knows that Amrapali will remain within Vaishali and that it won't take much for us to have her arrested again if he doesn't keep his word,' the King responded.

No further contestations were made and the Vajji council, with a rare unanimous vote, decreed in favour of releasing Amrapali from captivity and annulling all the charges framed against her. Senapati Chetak's was the last hand to go up in the show of hands, but he knew that irrespective of how he felt, the decision being arrived at was the most judicious one under the given circumstances.

There was a spring of purpose to his steps as Ajatshatru scuttled past the bronze ornamentations—vases and figurines—decorating the corridors of the Magadh palace at Rajgriha. He had arrived from the front late in the night, and knowing that Vihalla Kumar in all likelihood would be scaling some obscure plane of inebriation by then, had decided to shelve the meeting with his brother for the next morning and retire to his chamber instead. He had of course remembered to order an immediate change of the sentries stationed outside Vihalla Kumar's chambers, positioning his own loyal guards on duty instead—a precautionary measure of sorts—and instructing his personal attendant to summon his favourite concubine instantly. The war had forced him to lead a life of depravation for several months now, and given his father's absence from the palace, he could certainly permit himself some trivial liberties.

After a night of contentment and comfort, he had risen relaxed and ready to discharge the duty assigned to him by his father. Spending little time to freshen up, he had emerged from his chamber to head resolutely towards his half-brother's bedroom.

By Vihalla Kumar's standards, day was still a fair way from breaking and it took no less than a firm shake before he opened his eyes lazily. 'You? When did you return? And what are you doing here?' He was somewhat startled to find the familiar but unexpected image of Ajatshatru at his bedside.

'My apologies for waking you from your sleep brother, but the matter I am here to discuss is extremely urgent and could not be delayed any further,' he replied in a calm but stern manner. Sensing the urgency in Ajatshatru's tone, Vihalla Kumar sat up on the bed, struggling to acquire a basic level of composure. His eyes were bloodshot, not the red of disturbed sleep but that of the excesses from the previous night.

'The battle of Vaishali is over. Yesterday we undertook a decisive assault with all the men and beasts at our disposal and were finally able to breach the city walls. Our forces, as they marched into the city, did not face much resistance, and in no time we had the Magadh flag fluttering atop their royal palace,' Ajatshatru said, his gaze affixed on Vihalla Kumar's face and keeping tab of even the slightest crease that emerged as a reaction to his fabricated but well-rehearsed tale.

For some time Vihalla Kumar remained impassive, expressionless like a statue, but eventually his lips fluttered. 'That is great news. Heartiest congratulations, my brother, on yet another glorious feather of victory in your cap,' he said, his passive eyes belying his words.

'We were able to capture most of the Vajji office-bearers alive and among them was their Senapati—you might have heard of him, Chetak, he is known as. Maharaj personally undertook his interrogation and it is to him that he revealed the name of the traitor who had betrayed Raja Amanverma and his two accomplices,' Ajatshatru continued. And now his words suddenly seemed to be making an impression. Vihalla Kumar first turned pale and now his crimson eyes were widened with fear.

After a slight pause, Ajatshatru spoke again, his voice suddenly acquiring a sympathetic tone. 'Why, brother? Why did you do this?' he said.

Vihalla Kumar eyed him momentarily, as though trying to examine the sentiments behind his words, and then his lips quivered again. 'You have no right to question me and I don't owe you any explanations either... I am father's eldest son and yet, right from the days of our childhood you have been staking claim to everything that should have rightfully been mine. First, you get to lead the army in the battle of Anga and then, ignoring my very existence, father appoints you the Yuvraj of Magadh—the King in waiting.

And it doesn't end just there. We prepare for one of our biggest battles and while you are placed at its helm, I am not even informed of it, let alone allowed to make any sort of a contribution. You, Ajatshatru, will never know what it feels like to be shunned by your own father, and so you are incapable of understanding my emotions or the inner turmoil I am left to deal with for every breathing moment of my life.'

Though his tone had remained even, Vihalla Kumar's jaws had tautened, his eyes had turned redder and his breathing seemed far more labourious now than it had been. He was shaking with pent up rage and for once even Ajatshatru shuddered at the thought of all the hatred his brother had been piling within him for nearly his entire life.

'You could have spoken to father, or to me at least.'

'And done what, pleaded with you to hand me my rightful place in the eyes of our father?' Vihalla Kumar nearly screamed, but checked his tone instantly. When he spoke again, his voice had once again acquired its level pitch. 'I knew that the only way for father to become aware of my existence was through your failure, and when I overheard him and the Mahamatya discussing their plans for the annexation of Vaishali, I thought I had just the opportunity I was looking for. But alas, I failed yet again.'

Ajatshatru had got the information he desired, but the pain in his brother's voice had ignited an internal tussle within him. On one end was the dutiful son bound by his father's orders and on the other was the brother who had just come aware that it was he who had been at the root of all inflictions that his brother had to endure all through his life. He felt as though he was being torn in half and there was nothing he could do to save himself.

'But you know what this means, don't you? The punishment for what you have done could cost you your life,' he said, more a rhetoric than a statement. But his words only flared Vihalla Kumar even further.

He leaped towards the scabbard positioned against the wall to the left of the bed, screaming, 'and who is it that is going to kill me, you? Let me see what you've got. I shall end this right here once and for all.' But his flailing feet managed to find the edge of the side table, and stumbling, he fell, taking the table down with him. Following the noise, two of Ajatshatru's guards who were stationed right outside the room rushed in, their weapons drawn and ready.

Perhaps this was the moment that sealed Vihalla Kumar's fate, for this was all the time it took for Ajatshatru to arrive at a decision. 'Detain him and take him to the dungeons,' he instructed the guards. Then, pausing to lift a small metal container that was previously placed on the side table and had now found its way to the carpet, he added, 'here, take this. And ensure that he has had enough of these by the time I get there.' A guard extended his hand to take possession of the container that Vihalla Kumar used to store his opium pellets.

He emerged from the room, dabbing the moisture in his eyes with the back of his hand and once again began to tread the winding palace corridors, only, now his purposeful stagger had diluted into a cumbersome amble. He was heading towards the section of the palace which housed the royal women and he knew that the confrontation with Rani Nanda was going to prove a significantly tougher challenge for him than punishing her son for his crime.

'Greetings mother,' he greeted the Queen with folded hands once her attendants ushered him inside the chamber. She was visibly alarmed by Ajatshatru's visit and more so given the early hour of the morning, but she responded to the greeting without voicing her concerns.

'I come to you seeking your blessings and forgiveness for the task I have set out to perform. This, you must appreciate, is in line with the laws of the land which we have all vowed to defend and I am but discharging my duties as the Prince of Magadh,' he began, his voice unusually shaky and words imprecise. The Queen's bewilderment only increased with every vague word he uttered and eventually she had to interject and ask him to unhesitatingly state the purpose of his visit.

Ajatshatru obliged. He summarized, for her benefit, the dastardly deeds of Vihalla Kumar and informed her of his arrest and impending execution. Rani Nanda managed to hold her composure till Ajatshatru concluded his elucidation, but barely just. The moment his lips pursed, a stream of tears emerged from her eyes and she began pleading with him, amid incessant sobs, to spare her son's life.

This was precisely what Ajatshatru had been dreading. He stood motionless, head bent low, mutely witnessing the Queen's histrionics. It wasn't often that a mother was approached to pardon the slaying of her son while he was still alive and Rani Nanda's desperate hysterics, therefore, were not entirely unfounded. 'Speak up, say something, look me in the eye at least! He is your brother, you know that he means no harm; he would have done this in one his inebriated fits. How can you even think of taking his life? Wait till Maharaj returns at least. I am sure he will find it within him to forgive his son.' Her voice had scaled up a few notches and she was trembling and gesticulating wildly as she screamed her guts out. Ajatshatru remained unmoved by her pleas, preferring to stare at the ground between his feet than to answer back. Then suddenly, frustrated perhaps by his lack of response, the Queen flung herself towards him and clasping the bosom of his tunic in both her hands, began shaking him vigorously. Her attendants, catching a flick-of-an-eye command from Ajatshatru, were quick to intervene and pull her back.

Ajatshatru turned on his heels and exited the room, walking

away from the heart wrenching cries of a mother grieving her yet undead son, to finish his incomplete task.

As he stepped into the dungeon, Ajatshatru was somewhat relieved to find an insentient Vihalla Kumar sprawled on the stone floor. The guards had done well to infuse him with a liberal dose of opium, a blessing that was going to make him peacefully endure the last few breaths of his life. Instructing the guards to seat him on the stone slab protruding from the wall, he reached out for the dagger dangling from his waist band. One practised slice on Vihalla Kumar's neck was all it took and his head leaned lifelessly to one side, letting out a torrent of warm, crimson blood that bathed Ajatshatru's hand and smeared his clothes. Not surprisingly, to Ajatshatru its shade didn't appear very different from what he had seen oozing out of his own wounds in the past.

First a small drop on her nose, then another and yet another, the sky seemed to be opening up in celebration of Amrapali's return. It was late evening and the sun had long exited the horizon, leaving behind the tawny light of dusk to guide daytime revellers to the safety of their homes. Birds too, chirping and fluttering riotously, were making for their night-time dwellings, rushing to make good their escape before the falling drops gained enough momentum to drench them.

It had been a long day, longer than any she could recall having endured. The attempt to escape from the Old Palace and the ensuing massacre, the sad demise of Ballabh and so many other men who had valiantly staked their lives for her sake, her arrest and subsequent detention in a dark cell with an unbearably dank and putrid smell, it all seemed like a sequence of events from a nightmare she was yet to wake up from.

And then, suddenly, just as unexpectedly as the other events of the day, Senapati Chetak had made an appearance and ordered her release. He appeared to be avoiding Amrapali's gaze and she had not felt the need to engage him in dialogue or seek any explanations either. He had escorted her outside, where a chariot stood waiting. He had hurriedly doled out instructions, to a couple of cavalrymen for escorting her and to the charioteer to take her back to the Old Palace, before making a quick exit.

Of course she was desperate to get back to Vimal's side and nurse him, but as soon as the wheels of the chariot began to move, she found herself being drawn into a deep dark abyss of her thoughts. She sat still, unmindful of the falling raindrops which were rapidly gaining in intensity, thinking about what had become of her life. From the revered Nagarvadhu of Vaishali and a woman blessed with a healthy son with the man she loved, she had been reduced overnight to an alleged traitor and the mother of an illegitimate child.

Bindusen, the man she had secretly hoped to lead her entire life with, had turned out to be an illusion, and the only stable ally she had ever had—Prabha—had failed her too. She found herself unable to comprehend Prabha's motivations either. Something had strained her relationship with her friend and she could only hope that the damage was not irreversible. Barring little Vimal, every other thing in her life had become so hazy, so obscure, that she felt tremendously lonely. It was as life had taken a full circle and she was once again the unwanted child abandoned under a mango tree. Her heart felt heavy, as though it had suddenly metamorphosed to steel, and she also felt an uncontrollable urge to weep. Thus, resting her head atop her buckled knees, she opened the floodgates of her eyes and the saline liquid that emerged began to blend with the rainwater which had already formed a tiny puddle near her feet. And just like that Amrapali did not even realize when her chariot reached the last leg of its journey.

The gates flung open instantly and even before Amrapali could make any attempts to regain her composure, the chariot had begun sketching its way towards the palace veranda. The sentries, upon recognizing their mistress, had instantly relayed the news of her arrival to the other residents and even before Amrapali could disembark from the stationary chariot, she saw Prabha screaming and running towards her.

She swept Amrapali off her feet and swirled around excitedly, like a doting father returning home to see his child after a hard day's work. Once the spurt of exhilaration had waned, she clung to Amrapali, holding her in a tight embrace, unmindful of the falling rain. There were tears in Prabha's eyes, but this time they were a manifestation of her unrestrained joy. 'Please forgive me sister,' she managed to whisper into her friend's ear in between her sniffles. Amrapali nodded her head and was about to say something when a distinct sound drew their attention towards the gate once again.

'Bhiksham dehi,' a lone monk, sopping wet, clutching a wooden bowl was screaming at the top of his voice from the other side of the grill. Instinctively Amrapali gestured at the guards to permit him inside. The monk approached them, walking with a tranquil, dignified gait, the raindrops landing on his bald head before pursuing a course down his body, failing to perturb him to the slightest. 'He looks oddly familiar,' Amrapali thought, as the monk stood at an arm's length from her.

'Devi, bhiksham dehi,' he repeated, sparing a serene smile for the Nagarvadhu.

'Mahatman, it is raining heavily and you are soaking wet. It will be an honour if you would stay back and join us for dinner.

Once your clothes have dried and the rain abated, you could continue with your onward journey,' Amrapali said, folding her hands in obeisance.

'Devi, I am a bhikshuk and these vagaries of nature,' he said, lifting his hand towards the sky, 'don't mean anything to us. Just as they do their job, we are bound by our own callings, and neither of us interferes with the duties of the other.'

'I come to you not for alms, but to collect something that is mine. You might not remember Devi, but we have met once, many months back on a hot, sweltering afternoon. And it was then that I had given you a mango fruit for safe keeping. It is that fruit that I am here to collect today,' he replied, the calm smile still proudly positioned on his face.

Suddenly it came rushing back to her—the afternoon when they were returning from Raja Udit's Khanda after attaining Suraj and Parimal's release. They were all terribly thirsty and there was not a single drop of water in sight, neither a well nor even a house where they could hope to get some water, had been visible in the distance. It was then that the monk and his colleagues had emerged from nowhere and offered them the drinking water they had been carrying for their own consumption. Amrapali recalled having questioned the man on his purpose behind leading the life of a wanderer. He had said something, but she could not recall his words just then. The only memory she had of her previous tryst with the ascetic was that she had failed to comprehend his arguments back then as well. And yes, while departing, he had indeed given her a ripe mango for safe keep.

'Anand, wasn't that your name?' she said, stressing hard to recollect the monk's name.

'I am glad you remember Devi, and I am certain now that you would also recall the mango fruit I had left in your custody.'

'Yes, I remember. But you do know that it is impossible to preserve a fruit for so long. It would have rotten long back. However, if it is mangoes you desire, you could return in a few months' time, when the fruit on the trees is ripe, and you can have as many of them as you wish,' Amrapali reasoned.

'No Devi, I do not want your mangoes. All I seek is my fruit, the one I had given you for safe keeping,' the bhikshuk retorted.

Amrapali was getting impatient now. She wanted to rush to her chamber and cradle her son and the man was needlessly holding her back with his ridiculous demands. 'But that is not possible. The fruit you gave me was not beyond the ordained process of natural decay. There is no way that it could have lasted for so long. Hence, I urge you to put forth a demand that is practicable and I shall try and address it to the best of my faculties,' she said.

'If you so wish Devi, I will forget about my fruit, but in lieu of that you must answer a few simple question for me. Can you do that?' Amrapali replied with a brief nod.

'Just like the fruit's decay is inevitable, isn't everything else around us preordained too—the inexorable chakra of life and death, the people we meet and get separated from, and even the joys and sorrows that we experience? Why then do we feel pain on separation and joy when united with those we consider to be our own? Why do we consider anyone to be our own in the first place, when we know that they are nothing but souls trapped within the circle of mortality? Will the things that give us joy—our youth, our wealth, our friends and our family—forever remain with us? And if no, why do we grieve when they leave us as they are ordained to?'

The monk stood there smiling, but his questions had propelled the Nagarvadhu into a cerebral turmoil. She knew that the questions were a reflection of her own life and the monk, undoubtedly an enlightened man, had arrived not to collect a mere fruit but to pose them to her. After all, wasn't she, just a little while back, ruing all the losses she had been made to suffer—of love, friends, family, dignity and esteem? Was the monk right and her losses nothing but a set of preordained events that she had absolutely no control over? And if the events were indeed beyond her control, what use were her lamentations?

Amrapali felt her thoughts thrusting her into a surreal plane, one where she could detach herself from her own persona and objectively evaluate her position. And when she did that, she found a fresh volley of questions assaulting her.

'If I understand you correctly Mahatman, you are saying that our joys and sorrows are all unfounded since they depend on a sequence of happenings that we don't influence. So does that mean that we humans should not be feeling happy or sad no matter what situations we face? And if indeed there is some mystical power that steers our lives, how do you explain the glaring discrepancies in what each one us is bestowed with? Why are some people rich and some poor, some healthy and some frail, some good-looking and others an eyesore?' she queried.

'No Devi, neither am I suggesting that we exert no influence over the happenings in our life and nor do I say that happiness is a state to be abstained from. It is our karma, our deeds that are the cause behind all that we withstand—the good and the bad. We are all heirs of our own actions and it is these actions that are responsible for the divergences you allude to. These invisible causes, however, might not always be confined to the present life and can sometimes even be traced to a proximate or remote past birth, but over a period of time the difference between what we sow and what we reap is marginalized. As for happiness, it is a blessing that we are all entitled to and we must strive for it.

Only, we must understand the difference between the transient and the permanent and only then can we experience a joy that is truly wonderful and everlasting. It is only by circumventing the delusions of delight that we so often find ourselves entangled in— the joy of having eaten a hearty meal, the taste of which shall only linger momentarily or the happiness from being in the company of friends and accomplices who are there today but might not be tomorrow—that we can embark on a path to achieving the elixir of true and eternal bliss.'

'Tell me Mahatman, where does this path to attaining true bliss lie? And what does it take for one to scale it?' Amrapali probed further. Having lost all sense of place and time, she was completely immersed in the words of the ascetic now.

'I have revealed all that I was supposed to Devi, and when the time is ripe you shall find yourself drawn to the path on your own. Your will not need to search for your destiny, it shall find you. I must take your leave now, may Buddha be with you,' he said before abruptly turning on his heels and walking towards the gate. Amrapali, in a state of daze, remained transfixed to her spot till such time that his faint chants of 'Buddham Sharnam Gachchami' continued to reach her ears.

Meanwhile, just as the monk was exiting from the Old Palace, elsewhere, in the Magadh encampment outside the city gates, Senapati Prasenjit had been summoned by the King into his tent. Prasenjit had been experiencing incredulous pangs of omission of late from not being in the know of several happenings in and around the camp—the abrupt departure of Yuvraj Ajatshatru from the front, the messenger that Bimbisara had sent to Vaishali, without even bothering to consult him, and his subsequent return, carrying perhaps a reply to whatever message he had carried with him, and he had queries of his own that he wished to pose to the King. He was the Senapati, the man in charge of the battlefront, and it was well within his authority to question these seemingly curious activities, or seek an explanation for them at least. It was purely due to the order he had established within his ranks that he became aware of the King seeking out one of his best cavalrymen to ride to Vaishali. Bimbisara had surpassed him to summon the rider directly, a scathing insult to his sovereignty at the battlefront, and it was only through the commander who had carried out the Emperor's orders that he had leant of it. The messenger wouldn't have succeeded in riding out of his security cordon without his knowledge anyway, but the least Bimbisara could have done was to inform him to expect and allow passage to a rider heading towards Vaishali carrying a white flag.

Prasenjit had been in two minds about apprehending the man and seeking out the suspicious message, and had its originator been anyone but Bimbisara he would have done so unhesitatingly. However, even in his agitated state he was aware of the boundaries he could safely tread and those he could not, so he had allowed the messenger to leave and return, bottling his curiosity within. It was only now, when the opportunity had suddenly presented itself, that he was intent on seeking some answers from the King.

It was a gloomy day, cloudy and dark, and it had been raining all evening. The daylight had waned earlier than usual and the two flaming torches were struggling to adequately illuminate the insides of the tent. As Prasenjit stepped in he had to crease his eyes to adjust to the lighting, and when he did so, he saw the stern and daunting frame of Bimbisara facing him. At once his anger and all the questions he had been accumulating within his head evaporated and a greeting for the King with a crisp salute was all he could manage.

'Senapati, it has been several months since your men have been away from their families, fighting valiantly for their motherland and their king, and I have little doubt that they will continue to do so till their very last breath if so required. I am humbled by their loyalty and consider myself fortunate to have been the subject of their devotion. However, the time has come when we must rise above our esurient aspirations to think about the general good of those who serve us. The war has outlived its term and it needs to end now. So go Senapati, go and ask your men to get packing. We shall begin our retreat from the shores of Vaishali early tomorrow morning, so that all our troops manage to set sail before nightfall. And ask your men not to be concerned, there will still be enough rewards to compensate for their bravery and allegiance once we return,' Bimbisara said, without expending his words or indulging the commander of his troops.

Each word fell on Prasenjit's ears like a drop of molten lead. Something was amiss with Bimbisara, he gathered, but the instructions he had just received were beyond even his wildest dreams. The many months he had spent urging and rousing his men, the several sleepless nights he had spent dreaming about the glories of victory, was all of it going to end so callously, so unyieldingly? The rewards were one thing, but what would he say to the men he had coaxed to staking their lives for the sake of pride and honour? He couldn't just tell them that the war they had pledged to fight till their ultimate breath had been called off. He felt as though the ground had been pulled from beneath his feet.

'But Maharaj...' he began, uneasily attempting to word his concerns, but only to be cut short by Bimbisara's raised hand.

'I understand your concerns, Senapati, even before you voice them. But my decision is well deliberated, and it is best that we use our vitalities in implementing it instead of mulling over it any further,' he said. There was a sense of finality to Bimbisara's tone which discouraged further dialogue and the Senapati could only retreat with a submissive bow of his head.

14

The news that his father had returned from the front and was heading towards the palace came as a jolt to Ajatshatru and he rushed to greet him. The other piece of information he had just received, about the war having ended and the Magadh army being on its way back, he still could not bring himself to believe. He had been unsure of whether or not to order the celebrations—drummers, showers of petal and scented water, dancing women and other accompanying festivities—due for a victorious King returning from war. But the lack of time had made the choice for him and he had settled for a low-key reception with only the women of the household accompanying him for the customary aarti. Rani Nanda, who was grieving the recent loss of her son, had expectedly not joined them.

Soon Bimbisara's entourage, his gleaming chariot with the Magadh flag fluttering impudently on its dome, and the accompanying unit of mounted bodyguards came into view, steadily progressing towards the waiting reception party. Bimbisara, in a few quick steps, covered the ground from the chariot he had alighted from to the waiting party. Ajatshatru stepped forward to greet his father. As the Prince bent down to touch his father's feet and seek his blessings, he had a distinct sensation that the Bimbisara in front of him was different from the man he had left on the shores of Vaishali barely a couple of days back. There certainly was something playing on his father's mind and he could feel its strain by simply being in his proximity. It wasn't any remarkable variation in conduct or some stark change in his appearance, just the subtle, often indiscernible vibes that are exchanged between most fathers and sons, which was the cause for Ajatshatru's slight unease. He couldn't put it in words, but intuitively he knew that all was not well with his father.

Placing his hands on his shoulders, Bimbisara guided him back up and pulled him into an embrace. 'It is nice to see you again so soon father. I had supposed that only when I returned to the front in a few days would I get to see you,' Ajatshatru said, before Rani Vaidehi, his mother, and other Queens approached the King with the aarti platter. Bimbisara simply nodded in response to his words.

It was only once Bimbisara, after the conclusion of his ritualistic welcome, had stepped inside the palace and was heading towards his chamber when Ajatshatru caught up with him. 'Maharaj, there are some things I wish to speak to you about,' he said. Bimbisara eyed him and nodded—a cue for Ajatshatru to follow. He had refrained from asking Ajatshatru about the subject that warranted a discussion, an unusual omission by his otherwise strict standards. Was it possible that he knew already about the matter occupying the Yuvraj's mind and had deliberately refrained from bringing it up?

'You must have heard about Vihalla Kumar, Maharaj. I had dispatched a messenger to update you on the developments,' the Yuvraj began after they were both comfortably seated on facing chairs in Bimbisara's private chamber.

'Yes, I did receive your message, and what happened was nothing short of a tragedy. Clearly, opium had claimed his faculties, but not his ambitions. Only if he had made even the slightest attempt to mend his ways and realize his desires in the right fashion. A father's heart weeps, as I know yours does for the brother you've lost, but justice had to be delivered and you did well to carry out the task by keeping your emotions at bay,' he replied. This was the first time Bimbisara had addressed Ajatshatru since his return. And though the subject was a highly discomforting one, one that Bimbisara had even voiced his anguish over, Ajatshatru, much to his dismay, found his tone to be carrying a hint of relief. However, as the Yuvraj was soon to discover, the relief in Bimbisara's voice, if any, was to be extremely short lived.

'I also visited Mother Nanda to apprise her of her son's deeds and the consequent punishment he was to be served, and expectedly, she became hysterical, pleading with me to spare him—a clemency that was well and truly beyond my authority to exercise. She has taken her loss badly and a visit from you, if you so deem appropriate, might help her in coming to terms with it,' Ajatshatru continued.

'Of course I shall visit the Rani soon. A mother's heart rejects all rationality and logic when it comes to her offspring, a continuum perhaps of the nine months she carries the fetus within her womb. Nanda's agony is not unfounded and in me she shall find all the care and support she needs to recover from her trauma.'

'Your kindness and compassion are legendary Maharaj and I can only hope to imbibe a fraction of your virtues someday,' Ajatshatru said, bowing his head ever so slightly. 'And if I may seek your further indulgence, there is just this other little matter I wish to bring up,' he added. Bimbisara nodded, but once again Ajatshatru thought he saw a flicker of uncertainty in his father's otherwise domineering carriage.

'I hear that you have called off the war and that our men are already sailing out of Vaishali's shores. Is this indeed true?'

'Yes, it is true. The war had stretched for long and was consuming a significant proportion of the state's resources, so it was best for it to be called off,' Bimbisara replied dismissively.

'But Maharaj, wouldn't that imply that all our efforts that have already gone behind the war will go to waste? We have successfully managed to curb all external supplies into Vaishali for nearly a year now and they are bound to be reeling under the scarcity of essential commodities. It is only a matter of time before their insufficiencies mount to such drastic proportions that defending the city will prove impossible for them,' Ajatshatru argued. He was trying hard to control his tumultuous emotions, raging in response to Bimbisara's absurd step and equally strange justifications.

'True, but who can say with certainty as to when that would have happened. A harsh call, to cut our losses, had to be made sometime and the further we delayed it, the more it would have cost us.'

'I don't understand this. We could have backed out long back, when our first attempts to breach their walls had failed, so why did you advise us to persist back then? And now, when we have enfeebled them, understood their terrain and methods, and have the support of Devdutt's devastating weapons, why do we suddenly have to withdraw?' Agitation was now beginning to seep into Ajatshatru's tone despite his best efforts to keep it at bay.

'And what happens to your dream of expanding the Magadh rule through the breadth of land? Why Maharaj, why have you suddenly turned so frail that you are unable to justify even your own actions? I am your son Maharaj, the King in waiting, and this decision impacts me and my future reign as much as it does you. So, if there is something that my untrained eyes are unable to gauge, please guide me,' he continued.

'Enough!' Bimbisara roared in response. 'You are my son alright, but that doesn't give you the right to address your King in this manner. How dare you question my judgment and my actions? Or is it that all the adulation and praise I have showered upon you has got into your head?' Bimbisara, his face seething with rage, locked his gaze momentarily with Ajatshatru before turning his back to him. Ajatshatru remained unrelenting. He knew that his questions were legitimate and the least Bimbisara owed him was an honest answer.

'The decision to choose my heir is entirely mine, and if a simple whiff of authority can blind you to your basic etiquettes and mannerisms, I might have made an error that merits a reconsideration. Don't forget that the throne you dream of occupying someday is nothing but an ornamented chair without me. It is I, Magadh Naresh Bimbisara, who is responsible for the influence and power that the throne wields today. I have built this kingdom, stone by stone and territory by territory, and if any man, in his hauteur, dares to challenge my authority, he shall be made to bear the brunt of my wrath. And then it will not matter if the malefactor happens to be my own blood,' he growled.

Bimbisara had turned once again to face Ajatshatru and he appeared like an enraged bull, its sharp horns ready for gore and its colossal frame itching to ram into its adversary. Ajatshatru stood his ground, staring back into Bimbisara's eyes, almost defiantly, but managing to restrain himself from answering back.

'This discussion is over now, and you may please leave,' Bimbisara finally decreed. Without uttering a word, Ajatshatru turned on his heels and stomped out of the room. He had been circumspect and cagey while entering Bimbisara's chamber, a man hoping for answers to questions that had been troubling him, but he was an entirely changed man now. He was furious, frantic and somewhat fearful. Was it possible that the pressures had eventually got to Bimbisara, stressing him off his sanity?

Bimbisara watched his son exit the chamber, holding on to his stiff, formidable stance. But as soon as Ajatshatru was out of sight, he allowed himself to slump resignedly on the chair. Had he committed an error that was beyond remediation?

His heart, vetoing the suggestions of his mind, had guided him in favour of withdrawing his troops from Vaishali. He had expected some backlash from his closer aides, but he had been relying on them to help him tide over them. He thought he had done well to handle Senapati Prasenjit, but the dialogue with the Yuvraj had gone completely out of hand. Perhaps he too had been somewhat harsh on the young man—an attempt by his subconscious to shield his guilt maybe—but the Yuvraj too had remained firm, unwilling to accept his actions unquestioningly.

Ajatshatru's unwavering stance and his vehemence to stand for what he believed was right pleased the father in Bimbisara, but the opponent within him, on this one matter at least, was left nervous and fearful. He could not shake away the image of his son's amber gaze boring through his frame and he felt a slight shiver crawl down his spine. Then slowly, his thoughts began to meander towards matters he had been unable to brood over for as long as he would have liked—Amrapali and her loving presence, which was to forever remain an illusion for him now, and Vimal, his young son, who he had only once managed to set his eyes upon.

And soon he felt his eyes drooping and the fatigue of the long journey beginning to tell. His limbs, all in one gradual slide, withdrew from the services of his mind, and before he could even realize, his head resting against the backrest of the chair, he had fallen asleep.

Another man in Rajgriha who had taken rather badly to the news of Magadh army's retreat from Vaishali was Devdutt. The update had reached him a little after Bimbisara had arrived at his palace, perhaps at the same time when the discussion between the King and the Yuvraj was underway. He had felt betrayed and the excruciating pain from many years back, from the trauma of watching his father being lynched by a delusioned mob had come back to strike him like a sledgehammer.

The war had served as a personal medium for him to vent out his hitherto suppressed anger. He had fantasized about the Magadh army marching into the streets of Vaishali, pillaging and wreaking havoc upon anything that stood in their path, and it had acted as a temporary ointment for his sores. Each time he had conjured within his mind the image of a Magadhan sword slicing through a Vajji neck, he had felt his own blood enthusiastically surge through his veins. He had done whatever he could—evoking mystical powers for assistance and coming up with ingenious weapons that, he had little doubt, were capable of altering the course of battle—and yet, the war had been called off at the whims of one man.

He had sat brooding for a long time, but not meaning to allow his destiny to play its cruel hand unopposed, he had decided to grab the baton and do whatever he could to salvage the situation. The first mystery he set out to unravel was the actual reason behind Bimbisara's sudden change of heart. The King's action had been puzzling and Devdutt was certain that there was more to it than the flimsy excuse he had learnt Bimbisara to be propagating.

He had a vague inkling that the answers he sought lay concealed within the walls of Vaishali and that with their revelation he would find further illumination in his path. So he had instantly summoned two of his loyal men and sent them to Vaishali with the wide-ranging instruction to find out all that they could about the war and the possible reasons for its sudden termination.

The men, as they informed Devdutt upon their return, had struck gold within moments of entering the city. Vaishali, having just emerged from the clutches of war, had been doused in a spirit of unrestrained festivities, and among the many stories doing the rounds amidst the revellers were the ones pertaining to Amrapali's arrest at the hands of Senapati Chetak and Bimbisara's offer of withdrawing his troops to secure her release. Devdutt's men had stumbled upon the lead they sought and it didn't take much for them to unravel the entire sequence of events that had led to the withdrawal of the Magadh army.

Devdutt was infuriated on listening to their account, but as his temper eased, the flagrancy of the information in his grasp dawned upon him. Rewarding the duo handsomely, enough to prevent them for spilling what they knew elsewhere, Devdutt retired to his private chamber, his face alit with a candescent ray of hope. It was in isolation that his mind worked the best, and indeed so, for when he emerged from his chamber a while later, he had an unmistakable sparkle in his eyes. He knew exactly what needed to be done and he was confident that his ploy would yield the results he desired.

It was evening already and daylight was fast fading. But eager and impatient, he had instantly despatched a messenger to the royal palace, seeking an urgent and private audience with Yuvraj Ajatshatru. The messenger had however returned soon, bearing regrets from the Prince, asking Devdutt to visit him the next morning instead. He had grimaced at the response, but given the absence of alternatives, had grudgingly retired to the privacy of his room once again. He had remained there, sailing with the gushing waves of his emotions, ignoring the corporeal needs of food and water, for the remainder of the night. None had dared disturb him with a reminder for dinner and the bodily hunger had joined hands with the hunger within his heart to further his miseries for the night, most of which he ended up spending twisting and turning on his bed.

Now, with the advent of another morning, as he waited in the anteroom of Ajatshatru's chamber to be summoned inside, he could feel his heartbeat racing like a pack of wild horses. But when the moment arrived and the Yuvraj's sentries emerged to escort him inside, he was glad to find his confidence and poise returning. The situation would have been different if it were Bimbisara he was stepping in to confront, but this was only Ajatshatru and Devdutt was certain that he would succeed in influencing him just as he had so meticulously planned.

'It is the burden of my responsibilities towards the populace of Magadh that brings me here Yuvraj. And if you will permit me the indulgence, I seek your permission to voice certain concerns that have been weighing on my mind,' he said, following the perfunctory exchange of civilities. Eyeing the minister rather objectively, Ajatshatru accorded his consent with a slight nod of the head. 'You may speak freely Amatya,' he added.

'I am no expert on the nuances of warfare Yuvraj, but the sudden retreat from Vaishali baffled me as it did every other proud citizen of Magadh. It was inexplicable why, when within an arms reach of victory, would an astute strategist like Maharaj Bimbisara take such a step. Though my detestation for Vaishali and its people is well-known, I had resigned to this development as a possible manoeuvre that I wasn't equipped to comprehend or comment upon.

But just when I thought that the war was a thing of the past, I was confronted with some very disturbing news trickling in from not one but several quarters simultaneously. The abrupt end to the war, as you would be aware, has not only dented the confidence of our men, but also acted as a conduit for bolstering our enemies. Our retreat is being looked upon as a weakening of the Magadhan might and many of our foes are eyeing this as an opportunity to get even with us. The word is that several of our vassals are looking to combine their forces so as to forcibly break away from the Magadh Empire. And that is not all; some unconfirmed reports even suggest that Bhadra Naresh Ashokchandra has begun amassing a force that will allow him to march towards Rajgriha soon.' The minister paused for effect, only to find Ajatshatru's pupils dilating with his disclosures.

His words were not entirely fabricated and he had indeed heard whispers corroborating the beating Bimbisara's perception had taken in the eyes of his detractors as a result of this incident, but those had mainly been conjectures by concerned citizens of Magadh. He had only tweaked the facts slightly to make it sound as if the information he alluded to had been routed to him through some established medium of covert intelligence. Of course he had taken liberties in using Magadh's long standing animosity with the kingdom of Bhadra and also the obvious inclination of their vassal states towards their freedom, but these were merely to add credence to his arguments. He could see that his words were having just the desired effect on the young and impatient Yuvraj, who was clearly seething from within by now.

Satisfied, he continued, 'I tried to approach Maharaj with the information, but he has been keeping away from court ever since his return from Vaishali and has even issued a directive prohibiting anyone but the prime minister from visiting his private chambers. The matter at hand was crucial, and not meaning to dilute it by having it relayed, I persisted with my efforts to gain his audience. I spoke with Narsinh Dev and even some men among his personal bodyguards to seek their help in approaching him, but to no avail. While none of them could muster the courage to go against

Maharaj's wishes, one did confide in me the real reason behind his sudden desire for solitude—his fascination with that woman. And while that does explain some of his recent actions, it certainly does nothing to dispel the dangers setting in on Magadh today.'

'Which woman? What fascination?' Ajatshatru interrupted.

'Amrapali.'

'Amrapali, the Nagarvadhu of Vaishali? What does she have to do with my father?' Anxiety was writ large on the Yuvraj's face and he was desperate to curb his curiosity—all at one go, if it were humanly possible, like an instant dip in a pool of answers.

'Oh, you didn't know?' Devdutt began, mocking Ajatshatru's ignorance, as though Bimbisara's liaison with Amrapali had been a matter of common knowledge. 'Maharaj has been visiting Amrapali for long now—from much prior to the commencement of the war. He has even fathered a son with her, Vimal Kondana is his name. The boy was born sometime while the war was still being waged on the shores of Vaishali. It is only at Amrapali's behest that Maharaj agreed to call off the battle and withdraw our troops. I have even heard that Maharaj has invited Amrapali and his son to move to Rajgriha and stay here at the palace with him.'

'What? Do you even know what you are saying Amatya? You do realize the implications if, God forbid, your allegations happen to be untrue, do you not?' Ajatshatru burst out, unable to contain his reactions any longer. There was an ominous threat embedded within his words and its ring did not escape the ears of the minister.

'I do Yuvraj. And I beg your forgiveness, for it is not within my authority to comment upon the King's personal associations. It is only because you wished to know that I dwelled upon it, stating in your presence whatever I was in the know of. From highly reliable sources, I might add. I have come to you driven purely by my love for the land that embraced me when my own people brutally shunted me out. I am here to discharge my duties as a member of the Magadhan court, to fulfill my pledge of keeping the Magadh Empire's interest at the foremost of my considerations.

We face imminent threat from all quarters today Yuvraj, and Maharaj Bimbisara, in his present state of delusion is inept to ward it off. I am here to make an appeal on behalf of the people who look up to you, just as they do the rising sun—Magadh needs you today Yuvraj Ajatshatru. Magadh needs you to seize its reins and steer it past the looming menace, back to the pedestal it is rapidly sliding from. Rise Yuvraj, rise before it is too late else all that shall remain of the monumental Magadh Empire are tiny fragments that can never again be pieced together. Vaishali has been our bane, and it is only with Vaishali's seizure that we can regain our lost glories and give a fitting reply to those who arrogantly rise to question us today. It is the blood of those who rode to their deaths upon a single command of yours that seeks retribution from you today. Don't disappoint them Yuvraj, give them what they died for. Give them the pleasure of watching the Magadh flag fluttering over the fortress of Vaishali, and their souls shall remain eternally grateful to you,' he said, his voice simmering with alternating passions of pain, grief, rage and desperation. Ajatshatru remained transfixed, listening to the diminutive man speak like he had never spoken before, at least not that the Yuvraj had ever witnessed, and he found himself unable to react.

'And if in presenting this plea to you, I have committed a felony, I shall eagerly accept any punishment for my transgression that you please,' he added. After a brief silence, during which Devdutt's gaze kept searching unsuccessfully for Ajatshatru's to lock itself with, he bowed slightly. 'I have said what I had to Yuvraj, and I must now return. But in your contemplations, do think of the millions of Magadhan's whose hopes remain pinned to you and you shall find your decision becoming much simpler,' he said before turning on his heels and stepping towards the door.

Ajatshatru, who was still staring at something invisible in the distance, failed to take note of the faint smile that had fleetingly emerged on Devdutt's lips as he exited from the chamber.

Three days had passed since Ajatshatru had last seen his father. Bimbisara had, oddly enough, contained himself within the seclusion of his chambers since their minor altercation on the day of his return to Rajgriha. And just as Devdutt had pointed out, Ajatshatru had only seen Narsinh Dev, the elderly prime minister visit the King a few times ever since.

Ajatshatru hadn't intended on casting aspersions over his father's jurisprudence, all he sought were answers to questions that were troubling him. He had felt slighted and marginalized at not being consulted by Bimbisara before calling off the war that he had been delegated to spearhead. He knew he was well within his rights to seek explanations for Bimbisara's decision to end the siege of Vaishali and that is precisely what he had set out to do by seeking an audience with him. But the discussion had quickly acquired a riotous course of its own, and Bimbisara, in a rare display of hysterical rage, had shunted him from his chamber.

The Yuvraj had emerged affronted and hurt from the meeting, infuriated further by Bimbisara's uncomely behaviour. The King seemed intent upon abusing his authority and using the garb of aggression to elude him the answers he deserved, and Ajatshatru was finding it tough to shatter the screen of reverence he had always looked through at his father and demand what was rightfully his to know.

For as long as he could remember his father had been his guiding light, his beacon, and he had strived hard to emulate him, to embody the virtues that made him the mighty Emperor that he was. Bimbisara, too had not once let him down, nurturing and mentoring him not only as a worthy son, but also an able successor. There had been no formal ceremony, but somewhere along the way, everyone including the Maharaj had taken to addressing him as Yuvraj—the King in waiting. His heart swelled in eager anticipation each time he heard the salutation and he toiled to live up to his father's expectations in even the slightest of tasks he was entrusted with. An acknowledgement or a word of appreciation from Bimbisara had always been the stimulus behind his actions, up until very recently at least. But things had taken an unexpected turn since their confrontation and the more Ajatshatru pondered over the incident, the more detached he felt from his father. While the righteousness of his stance prevented the Prince from making any reconciliatory gestures, the King too had stayed away from any such efforts from his end. The causticity of time, it seemed, was eating into the strength of their relationship, and the lack of any reconciliatory initiatives was only acting as a catalyst for the tempest brewing within him. The venom of insult he had chosen to swallow was spreading across his soul, snapping thread-by-thread the bond of blood that secured him to Bimbisara.

Senapati Prasenjit, another victim of Bimbisara's authoritarian dictate, also visited Ajatshatru upon his return to Rajgriha with the last of the troops sailing out of Vaishali. The Senapati had been as perplexed as the Prince with Bimbisara's sudden and dramatic transformation and while he had been unable to address the Yuvraj's inflaming curiosity, he had left him with a further set of doubts to contend with. What was playing on the King's mind? Was it on purpose that he had despatched Ajatshatru to Rajgriha so that he could go about his plan unobstructed? If yes, just what exactly was the plan brewing within Bimbisara's mind and why couldn't he share it even with his own son, the successor to his throne?

The Senapati had also apprised him of the plummeting morale among their ranks, especially the warlords and chieftains—mercenaries who had joined the Magadh army with the lure of bountiful booties once the annexation of Vaishali was complete. Ajatshatru knew that the fiasco will prohibit him from approaching them to join his ranks in the foreseeable future, only corroborating the fears that the minister Devdutt had voiced. The Magadh Empire was indeed on the brink of disaster and if there was any one man to contain the slide, it was him—Yuvraj Ajatshatru.

The most striking among Devdutt's revelations had however been the news of his father's affair with the Nagarvadhu of Vaishali and his illegitimate son that she had given birth to. Undeniably, this was the most plausible among the reasons he had been contemplating to explain his father's actions. It is only when in the clutches of a woman that a man ceases to use his mind and becomes impervious to logic and reason, and Bimbisara, the Emperor of Magadh, was a man too.

The thought made his stomach churn in disgust. It wasn't unusual for kings to marry several princesses and also maintain harems-full of concubines, but it was never easy for a son, a grown up one at that, to accept his father's carnal exploits unflinchingly. The existence of a half-brother, young enough to be his own son, had come as an unbearable jolt to Ajatshatru and his rage was pressing against the brink of his containment.

Getting up from the chair, fists clenched white, he began pacing up and down the room, muttering his displeasures to himself. 'How could he, the mighty Bimbisara, allow himself to be manipulated by a woman of the market—a mere courtesan? Has age made him so senile that he didn't once think of his empire, his family, his people, his ambitions, before giving in to her demands? And what with the bastard son and his invite for them to shift to Rajgriha? How far can his obsession take him? Amrapali will obviously want the best for her child, perhaps even the throne of Magadh. Will he be willing to concede to such a demand as well? Or who knows, perhaps the deal has been struck already? After all, didn't he state that the right to appoint his successor rested with him and him alone?' His latent fears were acquiring the shape of words and oozing out uninhibitedly, discomforting even the Yuvraj himself. Therefore, with great effort, he began channelling his fury towards a more agreeable matter—his concern for the Magadh Empire. His incessant muttering did not cease, but the direction of his utterances underwent a mild deviation.

'The dangers that face us today are all but an outcome of his actions, and instead of facing them, he remains hidden in his chamber, conjuring who knows what fantastical images of Amrapali and him. The minister was right, Magadh Naresh Bimbisara is no longer the man he had once been, and if the pride and vanity of Magadh needs to be preserved, someone needs to rise to the occasion.'

Then, just as abruptly as he had got up from the chair, Ajatshatru turned to face the door and clapped twice. Instantly the two wooden slabs parted and a sentry stepped in, one hand on his chest and head tilting a touch towards the floor. 'Summon Senapati Prasenjit. Tell him that I seek his immediate audience. It's urgent,' he instructed the man before turning away from him. The confused anger in his appearance had now given way to a look of fierce determination and he appeared just as focused and resolute as he did before embarking on a military incursion.

15

An unusually dark night seemed to have descended over the royal palace of Rajgriha. Its protected chambers, its ornamented walls and its winding corridors, all appeared in deep slumber, completely heedless to the devastating storm brewing within their own containment. A set of silhouettes, six in all, were scampering across the palace passageway with a purposeful hustle to their steps. The sentries they encountered along the way first leered at them through the blackness of the night and then, once their identities were ascertained, bowed deferentially to allow them passage. Their unimpeded progress continued as they approached the most heavily guarded section of the palace, the part that housed the private chambers of King Bimbisara.

It was in front of the heavy, metal-lined door to the chamber that four of them paused, allowing the two men at their helm to step forward and approach the guards manning the entrance. Here, the faint glow of a lone torch resulted in a dim but definite blotch of lighting on the dark canvas of night and as the two men breached its periphery, allowing the luminescence to bathe their features, a spark of instant recognition flashed within the eyes of the alert guards and in near unison their heads bowed in regard for the two intruders.

Ajatshatru and Prasenjit nodded their heads in response and the Yuvraj stepped forward to whisper something in the ears of the man who appeared to be in command of the unit deployed for the King's security. The startling aspect of this encounter was that none of the guards exhibited even a hint of surprise on the sudden arrival of the Yuvraj and the Senapati at this unearthly hour. Their bearing gave the impression that the intrusion wasn't entirely out of the blue and that they had been expecting a visit by the dignitaries.

The commander of the guards unit, after listening to the Yuvraj's orders, stepped back and within moments emerged holding another flaming torch in his hand. His eyes locked briefly with that of the Prince and receiving his command in the form of a slight flicker of the eye, he gently pushed the door ajar and stepped in. Yuvraj Ajatshatru followed him, his right hand resting gently on the hold of the sword dangling from his waistband, ready to call upon its services within a fraction if the need ever arose.

'Who is it that dares to interrupt my sleep?' a thunderous voice emerged from the darkness ahead to greet them. They had only just stepped inside and the tawny light of the torch was but a hurdle for them to see beyond its periphery and survey the chamber's complete expanse. In spite of himself the Yuvraj found his steps glued to the floor and his eyes darting hither and thither, like that of a prey having sensed a predator in its vicinity, to spot the source of the voice. The brief rattle he had heard at extremely close quarters, he was certain, had come from the trembling knees of his companion and not the natural occupant of the room.

'When his subjects are distressed, a ruler cannot rest in peace—I hope you remember these words Maharaj, for they happen to be your own,' Ajatshatru said, drawing every sliver of courage within him to give his words the intended impact. He had snatched the torch from the guard's hand and stepped closer to the King's bed. Bimbisara's frame, frozen midway in the process of sitting up, his back sluggishly raised and resting partly on the headrest and partly on his hands, was clearly visible to him now.

'You have been an efficient and able ruler Maharaj, but even the best are known to eventually lose their sheen. Your luster has worn out now and your deeds are only causing irreparable damage to all that you have ever stood for—the Magadh Empire and its subjects. And it is for their sake that I urge you to step aside,' the Prince continued, even as he felt his father's cold, measuring gaze affixed on him. 'It shames me to even think that the man I idolized all my life would one day betray his own people, all at the behest of one woman. It is disgusting how, blinded by pangs of passion, you chose to disregard not only the interests of your motherland but also the ultimate sacrifice of those brave men who staked their lives in the battle of Vaishali. And today, when Magadh prepares to bear the brunt of your indiscretions, your sins, you choose to lock yourself like a coward and wait for the storm to pass?'

The venom within Ajatshatru was seeping out in the form of his words. His teeth were gritting together and even in the tawny light of the lone torch the amber of his eyes was clearly discernible. He had expected some reaction from his father, if not an attempt to justify his actions, at least a shout or a scream, a call for his sentries to intervene and bail him out, but he received none. Bimbisara remained impassive, the unwavering stare remaining his only response to the Yuvraj's words. Of course Ajatshatru had covered his ground well and even if the King had decided to summon help, he would have received none. All his close confidantes, including the prime minister, had already been relegated to the palace prison, and every guard, every weapon wielding man present within the palace premises at that hour had already sworn his allegiance to the Yuvraj.

An attempt to dethrone the mighty Emperor of Magadh had to be meticulously planned to say the least. And over the past couple of days Ajatshatru and Prasenjit had done just that, thinking and rethinking each aspect of their plan, identifying the most loyal among their men and deciding the responsibilities that each could be entrusted with, and debating every possible obstruction they could come to face. The two wars they had fought alongside each other had harmonized them such that they had learnt to function like two wheels of the same chariot, understanding each other's unspoken words and aptly covering for any oversights or lapses by the other. It was this harmony that had permitted them to shape one of the most astounding and yet bloodless coups of their times.

Today, with the first pehar of the night, their contrivance had crawled to life, gathering in momentum with each passing moment. Teams of armed men had scrupulously surfaced at pre-designated spots of the city, and at roughly the same time had begun advancing towards their respective targets—dwellings of those known to owe their allegiance to Maharaj Bimbisara. Over eighty arrests were made, of unsuspecting, stunned personnel employed in the service of the King in some or the other capacity—soldiers, generals, and administrative officers alike. Neither the elderly prime minister Narsinh Dev nor Bimbisara's personal astrologer, a man known to wield considerable clout within the upper echelons of the Magadhan society, were spared.

As the detained men were covertly herded to the palace dungeons, suitable precautions were taken to avoid any kind of commotion erupting due to their arcane arrests. Some among those apprehended were men of considerable influence and to prevent their kins from exercising this authority to fuel protests or rebellions, personnel from Ajatshatru's special task force had stayed back at the arrest sites, prohibiting them from leaving their houses and even forbidding the men of the house from grouping together. All paths leading to the royal palace were securely barricaded and the palace itself was cordoned off like a cocoon under several layers of security, all hidden from the eyes of the usual palace dwellers.

Within the palace, the scene, for an untrained eye, appeared like any other night-time—guards, impersonal and fixture-like, seemingly oblivious to the customary passersby, were stationed at every few paces. But if anyone had ever regarded the sentries as men with unique features and characteristics rather than mere appurtenance of royalty, they would have realized that these men, all of them, were different from those usually seen guarding the palace. The only uncanny thing worth a mention was Ajatshatru's unexplained absence from the palace. He hadn't shown up even around dinnertime, and his mother, Queen Vaidehi, after waiting on him till her maternal affection could no longer stand up to the corporeal need for food and sleep had retired to her chambers. The King's food was served to him in his room as usual.

It was just a while back that Ajatshatru had returned to the palace, flanked by Prasenjit and a horde of other stern-looking men. Instead of heading towards his own room or the guest chambers where he usually entertained his guests, he had resolutely headed towards a section of the palace he had been avoiding like plague over the past few days.

Darting his eyes briefly towards the open door, at the threshold of which the Senapati stood with his broad arms spread across the spacious breadth like a stamp of his domineering presence, Bimbisara returned his gaze to once again affix it upon Ajatshatru. His lips had remained pursed, not allowing a single word to slip out, adding to the Yuvraj's discomfiture.

'The legacy you had promised me, the burgeoning empire of Magadh, is on the brink of disintegrating into fragments and I must do what I need to for preserving its sanctity. Your shoulders have borne well their responsibilities, but they are clearly wavering now, and as your son it is my moral duty to relieve them of their burden—if not with your acquiescence, then without it. I am sorry father, but the time has come for you to retire and my men are waiting to escort you in this embarkation. You must leave with them now,' Ajatshatru commanded, the earlier sting of his words somewhat diminished by Bimbisara's dearth of response.

Bimbisara listened attentively, his face remaining expressionless, allowing the meaning of Ajatshatru's words to seep in gradually. Then, with a slight movement, he turned sideways, his gaze brushing the sword-hilt peeking invitingly from under his headrest, to flail his feet and land them atop the sandals placed at his bedside. With the languid gait of an elephant rising from slumber he got up and stepped towards his son. 'Come, let's go,' he spoke, his voice not betraying even a hint of the emotional explosions he was attempting to suppress.

Ajatshatru led the King outside the room and then stepped back for his men to escort him onward. Mechanically, four men, two with sheathed swords clasped to their waistbands and two brandishing lethal-looking spears, surrounded Bimbisara and led him down the corridor. The mighty Emperor of Magadh walked along unresistingly, steered within his own bastion by soldiers who had the very emblem he had designed engraved on the crest of their metallic helmets, to a destination he was unsure of. Ironic as it was, Ajatshatru was glad of the way things were progressing, for he knew that if Bimbisara had decided to put up a fight, the four soldiers, despite the weapons they flaunted, would have been biting the dust in no time.

Bimbisara was to be held hostage in a secluded outhouse within the palace compound, which, over the past few days had been readied specifically for this purpose. All his woes notwithstanding, Ajatshatru could not bring himself to imprison his father, the man who had made him what he was today, in the dungeons like the others he was holding captive. But since he could not allow the King to remain in his quarters, for who knew what deadly apparatuses lay hidden there—a concealed parchment with incriminating evidence against one of Ajatshatru's men or some precious treasures, which he could use to bargain or bribe his way out of confinement—so he had chosen the outhouse to serve his need, furnishing it sparingly and securing it to his satisfaction before the arrival of its latest habitant.

Originally he had planned to tail the soldiers as they led Bimbisara to his penitentiary, but content with the smooth flow of events, he had changed his mind. The matter had been dealt with and it didn't seem in the need of his immediate attention. On the other hand there were considerations, his proclamation as the King of Magadh for instance, that needed his urgent attention. Thus, gently patting Prasenjit's back, a gesture to delegate the task of safely securing Bimbisara in his ordained confine to the Senapati, he turned back once again to the winding palace corridors he had emerged from.

Kundali's deception, Ballabh's death, her own arrest and the unexpected visit by Anand, the Sakya Muni's acolyte—Amrapali's life had acquired a pace that her mental faculties were struggling to match up with. Her life had suddenly become an obscure hallucination and she, a mute spectator. There were several questions that the monk had left pounding in her mind, but they were simply too many and way too complex for her to even begin tackling. She appeared to have resigned to them and to her destiny, dragging the burden of life with the monotony of a bullock dragging a yoke through soft earth.

She seemed to have erected an invisible cocoon for little Vimal and herself to live in, with Prabha being the only other mortal permitted to breach its frontiers occasionally. Amrapali would not talk to anyone, her attendants included, and even when someone tried to make conversation, they would have to call out aloud several times before she emerged from her perpetual trance to dish out a monosyllabic reply. Her dasis too, after many unsuccessful attempts at initiating dialogue, had given up on her and taken to approaching her only when absolutely necessary.

Prabha was the only one, who, partly out of concern and partly due to the guilt that made her feel responsible for her friend's pitiable state, had doggedly persisted with her efforts to extract Amrapali from the veil of vacuity she had slipped beneath. On several occasions she had felt that she was talking to a quiet apparition rather than a living person, but unrelenting, she had continued to engage with Amrapali, talking to her, updating her on developments she hardly seemed to care about, clinging on to the hope of being able to revive her someday.

It was Prabha who had informed Amrapali about the reason behind her abrupt release from captivity. 'Maharaj Bimbisara, people claim, had made an offer to the Vajji council for withdrawing his troops in return for your release. And indeed, just the morning after you came back the Magadh army had begun its retreat,' she had said. Amrapali's face had remained deadpan, devoid of any reactions whatsoever. She had simply got up, not leaving Prabha with the opportunity to elaborate further, and slumped down on her bed.

Though Amrapali's appearance gave an impression to the contrary, her mind was working just fine and it had assimilated each one of Prabha's words. She had failed to respond perceptibly, but while she was glad that Bimbisara had kept his promise, the information had only compounded the burden of unanswered questions she was reeling under. Why did he make any effort to secure her release? Was it an act of mere compassion, since it was the information he had desired that had resulted in her arrest, or was there something more to it? Was it possible that he was speaking the truth while proclaiming his love for her? Did he still love her? And more importantly, had she truly managed to forget him and move on? Bimbisara's men had marched out of Vaishali's soil, but his thoughts had once again managed to invade Amrapali's mind and despite her best efforts she found herself unable to shake them away.

Today too she had been sprawled on her bed, her hands involuntarily tugging on to a string attached to the wooden cradle where Vimal lay asleep, when Prabha barged into her room. The morning had long passed and the noonday sun's rays were slanting in through the partly ajar balcony door. Vimal, after his morning ablutions and having consumed bellyful of milk had gently slipped into slumber, allowing his mother to transcend into her familiar zone of contemplation.

But Prabha's loud entry, the wooden door almost pounding against the wall with her shove, had startled both mother and son alike. Amrapali had instantly eyed Vimal, who, much to her respite, had only squirmed slightly and not opened his eyes. 'What happened?' she couldn't help but enquire from Prabha.

'Maharaj Bimbisara, he is dead,' Prabha declared without mincing her words. Her face remained contorted by a look of utter dismay as she stared expectantly at Amrapali, as though waiting for her instructions to divulge all that she knew.

'What?' Amrapali allowed a rare exclamation to slip out of her lips. She wasn't sure if she had heard her friend correctly.

'Yes, Maharaj Bimbisara died in Rajgriha yesterday night. This is what the whole of Vaishali seems to be talking about. People are out in the streets rejoicing and celebrating his demise,' she added.

'But how, why?'

'I hear that Ajatshatru, his son, infuriated by his decision to call off the war, conspired with some top Magadhan officials and put the King under arrest somewhere within his own palace. Today morning, while still in captivity, his body was found soaking in a pool of his own blood. His throat was slit open. While some say that the grief of being detained by his own son proved too much for him and he claimed his own life, others believe that Ajatshatru, in a move to eradicate all possible obstacles in his path of staking claim to the throne, had slain him.'

Prabha's words were hitting her like deadly blows of a sledgehammer. Even if she hadn't been with the man she loved, she at least had the comfort of knowing that he was out there somewhere, perhaps thinking about her and reminiscing the beautiful moments they had once shared together. And now, even that comfort had been brutally snatched away from her. To make matters worse, it was she who had unknowingly paved the way for his death. After all, wasn't she the reason why Bimbisara had ended the war, thereby enraging Ajatshatru into taking this radical step?

Her grief was so immense that for a moment she thought she couldn't breathe. Her innards were churning and the throbbing within her head was so intense that she feared her eyes would fall out of their sockets. And then, suddenly, everything fell silent. She felt as though a link of some heavy metal chain that had been containing her had snapped, setting her free of all her burdens. A gush of calm spread across her being as if her agony had transgressed its own frontiers to land her in a space where she was unable to experience pain anymore. She saw a blinding light, one that seemed to contain in itself the dazzle of a thousand suns, flash before her eyes and in that slight instance she felt as though all her questions had been answered and the mysteries of life had all revealed themselves to her.

It had all happened within the passage of a few palas, the advent of the unbearable anguish that threatened to blast her into shreds and its sudden evaporation, but to Amrapali it seemed as though a lifetime had passed between those moments. Prabha was still staring at her blankly when she emerged from the stupor and, taken aback by the sudden transformation in Amrapali's demeanour, her brows were quick to pucker into a frown. 'Are you alright?' she asked concernedly.

Amrapali nodded with a slight smile, further splaying Prabha's concerns, for this was hardly a reaction expected from someone who had just learnt of her lover's death. But it were the words of the monk that were ringing within Amrapali's ears, 'We must understand the difference between the transient and the permanent and only then can we experience a joy that is truly wonderful and everlasting.'

And it was an ovule of this infinite joy that seemed to have burst within her, slowly spreading through the complex of her veins to drench every alcove of her body. It was a feeling she could not put to words and certainly not explain to Prabha. So, stepping past her dazed friend, she reached for her wardrobe and pulled out the simplest, most austere garment it contained—a white cotton dhoti with silver laced borders. Her sudden enlightenment had not only relieved her of her past agonies, but also opened her mind to what she needed to do next. Where she was headed, she would have no need for her luxurious garments, her jewellery or any other worldly possessions that she had amassed.

Later, as she sat on her chariot, little Vimal idling in her lap, the only thought pervading her mind was, 'Budddham Sharnam Gachchami'. The chariot was racing through the streets of Vaishali—a city immersed in celebrating the demise of its nemesis, unmindful of the floodgates of disaster that had opened up for its citizens in wake of Bimbisara's death—heading towards the Sakya Muni's ashram on the outskirts of the city. Amrapali was consumed by a strange sense of exhilaration and could not wait to reach her destination and present herself in the service of the

Buddha, for she was now certain that it was in his feet that the path to her salvation lay.

At almost the same time, Ajatshatru returned to the royal palace of Rajgriha after cremating his father's body. He rushed to his chamber, and shutting the door behind him, pulled out a parchment from within his waistband. It was a letter he had found under the headrest of Bimbisara's bed in the room where the mighty Emperor had breathed his last. The letter was addressed to Ajatshatru and he had already read it a couple of times, but once again he was experiencing a strong urge to read his father's last words to him. Holding the letter in front of his eyes, he began reading it aloud.

'My son, I know not the circumstances under which you will find yourself reading this letter, but one thing is certain that when this letter reaches your hands, I will no longer be around to say these words to you in person.

'I am an extremely proud father today, for I see in you a man able in every sense of the word to take Magadh to the heights I had once envisioned. People might question your actions, they might accuse you of forcibly snatching the throne from your father, but don't let them deter you my son, for had I been in your place, I would have perhaps done exactly what you did. I have always taught you that the interest of the state and its subjects supersedes everything, even the bond we share as father and son, and I am glad that you found it within you to demonstrate that when time so demanded.

'I have indeed failed you and the citizens of Magadh, but sadly I carry with me no remorse or regret over my deeds. As our men were struggling to breach the vaulting walls of Vaishali, I found myself besieged by an internal battle of my own—a battle between my mind and my heart, and the heart didn't take long in establishing its supremacy over the mind. Even though I knew that the subject of my affection, the very reason behind this internal tempest—Amrapali—would never be mine, I allowed my heart to guide me, and in doing so I found a sense of contentment that is difficult to explain in words.

'I was aware that in calling off the war I was perhaps deviating from my sworn duties as the Emperor of Magadh, but in doing so I achieved a sense of satisfaction that I have never experienced before, not even with the many successful campaigns I have led our men through. I am not sure if you will find yourself in a position to comprehend this, for I am myself struggling to put my feelings into perspective till this day, but I have little doubt that you will undo any harm my actions might have caused to the Magadh Empire and its citizenry.

'While I know that you will bring laurels to Magadh and to our dynasty of an order that will surpass my own realm, the last advice that a father wishes to leave for his son is that while following your ambitions never be ignorant of the seemingly small desires that sprout up every now and then, for it is in one of them that you might stumble across the true purpose of your life. Amrapali could have been mine had I not allowed my ambitions to shroud my desire for her at the opportune time, and that my son is the only regret I shall carry to my death bed. We are all mortals and if we suppress any of our desires, we might never get another chance of fulfilling them. And a life of regret, as I can now vouch, is certainly not worth living.

Your loving father—Bimbisara of Magadh.'

The word 'Emperor' was conspicuously amiss from Bimbisara's signature. As he read the last words of the letters, Ajatshatru's amber eyes finally let loose the stream of tears they had been containing all along.

EPILOGUE

Ajatshatru succeeded Bimbisara as the Emperor of Magadh and ruled between 492-460 BC. He followed in the footsteps of his father, using conquest and expansion to make Magadh one of the most powerful kingdoms in northern India.

One of the first and most ferocious battles of Ajatshatru's reign was the war he waged against the neighbouring kingdom of Vaishali. In this war Ajatshatru is said to have deployed innovative weapons of mass destruction—a war engine which, like a catapult, was used to throw stones upon the enemy ranks from a distance, and a chariot to which a mace or blade was attached on both sides, enabling it to plough through enemy formations, crushing hundreds and thousands of soldiers at one go. The war lasted for sixteen long years, ending with the annihilation of the Lichchavis of Vaishali and annexation of the kingdom by Ajatshatru.

It was to facilitate the conquest of Vaishali that Ajatshatru is said to have shifted the capital of Magadh from Rajgriha to Patli Grama, a small town on the banks of river Ganga. Later Patli Grama developed into a city, gaining popularity as Patliputra, now known as Patna, the capital of the present day state of Bihar. After conquering Vaishali, Ajatshatru conquered Kasi, Kosala and thirty-six other republican states surrounding his kingdom, firmly establishing the predominance of Magadh Empire.

Amrapali, influenced by the Buddha's teachings, is said to have become an arahant (spiritual practioner). Her name finds mention in ancient Buddhist traditions, especially in conjunction with Buddha's stay in her mango grove which she later donated to his order. It was in this grove (Ambapali Vana) that Gautama Buddha is said to have preached the famous Ambapalika Sutta. Amrapali's son with Bimbisara, Vimal Kondana, is also said to have followed the path of his mother, becoming a monk of the Buddhist order.

At a distance of about seventy kilometres from Patna lies the modern-day Vaishali, a predominantly rural town surrounded by rice fields and banana and mango groves. It is here, within the folds of its quaintness that one can catch glimpses of the past glories and splendour that made up Vaishali, the capital city of the Lichchavis and the blessed motherland of Amrapali. Here, among the stupas and pagodas, each with an enchanting history of its own, one can also see remains of the Abhishek Pushkarini or the coronation tank, the sacred waters of which were used to anoint the elected representatives of Vaishali's Governing Council.

Made in the USA
Monee, IL
07 July 2026

56552378R00173